LEG THE SPREAD

LEG THE SPREAD

A Woman's Adventures
Inside the Trillion-Dollar Boys'
Club of Commodities Trading

Cari Lynn

BROADWAY BOOKS

New York

Names and identifying characteristics of individuals in this book have been changed to protect their identities. The book makes occasional use of composite characters as well.

PRINTED IN THE UNITED STATES OF AMERICA

BROADWAY BOOKS and its logo, a letter B bisected on the diagonal, are trademarks of Random House, Inc.

Visit our website at www.broadwaybooks.com

First edition published 2004.

Book design by Caroline Cunningham

Library of Congress Cataloging-in-Publication Data
Lynn, Cari.
Leg the spread : a woman's adventures inside the Trillion-Dollar Boys' Club of Commodities Trading / Cari Lynn.—1st ed.
p. cm.
1. Commodity trading advisers—United States. 2. Women in the professions— United States. 3. Brokers—United States. 4. Chicago Mercantile Exchange. 5. Commodity exchanges—United States. I. Title.

HG6046.5.L96 2004
332.64'4'0820973—dc22   2004045837

ISBN 0-7679-0855-4

1   3   5   7   9   10   8   6   4   2

What sane person could live in this world

and not be crazy?

—Ursula LeGuin

Contents

LEG THE SPREAD

Leg the Spread

In the Futures market, it's all about minimizing risk and maximizing your wallet. Buying something gives you one leg, but you've got big potential to lose unless you sell something to get the other leg. If you can come full circle, and you've got two legs to stand on, that's your spread. This takes expertise and guts, and it shouldn't matter whether you're male or female—but it does. It's a man's world in trading; as a woman you can make your money by legging the spread, or . . .

efore I officially set foot on the Futures trading floor, I was told a cautionary tale about a young woman trader, whom I'll call Anne McKenzie. When I asked her real name, the veteran trader who was confiding in me became squirmy. "I don't want to say, besides, you'll never find anything on her anyway." He stressed *never*. Unable to resist, I asked why. He writhed some more. He was merely an acquaintance of a friend of mine whom I'd just met, so he owed me no further explanation. But he offered me an ultimatum: "I will tell you this story if you promise not to ask anything more about it." I promised.

It was in the late 1980s, and Anne McKenzie lived a few blocks from my apartment, in a cluster of condominiums called Sandburg Village. Hers was a high-rise like most here in downtown Chicago: a tower with dozens of floors, a doorman, a swimming pool, and a view of Lake Michigan—the coveted lake view. A half turn southeast and you'd see the solid black-beamed Hancock building and contrasting marble Water Tower Place grazing the skyline. If you looked due south, to the Loop, you could see the Sears Tower—the country's tallest—and all the other skyscrapers in its shadow, including the world's largest and busiest Futures trading forums: the Chicago Mercantile Exchange, where McKenzie worked, and the neighboring Chicago Board of Trade.

On a blustery night McKenzie stood on the top floor of Sandburg, named for the Chicago writer Carl Sandburg, whose first published work was entitled "In Reckless Ecstasy." I imagine she still felt that ringing in her ears from all the shouting and commotion, and that fluttering in her chest from the fear and the awe, from the challenge of a volatile market, and the challenge of being one of the few females to try to play the game. McKenzie was around my age, early thirties. Her brand-spanking-new car—a Porsche, perhaps, that one trade alone had bought—was in the garage many stories below. Her condo, without a doubt, looked over the lake. She had been making the money, standing next to the men, enduring their taunts, their come-ons, their doubting her. She had earned their respect, at least enough so that they said hello to her, even though it was often just a breezy nod as they dashed past her to the inner circle of the pit. McKenzie had yet to make it to the inner circle, but she had the taste of success on her lips—and it seemed the sweetest sugar there was.

And then: Monday, October 19, 1987. The ticker scrolls by. The numbers are starting to drop. For the first couple of minutes, it's just a slide. It's like you're skidding on ice, but you still have your balance, you're still standing. McKenzie watches $5,000 disappear. It's going to be a bad day, she says to herself. In a minute, $5,000 turns to $20,000, and a bad day instantly turns into a bad month. But this is only the beginning.

The numbers nose-dive. Traders are yelling out quotes, and the yells are accelerating into bloodcurdling screams. It's sheer panic—a room full of hundreds of men and less than a handful of women, all in hysteria. At first, it's luxury that slips away—that new candy-colored BMW convertible you had your eye on, the A-frame condo in Aspen. A few minutes pass—minutes that seem like half seconds, flashing by like the ticker, all bright lights, there, then gone. The Dow is flashing: down 100, down 200, down, down, down. Chaos breaks out, men jump over one another, pushing, kicking, cursing the air—it's like war; every person for him- or herself. The rules don't matter much anymore. All eyes are glued, in disbelief, to the electronic price-reporting boards. The numbers flip at a dizzying pace. It's as if each board were a clock and some little devil has got hold of the levers and is twirling the hands round and round. Usually the numbers tick off with a sort of rhythm; they now are plummeting too quickly for the boards to even keep up.

Now it isn't only the Paris vacation you've lost, it's the second car in your garage—tick—it's your retirement savings—tick—it's your kids' college fund—tick—it's your only remaining car—tick—it's your mortgage. You're watching it all slip through your fingers—five minutes ago you were trying to make it better, trying to still play the game; now you just want to get out. But it's way past too late.

Right next to you, a man in his early forties, father of two, has a breakdown. He's a seasoned trader, had purchased his seat at the Mercantile Exchange ten years ago for $700,000. He was trading against it, as many traders do, using the seat as collateral. In less than a minute, he has just watched his seat, plus everything else, disappear. He is now bankrupt, he owes money, and he's lost the right to trade. In less than a minute. He sinks right there on the steps of the pit, his head collapsing into his hands, and sobs. On the other side of you, another trader grabs his tie and lifts it above his head as if he's hanging himself. Across the pit, a big-shot new guy lurches over and throws up on his $600 pair of Bruno Maglis. He, like everyone on the trading floor, had tried dumping everything, his whole position in the Market. But you can't, not when everyone's dumping and no one's buying; the bid-ask spread isn't just huge, it's nonexistent. People are wiping themselves out on a single trade, because once you're in a spot like that, it's like standing in front of a speeding train.

Now you hardly remember all those days when making money seemed effortless. One trade—boom! Three thousand!—it took less than a minute. Five thousand dollars! Ten thousand, thirty thousand! And now, losing it seems just as easy, sand through your fingers. One second it's a handful, the next it's gone, taken by the wind.

Only, you never realized that losing everything after you've had it is worse than never having had it at all.

It's all over the news—Crash! Dive! Meltdown! Massacre! The newspapers will run it as the cover story; each front page, the *New York Times*, the *Wall Street Journal*, the *Chicago Tribune*, the *Los Angeles Times*, will show similar photos: the average trader—a thirty-year-old white guy— overcome with rage, terror, even tears. They'll term it Black Monday; it will go down in the books as the day when $1 trillion evaporated in the single largest stock market drop in history.

It didn't matter to Anne McKenzie that everyone was feeling it. Self-absorption was part of the business, and so was greed. And here it was, in all its manifestations: it was only she who mattered, and money.

Trading is about making money. A job well done is not indicated by a problem solved or a task completed, nor by a promotion or the degree to which you've helped someone else. A job well done is indicated by money, and money alone. Money is the measure of your worth.

Not only was McKenzie out of money, but she, like thousands of other traders, received a margin call. It was just as if she had maxed out a credit card. Those faceless, nameless people who ran the show were coming to claim what seems like yours, but is rightfully theirs. For a Futures trader, the IRS-like figure is the clearing firm. They can be your best friend when they back you and enable you to start trading, or they can be your worst enemy when they're coming for you. Somewhere in the clearing firm that represented McKenzie, a notice went off on her account. The red alert: she owed money.

"Hello, Ms. Anne McKenzie, you have a margin call of $80,000. You need to wire the money to us within forty-eight hours or else we'll be forced to liquidate your position. You will be liable for any resulting deficit. Thank you."

On the next call, the voice wasn't as friendly. "Ms. McKenzie, you now have a margin call of $1 million. You must wire this money immediately or we will be forced to take action." That day in October was a busy one for clearing firms. Some clearing firms even had to resort to sending a representative to the trading floor to drag the blown-out trader off. Those were the traders for whom the gambler's last-ditch mentality had taken over, *If I can just keep going I can make back something, anything!* But the clearing firms knew better. The clearing-firm representatives had the loathsome task of recovering these corpses, corpses that were still warm enough to do lethal damage in the trading pits.

For McKenzie, the third call was the charm: "We've implemented our right to increase the margin requirement. You have a margin call of $3 million." Three million dollars? Unlike other traders, she had never even *had* that much money, and now she owed it. So if having zero made her nothing, what in the hell was negative three million? She was shit. Lower than shit, and how do you face that?

She decided that you don't.

Anne McKenzie took a forty-story swan dive from the top of her Sandburg Village condominium—in reckless ecstasy.

$ $ $

The veteran trader who told me about McKenzie turned out to be right—I'd find nothing on her. The day I heard the story, I was unexplainably entranced. I began scouring old newspapers. I combed death records and obituaries. I spent hours on the Internet searching every possible keyword I could think of. Nothing. How could someone leap off a high-rise and there be no mention of it? Anywhere? I began to wonder if my confidant was fabricating the whole story. Aside from the fact that there didn't seem to be a logical motive for him to do that—he was a well-respected trader who also taught and wrote about technical aspects of trading—his discomfiture made me believe he was telling the truth. Almost immediately after mentioning he had a story for me, he'd acted as if his better judgment had kicked in and that he wanted to take his words right back. He ended up drilling into me the "you didn't hear this from me" defense, only he seemed to do so not out of a need to be secretive, or private, or even dramatic, but more in an uneasy, backpedaling, fidgety way that, I believe, stemmed from the edges of fear.

I didn't understand it at the time; what possibly could he be afraid of? Of course, this conversation took place when I was a wide-eyed neophyte in the Futures trading world, before I had spent two years on the trading floor; before I really understood how money—just the very allure of money—could make people do very strange things; before I learned that McKenzie was far from the first trader to choose such a final option, and would likely be far from the last; and before I came to realize that fear was something that existed everywhere on the trading floor, encircling every trader in every pit. For fear was the only force that offset greed, and greed seemed to come stitched into the very polyester fibers of a trading jacket. Even people who weren't necessarily greedy in any other aspects of life, once they slid their arms into the trading jacket, once they affixed their badge with their acronym, the transformation was, dare I say, inevitable.

Anne McKenzie's tale was my dubious welcome into this world. Perhaps she had been welcomed in the more traditional way of being handed a roll of toilet paper and told, "This place is not for weak stomachs." It would be more than two years before I would finally stumble upon McKenzie's real name—and it would happen under similar circumstances, laced with discomfort and fear. The veteran trader had told me the truth all right—just not the whole story.

$ $ $

A typical trader—a male in his early thirties, golf shirt, khakis, sneakers, and the telltale brightly colored polyester trader's jacket—was extolling his philosophy of Futures trading to me. He emphasized his enthusiasm with dramatic hand gestures: "I make money on the Up," he swooped the air with his arm. "And I make money on the Down." He sliced the air the other way. His eyes were glowing. It was the glow of making thousands of dollars in a minute flat. The glow of hitting a million a year—when you're twenty-five years old. It's the Life Is Good When You're Me glow. And many Futures traders here, on the trading floor of the Chicago Mercantile Exchange, have it.

Today, like any typical day, the Floor resembled a Super Bowl stadium: a 70,000-square-foot arena where everyone was on their feet, screaming, pushing, shoving, anything they could do to get the trade; they were all dressed in vibrant colors, as if they were supporting teams; digital boards—scoreboards, for the sake of the analogy—lined the walls, blinking, flashing, dipping, rising; and the testosterone was almost tangible. The energy of the trading floor was undeniable, everything moved fast, fast, fast, watch out, or you'd get trampled! Several thousand people worked here, and they all seemed to be racing in different directions. It was like this five days a week, all year round. I still find it amazing, actually, that this apparent insanity works as effectively as it does, but Futures trading has been efficient for over a hundred years.

And not just efficient—but, potentially, downright lucrative. Some of the wealthiest people in the world stand in these trading pits. But what the trader didn't admit to me at that moment was that when the glow was not there, when you'd bet that the Market was going to rise, but instead it plummeted, when you *lost* money on the Up, as well as the Down, that's when you were caught. And the money always seemed to disappear faster than it had come to you. And then, the only dramatic gesture you were making was the invisible slit to the throat. For every glowing eye, there is an accident site. And the trader is bleeding money.

I suppose my journey began with a romanticism along the lines of, "What's a nice girl like you doing in a place like this?" and I'm still not entirely sure how it is that a young, soft-voiced, rather nonmaterialistic, rather introverted writer found herself on the trading floor. But there I was, in the midst of the opposite of everything that made me feel comfortable, the opposite of everything that I defined as my ideals.

I had grown up in a suburb of Chicago, and then moved back to the city after finishing college and graduate school on the East Coast. One would think that after spending two-thirds of my life in and around Chicago, I'd have been familiar with its famously lucrative Futures Exchanges, but I wasn't. I had seen them depicted in two movies, *Trading Places* and *Ferris Bueller's Day Off*. I had wondered at the apparent chaos and had been amused by the strange hand signals. I knew it all had something to do with money—and right there was where my interest ended. Money was something I was conscious of only to the extent that I knew I couldn't spend more than I had. I had grown up this way—in my family, there was neither an excess of money, nor a shortage. Throughout my childhood, my parents volleyed back and forth, one would work while the other pursued graduate degrees, then they would switch roles. There were undoubtedly times when money was tight, but there never was a sense of panic. I learned that you didn't waste money, you bought something if you really needed it, and you made it second nature to check out the on-sale rack.

I first realized that some of my friends' families had more than we did when a gated community went up and they moved out of their aluminum-sided houses that looked like mine and into expansive brick, wood, stone, and even stucco houses that were custom-designed according to their tastes. However, my town still maintained a large blue-collar segment, and to my 1970s generation it didn't seem as obvious, or as important as it does today, who was who. To my school friends, the concept of money was really relevant in only one situation: the type of vacation your family took over winter break. In this department, I lucked out: my dad had a rich uncle, and that uncle in turn passed everything on to his son, my cousin, who spared no expense on lavish Florida island beach houses, where we spent our holidays.

It was through my great-uncle and cousin that I came to understand how money could define a person. On one of these early cross-country road trips to Florida, my dad taught me the word "millionaire." "What are we called?" I asked. My dad muttered something that was inaudible to the backseat, but that made my mom laugh with sardonic ha, ha, has. It was likely on the next year's trip that I learned my relatives weren't just millionaires, they were *multi*millionaires, and I pronounced the word with emphasis on every syllable as I reported to my friends over cafeteria franks-n-beans how wonderful my trip had been. And yet, some twenty years later, the initial images that come to mind of those privileged vacations are somewhat startling: I remember our private beach, where I could walk for what seemed like miles, hoping, wishing, that I'd see another sign of human life, another family somewhere on this island who had just one child I could play with. I remember the bedroom that was designated as mine, filled with antique mahogany furniture shipped from France, the bed so grand and regal that even adults needed to use the matching stepstool to crawl in, and I remember lying awake at night, scared I'd fall out. I see the marble master bathroom, bigger than my bedroom at home, and the glass-encased marble shower complete with a solarium, and I remember how the water would smart and sting my sunburned shoulders. Oddly, these dreary blue images are the ones I've kept of the times my family lived like multi-millionaires.

While money was what drew most people to the trading floor, that obviously wasn't what interested me. My first inspiration for delving into the world of Futures trading came in April 2000, when the stock market took a historic plummet. My friend Tara Kim had been, throughout the late 1990s, day-trading stock options from her apartment, gleefully bouncing along on the bubble from one high-flying stock to the next. And then, one day, it all blew up in her face. Tara lived three floors below me, and on a particularly vicious afternoon, I brought her tea to try to calm her as she watched her portfolio disintegrate. Tara had had good days and bad days before, so it wasn't until the next morning when the indelible headlines landed at my door—MAUL STREET . . . MARKETS SUFFER WORST DAY EVER—that I realized the scope of the impact. It certainly wasn't just Tara who was having a bad day.

On Wall Street, dark-suited, slicked-hair big shots were right there with her. So was an attorney in Los Angeles, who had been banking on his sale of two blue-chip stocks to cover his taxes. Add to the list a sixty-nine-year-old grandmother in Fort Lauderdale named Harriet who would spend twelve hours a day trading from her home. From behind computer screens all over America, thousands of T-shirt-and-boxer-clad day-traders were also suffering. In Seattle a computer geek who, at the age of twenty, had sold his start-up company for exchange of stock shares, was getting squeezed. And, in hundreds of trading firms around the country, traders anxiously recalling the recent massacre at an Atlanta firm, where an employee opened fire after a market drop, were sharing her bad day, too.

It fascinated me how all this somehow circled around to a studio apartment in Chicago's Old Town neighborhood, where Tara, a young, pretty musician and former University of Michigan gymnast, got burned selling stock options called Puts.

After finally tearing herself from the computer that day, Tara took a cab to the gym. She ran on the treadmill for a few minutes before the feeling snuck up on her again—spinning head, racing heart, cold sweat. She had to get off the machine and lie down right there on the floor. "I'm a trader, just had a bad day," she said. No other explanation was necessary—everyone felt her pain. The reality was, most people at her tony gym had shared her bad day.

I, of course, had missed the stock boom completely. Because I was a full-time freelance writer, any money I had was earmarked for something specific and vital, like rent or food. On the rare occasion that there was an excess of money, it went into a savings account for the day (or month, or year) when checks I was owed experienced the severe delays that are commonplace in the world of publishing. While my lack of presence in the stock market made me exempt from the carnage, I still felt as if I had missed out—and that feeling intensified the more I began hearing the staggering figures of just how much everyone had lost. I—perhaps naïvely— formulated the view that I was exactly the type of person who *should* have been in the Market, for my lack of greed would have allowed me to get out well within the nick of time, with some much-needed spending money to show for it.

This was precisely when I began to realize that just a couple of miles from my apartment were two of the world's largest trading institutions where thousands of traders were packed in trading pits, yelling and screaming—and, if they had called it right, were actually *profiting* from the infamous turn of events. Because they traded Futures, they had the ability to hop on the crashing tidal wave and ride it straight down, mounting up cash every inch—every tick—of the way.

Although Tara day-traded from home, she also owned a seat on the Chicago Board of Trade, an investment prompted by her boyfriend, Tom, who had been trading Futures for the past few years. An Exchange "seat" wasn't really a physical seat, but rather the status and the badge that allowed you to trade from the trading floor, in the trading pits. Tara's status allowed her to trade in the Dow-Jones Futures pit. But she had never once utilized it.

Around the time the bubble burst and Tara's small fortune vanished like a white rabbit in a magician's hat, I began asking why she didn't start trading Futures on the trading floor. As an answer to my question, Tara, Tom, and I ventured to the Chicago Mercantile Exchange, where Tom leased a seat. He signed us in at guest registration, led us through the security checkpoints, and onto what, in its otherworldly, all-encompassing personification, was simply referred to as the Floor.

At first sight, I understood Tara's trepidation. The Floor was laid out like a jungle gym—all metal rails and rubber floors, winding steps and multiple tiers and narrow walkways that weaved around the raucous, roaring pits and up through the stadiumlike rows where those trading on the electronic system were at their computers. The Exchange was divided into two levels, each with numerous different trading pits. On the lower Floor, where Tom took us, were the Stock Market Index Futures—the Nasdaq and the S&P 500—and, across the Floor—what the financial guys viewed as Siberia—were the original Commodities: Pork Bellies, Cattle, Lumber. Upstairs was the massive Eurodollar pit and the various Currencies.

To my novice eye, this all seemed nothing short of chaos. But even when you perfectly understood the workings, it was still a predatory place, hardcore survival of the fittest; but perhaps most strikingly, it was one of the last male bastions—truly, the ultimate men's club. Only a handful of females had ever made it into the trading pits, and of those who did, only a select few had survived. Despite women's equality in most every other field, Futures trading remained a testosterone-saturated world where the men were sometimes monsters and there was no room for boys, let alone women. Indeed, the few women down there, screaming over the low-pitched rumble, pushing and shoving to be seen, to claim a spot, to not get trampled and lost and berated, these women had to have some balls.

"I don't like the way I feel in here," Tara said, as a man conspicuously eyed us up and down.

"Is the Board of Trade any better?" I asked.

"No," she admitted. "I don't like the way I feel there either."

When Tara had initially begun looking into purchasing a seat on one of the
Chicago Exchanges, her first stop was the membership department at the
Mercantile Exchange. Perhaps because Tara looked like she could pass for a
college sophomore, or perhaps for the simple fact that she was a woman,
she was immediately sent to an office that ended up being human
resources, where they handed her an application for a job as a clerk. She
tried to explain the oversight, but was still met with resistance. Finally,
the man from membership whom she needed to talk with was paged with
the message that a young woman would like to see him. He wouldn't come
out of his office, and when Tara insisted she needed to talk with him, she
was instructed to call him from the front desk.

Over the phone, Tara introduced herself, but he cut her off. "I'm really
busy right now," he said. "Well, when would be a better time?" Tara asked.

"Why don't you visit human resources?" he offered. Tara, at this point,
was exasperated. "But I want to become a member, not a clerk, a *member*."

Suddenly, the tone on the other end of the phone changed. In a few seconds, he'd bounded from his office and was effusively shaking Tara's hand,
then leading her back.

Tara ended up purchasing a seat on the neighboring Board of Trade,
which housed Commodities such as Wheat, Soybeans, and Corn, along
with the Dow-Jones Futures Index and the Bond Futures. She enrolled in
the necessary courses to gain a membership, then passed the required test
and paid the required dues. But when she went to the Board's membership
office to pick up her ID badge, the woman behind the counter kept trying
to give her a clerk's badge. "I'm a member," Tara kept saying, and finally it
sank in.

"Oh, you've got a seat?" the woman said, still with disbelief. "But you're
so young . . . and so pretty."

$ $ $

If stock trading is table wine, then Futures trading is moonshine. Also
termed Commodity trading, Futures trading was initially set up for the
purpose of protection—or hedging—for farmers so that they could lock in
a substantial payment for crops before delivering them at market, thereby
reducing the risk of price fluctuations from surplus or drought. The first

recorded example of a Futures trade dated back to 1697 in the Japanese rice market. Even mentions of such Futures-like hedging had been noted in the ancient mathematician Thales' recordings of Egyptian wheat trade during the flood of the Nile. In the mid-1800s, Futures trading became a necessity for farmers in the midwestern United States, bringing the largest Futures trading mecca in the world to Chicago with the development of the Board of Trade in 1848 and the Mercantile Exchange fifty years later.

To picture the Futures market, take your image of a Stock Exchange trading floor, such as the New York Stock Exchange, and double—triple—the volatile free-for-all. In its own way, the chaos was organized; in the midst of the mayhem, everybody amazingly knew where they were. But this didn't stop the anxiety attacks on the Floor (almost every trader admits to having them); or the occupational hazards—traders in their early thirties getting fitted for hearing aids and having throat polyps removed; or clerks getting verbally (and occasionally physically) slammed by traders taking out their frustrations on the nearest and easiest target; or the fistfights in the pit that would break out with surprising regularity. It was a tough place, indeed—they say if you have a heart attack on the Floor, the others will step on you. Or, at best, do nothing. "When one guy I used to signal to had a heart attack and fell down in the pit," a retired woman trader recalled, "no one stopped trading. No one even stopped! This isn't an exaggeration." Another trader confessed to me, "Money makes you do stuff you wouldn't otherwise do."

To really grasp the concept of Futures trading, you need to erase from your mind everything you know about Stock trading. Futures is faster, chancier, and the amount of money you can make or lose, especially when the Market takes a surprise leap or hit, is ridiculously greater. Futures isn't about shares or companies, and it isn't the one-way street that Stock trading is, where you buy a stock and bet (hope) that it goes up. Futures is a two-way racetrack—you bet that the Market as a whole is going to go either up *or* down, and you can buy it or sell it. But if your bet is wrong, you're not just out the money you invested, like you are with stocks; rather, you're at risk to lose far more because you're so highly leveraged. In Futures you can theoretically lose until the Market hits zero. It is the Futures traders' role in the economic system to assume risk, which thereby creates liquidity in the Market.

Futures trading, however, originated from humble origins. Here's the scene: the early 1800s, a desolate prairie, dusty and dry, the hot August sun beating down on the vast emptiness. Coming up on the horizon, a slow-moving speck—a wagon, hauling a full load of wheat. It's been tumbling across the plains for days, and there you are, the farmer at the helm, a thick layer of dust and grime caked on your sweaty face, your hands raw and callused from the weeks you've spent harvesting your crop. After several more hours of nothingness, you finally glimpse a sign of life up ahead—you've reached the big city, Chicago.

The open-air market is swarming with people. It smells of cattle and raw fish and ripe fruit, and everyone is scurrying and shouting and bartering. You lift your aching body from the wooden slab of a seat, and begin to try to sell off your wheat. This is your one and only chance to make your living for the year, and you have a good crop to show for yourself. The weather had been favorable and the harvest had come to plentiful fruition. However, you are not the only wheat farmer who has reaped a bountiful harvest. In fact, there is a surplus of wheat, and the few buyers who are still biting are offering ridiculously low sums. You want to laugh them out of their britches, but you know that if you don't take their offer, there are a dozen other farmers who will, and your crop, which you toiled over—your blood and sweat—will be left to rot. So you sell your wheat for half of what it's worth. You have a wife and five kids to provide for, and you've promised them new shoes, yet you can't even afford to buy kerosene.

Fast-forward fifty years, after the implementation of Futures trading. This time the scene is different: a babbling brook, the August sun diffused by shady trees. You are a farmer, and with the harvest just come to pass, you're resting your raw and callused hands, dozing off as your fishing line bobs in the water. Many months earlier you had sold contracts to buyers guaranteeing that you would deliver wheat to them at a specified price. The price was quite satisfactory to you, it covered your expense of running a farm, and it provided for your family. And it worked out well for the other side, too—there had been very little rain this season, resulting in an under-supply of wheat, so the price went up drastically and your buyers were happy that they had already locked in at a lower rate. One of your buyers even turned around and sold some of your crop to someone else at a higher price. You'd caught wind of others coming in and doing this, they were calling themselves speculators, and they had no interest in buying the crop themselves, all they were looking to do was make a little money off the difference in price. They were buying contracts for future harvests and hoping that the value went up so that they could sell the contracts at the market for a profit. Imagine that! All these middlemen trading wheat contracts when they didn't even want any wheat—some crazy fellas to be sure.

You're also glad that you didn't have to haul your crop across the state; rather, you and the buyers arranged for different delivery dates and places. Besides, you never did like the chaos of the market, all those people bartering; it was a madhouse. And now, with these future contracts, people gather in special little circles for trading different goods. You've got some people trading cattle contracts, and some people trading bean contracts, and there's a circle just for wheat contracts, and they buy and sell these things back and forth, and they're screaming and shouting; it's no place for a country boy.

In a way, not much has changed in the Commodity Futures market since. The market has moved indoors, but the traders still stand in a circle, in a tiered arena called a pit. In a sense, they're still bartering—they're buying and selling contracts and trying to get the best price, and it's all done through the age-old system of shouting at the top of your lungs. "Open outcry" is a fancy term for the yelling and screaming—Sell you five! Buy one! Buy ten! Sell two! There still exists a large Grain market, plus numerous other Commodity markets: Pork Bellies, Soybeans, Cattle, Lumber, Corn. Farmers still hedge their harvest in the Futures market, although the major players are large institutions and banking firms, like Merrill Lynch and Goldman Sachs, who have no interest in the product, only in making money off it. Brokers from these firms execute customer orders in the pits.

The speculator, that businessman in the pit who also has no want for the product, is now called a Local. Locals trade from their own accounts, using their own money and their own discretion—in the big economic picture, the Locals provide liquidity to the Market by being the source with whom the broker can trade.

While the basic mechanisms of Futures trading have remained remarkably static, what has changed—and only in the last thirty years—is that the

Futures market has morphed into something far beyond a Commodity Exchange. In the early 1970s, a savvy trader named Leo Melamed, who worked his way up from humble, immigrant beginnings to become the chairman of the Chicago Mercantile Exchange, enlisted the direction of renowned economist Milton Friedman to apply the Commodity-trading principles to numerous other facets. They came up with one basic rule: if the "product" can be standardized, it can be traded. And so was born the International Monetary Market, where world currency Futures are traded. In raucous trading pits in downtown Chicago, you can make your living betting that the Swiss Franc is going to go up or down, or the Japanese Yen, or the Australian Dollar, or the Canadian Dollar, or the British Pound—or any of the dozen Currency contracts traded there.

Initially, expanding Futures trading beyond straight Commodities was met with much reservation. Business-news journalists tossed out hard-hitting questions along the lines of, "What do a bunch of cigar-chomping, Pork Belly traders know about all this financial stuff?" The answer was straightforward, according to one such trader in the Mercantile Exchange's Pork Belly pit, who retorted: "Numbers is numbers!"

Ten years later, the chairman and the economist put their heads together again and slightly altered the definition of "product" so that not only did it apply to things that could be standardized, but it went a step further—the product didn't even have to be tangible. Thus, the Eurodollar Futures (which is based on interest rates, and which is now the most actively traded Futures contract in the world) and, later, the Standard & Poor's 500 Index and Nasdaq 100 Index Futures contracts were created. With such a broad definition of what constitutes something as tradable, the doors have been opened to trade virtually anything that can be quantified—which makes Futures trading, well, the wave of the future. It also makes things such as wine, weather, energy, electricity, chemicals—the list goes on—into tradable gold rushes.

$ $ $

After my first visit to the Floor, I desperately wanted to return. This seemed odd, even to me. I was accustomed to working alone, from my home, with just my computer, a mug of tea, and a stack of books and periodicals that I'd delve into during my writing breaks. The Floor was the antithesis of my quiet, pensive environment. But therein, perhaps, lay the attraction. I was gripped, just as thousands of others had been gripped. I'd heard the stories—the tale about the cabdriver who was always shuttling people to the Merc, and who one day decided to see what it was all about. He went to the viewing gallery and it was instant attraction, bye-bye yellow taxi. He got himself a job as a runner, worked his way up to be a trader, and was now a millionaire. Substitute "cabdriver" with any profession—dentist, lawyer, teacher—and the stories will pop up of people who impulsively chucked stable, often lucrative, careers for a tilt-a-whirl ride in trading.

With no background and no prior interest in finance, I suddenly found myself collecting books about the Futures market: *Market Wizards, The New Gatsbys,* and *Reminiscences of a Stock Operator.* In the back of my mind I entertained the idea that maybe, just maybe, I'd stumbled upon something I could do a few hours a day that would supplement my income and allow me to continue my writing career without the pressure to sell, sell, sell. That, to me, seemed the ultimate: to be able to pursue my passion for the sheer fulfillment of it, and to not have to take lousy assignments or make pride-swallowing compromises. The beauty of my plan, I reasoned, was in the irony of it all—I would be stepping into a new world that was solely about money, so that I could step out of the fiscal aspect of my existing world. It seemed a gorgeous paradox.

I ordered a subscription to the *Wall Street Journal* and one to *Fortune* magazine. I borrowed Tara's textbooks from the trading courses she'd taken, *How the Futures Markets Work* and the *Commodity Trading Manual,* and, with CNBC muted in the background, I set to work. One of the first lines that struck me was from a pamphlet I'd picked up at the membership office, entitled, "The Merc at Work: A Guide to the Chicago Mercantile Exchange." It stated: "Investors trade Futures for only one reason: to make money. They don't always succeed, but they try." I couldn't help but marvel at the boldness of it—no apologies, no sugar-coating, we're in this for the money and that's it! I reread the line, trying to get comfortable with the fact that, apparently, this was not just an okay ideal to hold, but an okay one to promote as well. I was five minutes into my new studies and already I was questioning principles. Of course I knew the job was about making money—after all, that was my motive, too—it just felt odd to admit that it was only, *only* about money. But I needed to get used to it; besides, as one of the guidebooks informed me, one of the worst habits a trader can have is to overanalyze. From here out, I told myself, no more thoughts about morals or ethics; no more thoughts about all the parts of the world that were destitute, or all the people who didn't have money for food. No, from here on out, money would be like points in a game, and at the end of the day, all that would matter would be the final score.

The first and foremost concept to know regarding modern-day Futures trading is: there is unlimited profit potential *and* unlimited loss potential; in other words, huge payout, huge risk. Huge fortune, huge misfortune. Thrill, excitement, adrenaline; stress, pressure, debit. It's a game of You versus the Market. Some say, like the House in any casino, in the end the Market will always win. Of course, the thousands of raspy-voiced men and the handful of gutsy women in the pits don't buy into those odds, and many of them have bank accounts sizable enough to prove their point. Like the glowing-eyed trader said, they make money on the Up—swoosh!—and they make money on the Down—swoosh!

The logistics of Futures trading are actually quite simple. So simple, in fact, that I initially had difficulty grasping it all because I kept looking for some complex strategic formula. There isn't any. If you think the Market's going to go up, you buy a contract, which is called going long. If you think the Market's going to go down, you sell a contract, this is called shorting the Market. That's basically it—nothing more than a double-sided version of "buy low, sell high."

If you have a position—that is, if you've traded at least one contract in the Market—you're either long or short, you've either bought or sold the Market. Now don't get all confused by the word "sell"—you're not selling in the way you'd sell shares of stock. What you're doing, in a sense, is *creating* contracts that you're obligated to buy back at a later point (hopefully after you've made some money). Buying and selling in the Futures market is really like placing a bet. Futures, for the most part, has become a monetary game—unless you truly are in the Market to take delivery of 40,000 pounds of frozen pork bellies, or 5,000 bushels of soybeans. Otherwise, you're not *really* buying or selling anything, because you're not trading anything that you're ever going to see, and in some cases, like with the S&P and Nasdaq Futures, it's nothing that's even concrete.

So let's say you think the Market's going to go down. You bet this by selling a contract at or near the Market price, which, for the sake of this tutorial, we'll put at 5. What d'ya know, you're right, and the Market tanks! You decide to take your profit when the Market hits 2. So you buy back your contract at a price of 2, and this action—selling a contract initially, then buying it back—cancels the other out. You no longer have any contracts, just your profits or losses. In this case, you've earned, in trader talk, 3 handles, and how much money you've made depends on what you're trading. Tara's boyfriend, Tom, walked me through a recent volatile day in the Futures market: in Bond Futures, if you bought one contract, which is the smallest amount you can trade, and you bought it at the lowest point of this particular day and then sold it at the highest point, you would have made $312; in the S&P 500 pit, if you did the same—bought one contract at the day's lowest point, then sold at the highest—you would have made $3,000; and in the Nasdaq pit, you would have made $8,200. Tom traded the S&P Futures, a job he often termed "a wild ride." Despite this, he chuckled. "The Nasdaq pit makes everything else look like kindergarten."

One night, while flipping through cable channels, I caught a short documentary about the history of the Market that summed it up this way: "Charles Dow put us on the wildest roller coaster. We laugh nervously all the way up, we scream like hell all the way down. And then we line up to do it again." This was around the time that I had learned just enough about trading to start becoming scared. Trading is an elaborate poker game. At its core, it's a study in human behavior. It's about being able to read and predict others. How will the Market—the public—react to breaking news? To economic reports? To weather conditions?

In theory, the Market should be determined by supply and demand, and perhaps it used to be, but now it's about two things: good old Fear and Greed. The powers vie against each other like a tug-of-war. As a trader, it's like pushing your right hand against your left. Greed and Fear. Fear and Greed. Will one arm ever overpower the other? There most definitely is an art to trading, and it lies somewhere between these two emotions.

But one thing connects the two: if, on a spectrum, Fear is on one end, and Greed the other, what occupies the place in between is Risk. This is the area where most traders reside, most of the time. Futures traders are people who are willing to risk everything for the chance at hitting it big—every day.

Trading is an ode to true capitalism. And, to many, an ode to self-destruction. With Futures if you're making money, you're making more; if you're losing, you're losing more. And because of this, there's a spark on the Futures Exchange trading floor that I have never felt anywhere else. It grabs you. It also scares you to the bone—man or woman. But as a woman, you have to really want it to be able to survive. Ironically, for all that behavioral science tells us, the makeup of a woman—the way she makes decisions, the way she sees the world and its consequences, and the way she rationalizes— stands to make her a better trader than a man. Yet, the good ol' boys' club that's the pillar of the trading world stands to keep her out, or at least to intimidate her to the point that she won't want to come back.

Take, for example, the male trader's philosophy on standing his ground: if you want to be respected as a trader, you have to throw a punch or two. They all agree, it's worth getting fined. They have all, at one point—or at many points—punched, elbowed, spat on, kneed, pushed, shoved, cursed out, tripped, or stabbed another trader with a pen. They've all been fined. They readily admit they'd do it again if the situation—such as someone stealing their trade—ever called for it. A few-hundred-dollar fine—even a few-thousand-dollar fine—to show everyone who's boss, that you won't take anything from anyone, was well worth it. Chalk it up to a business expense.

I also detected a lot of resentment toward those women who did stick it out in the pit, and the men liked to credit these rare successes with "unfair" advantages, such as the fact that a woman's voice could distinctly carry over the din. Especially one woman, whom I'll call Mega, as in megaphone. "Hers wasn't a voice, it was a nauseating screech, fingernails raking across a blackboard," a trader told me. "That voice would ride up above the pit, you could almost see it."

"If [Mega] was a man," another trader said, "I would have punched her."

But Mega made quite a living off this voice. She used to get trades just to shut her up. She'd be screaming prices and traders would turn to her and say, "Fine, I'll give you the trade, here, take it, just close your mouth and keep it closed."

Of course, the men also felt that women had other opportunities for leverage on the trading floor. As one man said: "You show up in a push-up bra, and you'll get whatever you want."

I had no choice but to marvel at the degree of unrefined brutishness that marked this male-driven world. I viewed trying to break in as a personal challenge that, theoretically, I—as well as any woman in this day and age—should be able to accomplish. And yet, I couldn't help but question: did I really have it in me to make it in this world? The truth, while provincial-sounding, and certainly not politically correct, was that I honestly didn't know.

TWO

Get into a Position

When you enter an order into the Market—that is, if you buy or sell at least one contract—you are taking on a position. Once you're *in*, your goal is to pick the most opportune time to *get out*. You can hold or ride a position, and if you're making money, you've got a winning position. Of course, that can change in a matter of seconds.

The entrance to the Futures Exchange has always been viewed as the golden door. Aspiring traders look upon the Mercantile Exchange much the way immigrants do America: inside, a better life awaits. But the world of Futures trading is rather insular and, for the most part, you need to know someone to get in. Sure, there are those who winged it, but typically, you need some sort of connection, even if it's loose—as in the case of the maintenance guy at the Mercantile Exchange, who, after gleaning enough knowledge from observing the pits while sweeping and changing trash bags, began to call in trades to a broker. In a short while, he made enough money trading to quit his janitorial job and trade full time.

Mostly, though, everyone who works on the Floor knew somebody—a cousin, a friend, an uncle, a neighbor—or they're second generation. Nepotism is a way of doing business in this world: seats are handed down, given as gifts for birthdays, graduations, or, in the occasional instance, to the wife as part of a divorce settlement.

A few women traders I'd later come to know got their *in* by being "discovered," oddly enough, through their jobs as bartenders. One such woman, Denise Hubbard, a former model, was spending her summers at the wealthy resortlike town of Lake Geneva, Wisconsin, teaching tennis during the day and bartending at night. A lot of traders keep summer houses in Lake Geneva, and Denise got to know them through the bars, one of which was owned by a Pork Belly trader and aptly named "Hogs and Kisses." The bar Denise worked at was a tiny place on the outskirts of town that was charming in its outdatedness—there wasn't even a cash register. Denise would have to add up the tab in her head. "The traders would always get on me about how the bill wasn't right," she told me. "But I'd add it up right in front of them and it would be right to the penny. They were impressed and said I should come clerk for them." The traders invited Denise to visit the Floor. She made the quick trip with them in their private jet and watched them trade for just a few short hours before they took her to lunch, and then hopped back on the plane. How could she pass up a workday like that? One of the traders recommended Denise for a job with his firm, which was hiring clerks whom they would train to become Options traders. Not only did Denise have no idea what an Option was, but the firm had never before hired a woman. But Denise proved she was smart and a quick learner. She was given the job and went on to become a successful trader in Deutschemark Options, earning her firm, and herself, a lot of money.

Another woman, Jen Klehr, was bartending at a restaurant in Union Station, down the street from the Exchanges. Traders would often stop in before catching their afternoon train to the suburbs. "The traders would give me $50 tips," Jen told me, "but they think because of the money they can treat you like shit." One trader in particular always harangued her, and one day she snapped, spun around, and shouted at him, "If you don't like my fucking service, go elsewhere!" Right on the spot, he offered her a job as his clerk. Jen, in her black trader's jacket, badge JNN, now stood on the Floor, just outside the S&P Futures pit, placing trades through a pit broker.

My *in* was Tom, who leased a seat at the Mercantile Exchange. When he offered me a position as his clerk, I jumped at the chance. Tom, like most traders, had also started off as a clerk, working for a friend of the family. He then got his own badge and traded for a brief stint in the S&P Futures pit. These days, he traded the computerized version of the S&P Futures from home, on a system called Globex. He had a vast setup: four computer monitors to display different charts and graphs, and two TVs, one tuned to CNBC, the other to CNN. Tom could trade from the Floor if he wanted to, and there were tiers of traders on Globex machines who did. But he preferred his method, where, rather than watch the action in the pit, he could trade off the news and could do so in sweat pants. Besides, with the influx of computerized trading, there were currently no available Globex terminals on the Floor, and a six-month wait list was dozens of names long. But Tom was doing well at home. He was twenty-eight years old and, working between the Stock-Index Futures hours of 8:30 a.m. and 3:15 p.m. (although he often trimmed it to more like 8:30 to noon), he typically netted over a thousand dollars a day.

My responsibilities as Tom's clerk would be to call him from the Floor and give him a read about what was going on—Was it quiet? Was the pit full? Half-empty? Who was in there, was it the big guys? And also, he added, I would need to keep him up to date on Floor gossip. "I'm just a dull guy who sits in a box all day swearing at a bunch of machines," he said. "I need a little vicarious excitement."

Tom's reference to "swearing" was an understatement. Tara had heard his rambling, high-decibel dialogue from all the way down the hall, and couldn't bear to fathom what the neighbors in Tom's Evanston apartment building, just off the Northwestern University campus, thought. "You cocksucker! Go up, go up! Screw you! Fine, you want it, here, take it. Take it! Now come on . . . Come! On! Give it to me, come to Daddy. Noooo! You stupid bitch! Fuck! Shit! Fuck!" To Tom's credit, that was a bad day. A good day went something like this: "There you go, that's right, gotcha! And thank you very much! Now what's that you think you're trying to do? You just listen to me. You listen to Daddy, bitch! Yep, there it is! There! It! Is! It's mine! All m-i-i-i-ne!" He'd howl with a Dr. Frankenstein laugh.

Tom's demeanor was strikingly different when he was not trading. He was quiet and reserved, shy even, in most social situations. He was tall and lean, with dark brown hair parted conservatively on the side, and a clean-shaven, pale complexion. Tom was actually descended from a long line of traders. He could trace his maternal roots back to Robert Morris, a wealthy land trader who had financed the Revolutionary War. Apparently, Morris (whose signature appears on both the Declaration of Independence and the Constitution of the United States) was quite a character, putting himself in many a precarious situation—the money he gave to George Washington was money he had borrowed from France, the loans guaranteed against his own land. He was also a top candidate for execution by the British and, to top it off, was known to be a womanizer and philanderer—

he once broke his leg jumping from a second-story window after the husband of one of his lovers returned home unexpectedly. As the story goes, Morris somehow lost all his money and was tossed into debtors' prison, where he died without any of the wealth he had once accumulated.

On Tom's paternal side, his great-grandfather was an inventor and patented the bumper and the fuel gauge, although he missed the patent on the key starter by one day. He took the money earned from those ventures and started trading. In the beginning of October 1929, he sold the Market short, speculating that it was due for a downturn. Little did he know just how lucrative this move would be. When everyone was floundering in the Stock Market Crash, he walked away with enough money to fund a lavish life, and to set up trusts so that his family could continue to do so for generations. During the height of the Depression, he took his wife and six children around the world on a luxury liner. Back in the States, they lived ostentatiously, despite the country's economic despair—every day Tom's grandmother was chauffeured to school in a 1930s version of a limousine. As she grew older, she too became interested in the stock market. Her father taught her about it, and she ended up buying and selling stocks on her own, an unprecedented feat for a woman at that time.

And now, generations later, Tom had heeded the trading gene, the fire of risk that coursed through his veins, the pulse of the free market that echoed deep within him. He was compelled, driven, it was what he was born to do. And there he sat, shrieking at a bunch of screens.

$ $ $

"The Mercantile Exchange at Wacker and Madison, please," I said. "On the southwest corner." The cabdriver gave me a sideways glance. "Honey, you just say the Merc, everyone'll know what you mean."

I sank into the backseat. Lesson number one, from the cabbie (which would turn out to be more far-reaching than I'd ever have imagined): leave all formalities at home, it was *Merc* culture now. I watched the sights as we barreled down Wells Street toward the Loop. Chicago is a city rich with culture and tradition. It's a sports town, a blues town, a big, juicy steak town. It's known for its brutal winters and vicious winds; for Oprah and Jerry Springer; and, of course, Al Capone. It's carried the term "The Second City," and, in the financial world, it's considered the second Wall Street. But in Futures trading, Chicago is number one. While there are some eighty Futures Exchanges throughout the world—almost every major city has one—Chicago's Futures forum is the largest and the busiest. Take, for example, the Eurodollar Futures contract, which trades at the Merc: on an average day, the traders in the Eurodollar pit will trade roughly $1 trillion worth of contracts—*a day*; compare that to the Gross National Product, which is $1 trillion a year.

The traders in the pits, for the most part, are pure midwesterners with humble beginnings. You're not going to find many silver spoons; there are a handful of rich kids who come in with Daddy's money, though many of them quickly burn through it all. But the majority of the Floor's oldest generation are from the blue-collar Polish and Irish immigrant-laden southern reaches of Chicago, simply known as the South Side. Chicago's reign of Mayor Daleys are from the South Side, and so is the stereotypical Chicago accent, where "th" doesn't exist (it's "*Sout* Side"), and "the" is "da"; S's are Z's (as in *da Bearz*); the A's and I's are long and whiny; and the word for any kind of soda is *pop*.

I felt lucky to have Tom as my ticket in—only I severely underestimated the difference between having a connection to the Floor and having a connection who was *present* on the Floor, and who knew the workings of the place and could help me acclimate to the unfamiliar craziness. After all, I was used to being independent and doing things on my own, and I almost preferred it that way. Just the summer before I had traveled Europe by myself, and really, I thought, how much more difficult could a trading floor be than navigating a foreign country?

The process for becoming a clerk seemed rather simple: fill out the forms—name, social security number, d-o-b, any arrests or convictions—then have the trader or firm hiring you pay the $100 registration fee. However, I quickly learned that, in actuality, nothing at the Merc was simple. For such a powerful, important financial institution—the cornerstone of the trading world—it was amazing how disorganized the inner workings were.

At the main lobby information desk, a man in a security jacket directed me to where I should go to register: "Take the south bank of escalators to the North Tower. Don't take the elevator because you'll wind up in the South Tower. Then, turn west. Take the far bank of elevators to the ninth floor. Head south."

Riding on what I thought was the south escalator, I couldn't help but hear the conversation of the men on the steps behind me. They talked in their booming trader voices; they were loud, but at the same time raspy from years of shouting at the top of their lungs for six hours a day. One trader announced to the other: "I am going to go home, and I'm going to jerk off." I didn't turn around.

I watched trader after trader standing on the down escalator. They eyed me right back, a confident "I'm a Trader and there's a new *female* face headed toward the trading floor." The escalator was also punctuated by clerks, but somehow I'd already trained myself to look right past them. Instead, I saw the jackets labeled with the coveted trader ID badge: a big plastic pin engraved with a trader's two-, three-, or four-letter symbol, along with their name in smaller print. Usually the symbols have a connection to the trader's name—initials, which was what Tom chose; first letters of the first name, last letters of the last name; acronyms; anagrams. A trader is most often referred to by his badge—sort of like a throwback to his fraternity days when he was branded with a nickname that would have driven his mother crazy had she found out that her precious little boy was Budmeister, or Itch, or Alky (as in Alcoholic) to all who knew him.

Some ID badges I noticed were: BZRK "Berserk" (Bob Krzinsky); MOSZ "Moses" (Zak Moser); LOCO as in Spanish for "crazy" (Laurence Collins); BRU "Brew" (Becky Rudman). I glimpsed others that I tried to figure out, like a game of interpreting vanity license plates to determine how witty the holder: TITN, KID, TRZN, ADNS, KOJK, KRMA, UBET, BRVO, OHNO.

I finally reached the ninth floor of the south side of the North Tower. I saw one lone person there. "No English," he said, twirling a dustpan.

It took a couple more tries before I found the registration office. Tom was waiting for me, his hands in the pockets of his red trading jacket. He was understanding—he knew the way they gave directions around here.

In the registration office, a woman was smacking her gum and filing her inch-long fingernails. "Whaddya need?" she said without looking up.

"I need to sign her up to become my clerk," Tom said. The woman shoved a clipboard at us. She didn't raise her eyes, not even for a glance of acknowledgment. "Go in the hall, sit in a chair, fill it out," she said, filing away.

A row of classroomlike desks lined the hallway wall. All but one were made for left-handed people. "Is there some trader/lefty correlation?" I asked. Tom shrugged. "I'm a righty."

I completed the forms, and Tom and I signed on the line. I returned the clipboard. "Go down to three. That's where you need to be fingerprinted," she smacked.

We rode down to three. There, we were told the fingerprinting person was only in on Wednesdays. It was Thursday. We rode back up.

She was still filing. "They told us the fingerprinting person is only in on Wednesday."

"I know," she said. It didn't seem worth it to question what had possessed her to send us down there. I scheduled a fingerprinting time for the following Wednesday, 11:10 a.m. "And you can't be late!" she warned. "And you can't miss your appointment or you'll be fined! And if you need to change it you have to do that in person!"

"Just nod," Tom muttered to me. He'd learned the hard way. He had been given the same sort of runaround when he was trying to register to receive his Globex machine. He was sent back and forth from the North Tower to the South Tower, from the thirteenth floor to the third floor to the seventh floor, and three hours later—three hours, all so that he could sign a few sheets of paper and write a check—he'd lost it. He gave the office administrator a piece of his mind.

"I've been running all across this entire godforsaken block! No one here knows up from down! Isn't there anyone here with half a brain who knows one iota of what is going on?"

Apparently, the woman who got the brunt of Tom's frustration knew how to do one thing: hold a grudge. Numerous times, Tom's monthly checks have been "lost" or "misplaced" or "never received," even though Tom has hand delivered them. Because he depends on that machine, and has trades riding, any interruption in service could be lethal to his career. So now the attitude was plain and simple: Just nod.

Next up was the photo. I sat in an empty cubicle and stared at a digital camera. "Raise your head higher," came the voice from the other side of the partition. I lifted my chin. "A little higher." I lifted a little more, and presto!—there I was on a plastic ID card, chipmunk cheeks and squinty eyes, looking like I was caught in the upswing of a nod. But I now had my proof that I was a clerk of TPW, Tom Price West. However, I still had to watch a mandatory video before I could get my clerk's jacket. I was placed in a closet-sized room with one chair, a TV, and a VCR.

"Welcome to your first day," announced a former head of the Merc. He dated the video with his plaid suit jacket and glasses that took up half his face and magnified his eyes. The picture on the television was terribly grainy from the tape having been rewound and played hundreds of times, and the cast of speakers, aside from dripping with polyester and wide collars, were stiff and unrehearsed, with Deer Caught in Headlights stares and halting monotones. They introduced the rules:

- You must be neat, clean, and presentable.
- Your tie must be knotted above the second button of your shirt. (Again, dating the video—this rule had since become obsolete; men no longer have to wear a tie, but must wear shirts with a collar, although golf shirts do count.)
- You can wear tennis shoes, but you must wear socks.
- For women, no overly fitted stretch pants, no skirts shorter than two inches above the knee, no harem pants, no denims, no leg warmers.
- For men, no turtlenecks.

Next, a representative from the Security Team took center stage to outline conduct rules and violations:

- You must show respect for others and respect for all property.
- No throwing of objects.
- No excessive speed.
- You must not use speech that's intimidating to others.
- You may get hungry or thirsty, so you may chew gum or hard candy, but no other food or drink is allowed on the Floor.
- If there's an accident, you should be specific—you need to call security and tell them in a clear, calm voice that you saw someone fall and bump his head in the S&P Options pit.
- You must protect integrity and security.
- Clerks cannot trade.
- And, just a reminder—there's a ban on giving advice to nonmembers; it's against federal law.

After the video, I was entitled to my jacket. The jacket department looked like a huge dry cleaner's with racks of jackets, each grouped by color: rows of yellows, reds, light blues, navy blues, blacks, greens, turquoises. Red, the official color of the Merc, is the standard trader jacket. But often, traders like to personalize their jackets. They can pay a bit extra and choose a different polyester color, or pay a bit more extra and have the jacket made out of a mesh fabric that is more comfortable. They can also special-order a jacket with fabric they supply—plaid, stripes, polka dots, black-and-white checkerboards. Some traders view it as an asset to have a loud jacket. It helps them get quick recognition—"Yeah, I know him, the guy with the jacket with Froot Loops dancing all over it." A jacket also helps distinguish a trader in the pit. When you're among ten black and navy coats vying for the attention of one guy way on the other side, it doesn't hurt if you're the lone one in the crowd wearing fluorescent green. The jacket that I'd already determined took the prize was one made entirely out of silver sequins. Perhaps not coincidentally, the traders with the loudest jackets—the smiley faces, the multicolored patches, the sequins—seemed to be the loudest traders.

Clerks, however, have no choice when it comes to color or style. Every clerk is relegated to a basic, mustard-colored jacket. The woman behind the counter slid over a couple of clerk's jackets for me to try on. There were no S, M, L here. No, this was a man's world, so it was 40R, 42R, 42L. The 40R (the smallest they seemed to have) was the closest fit, although the sleeves dangled past my fingertips.

"You'll be glad the jacket's big," the woman behind the counter told me. "You're going to want to wear a sweater and you'll be able to fit a big sweater. It gets cold in there. All those men, they like it *cold*. Trust me."

My jacket looked quite worn, the fabric was softer than that of some of the others, but the color was washed out. I rolled the sleeves, their edges slightly frayed. I wondered how old my jacket was, and how many aspiring traders had slipped it on and suddenly felt a sense of belonging. The jacket held a definite power. I felt it as I did a little pivot so that Tom could tell me if it looked all right.

"Yep, you're officially a clerk," he said. I felt oddly proud. The yellow jacket gave me an identity, immediately placing me in a microcosm, a subset, a subculture. It was just a simple polyester piece of clothing, in the most drab—and unflattering—of colors possible, yet it would enable me to work at one of the largest financial marketplaces in the world. This jacket would allow me to stand next to those who were part of an elite group with the country's finances riding on their shoulders. With this jacket and my ID card with Tom's acronym, I not only could step onto the trading floor, but I could enter the pit. I could stand directly at the center of it all.

I wondered who had worn this jacket before me. A slight man? A woman with a sweater? Had she decorated the lapels with pins, as many of the clerks and traders do—good luck charms, buttons with sayings, smiley faces? Was she a clerk with the intent of becoming a trader? Or was she a clerk with an eye out for snagging a trader? Did she, as the rumors went, wear slinky tops that would be revealed when she slid off the jacket after hours in a private, upper-floor office?

"Cleaning's on the first Tuesday of every month," the woman behind the counter informed me. "You can keep your jacket here if you want, or you can take it home with you. Just don't lose it. The fine is $250." A rather hefty price tag, I thought, for a dingy jacket. But it wasn't about what a bolt of yellow polyester would cost to replace it, it was about the price of the privilege to be here.

And now, my big moment. I followed Tom through the metal detectors and slid my new ID card at the turnstile. The green light flashed. We headed through the entranceway onto the Floor.

Commotion was in full swing, and even though this was now my second time on the Floor, I was still overtaken by the sheer pandemonium of it: this Roman Coliseum, where it was kill or be killed; this human ant farm, this beehive, where everyone had a task and they'd crawl right over you to do it.

One of the rules I'd just learned from the educational video was: no throwing paper. Hurling a trading card in the air was a $50 fine, if you were caught. Yet, the pit was covered. The whole trading floor, for that matter, was covered with a mass of paper and trash. With the pace so frenetic, people simply threw anything unwanted—trading cards, computer printouts, newspapers, candy wrappers, Kleenex, half-eaten sandwiches (a violation of the No Food rule)—to the floor. No one had the time to do something as trivial as find a garbage can, and your hands needed to be free to furiously wave them overhead and signal the contracts you wanted to buy or sell. Everyone on the Floor walked with the newspapers and all the other crap collecting between their feet. It was impossible to try to step over it so you just dragged it right along with you. After the Market's close each day, janitors with oversized, swiveling mops typically filled eighty large trash bags. And then, the next morning, three minutes into the trading day, the Floor would be covered again.

Tom had his own jargon for the Floor. "Ah, look at all the Merc jerks," he said, breathing in the sweaty-gym odor of the place, and oddly loving it. "Over here we have the Spits and Pukes, or the Spooz." He pointed to the S&P 500 pit. "And back there is the Spazdaq." Otherwise known as the Nasdaq pit. "Now," Tom said, "are you ready?"

I followed him as we weaved in and out of the swarm. In a few steps I was past the row of clerks who were positioned along the outer rim of the pit. I was past the metal rails, and past the pulpit with the price reporters. I was, suddenly, smack dab in the middle of one of the busiest trading pits in the world.

We stood in what's referred to as the soup—the lowest level of the pit, and the most undesirable spot, where all newcomers must start out. In the soup, you have no sightlines, which means you can't see who's trading and they can't see you. Sightlines are essential in the age-old system, where trades are initiated by eye contact and finalized by a bunch of rapid-fire hand signals and a nod. The ascending steps of the pit that surrounded us are designated—although unofficially—for brokers or those traders who have made it to the top leagues.

We were all shoulder to shoulder, the traders jumping and screaming and furiously waving their arms above their heads, twisting and shaking their hands in odd gestures. Spit spewed forth as they shouted orders: "Thirty on ten!" "Half on one!" "Seventy on five!" "Seventy on twenty!" "Sold!"

There must have been two hundred people in the pit, although Tom said it was a relatively quiet day. To me, it felt like a mob scene. Already I was being pushed and elbowed and bumped. I felt eyes on me. *Who's she?* You can't possess one ounce of claustrophobia in this field, or you're done for. I tried to imagine what the pit would feel like if there was a rush, if the Market took a sudden dive and mass hysteria broke out. I wanted to shield my head at just the thought of it.

I'd heard a story about the level of insanity that could be reached in the pit on a busy day. In the mass of elbows, arms, and bodies, a broker—who'd come to be infamously known as the "Pit Viper"—had his trading deck knocked from his hands, and all the cards with his customers' orders scattered across the pit. For a broker, this was not a good situation—his customers had buy and sell orders that he was contracted to execute, only now the orders were under everybody's feet, and the Market was zipping past the customers' specified points. The broker was crazed, his career was littered across the floor, nothing more than trash under shoes. Frantically, he crouched down, trying to collect the cards, dodging legs and pushing people to lift their feet up. No one was being very helpful—how could they, they had their own careers, their own fortunes on the line; and besides, if it was someone else with this bad luck, would *he* have been squatting down to offer assistance? Would he have even noticed? But it wasn't someone else, and he decided to hell with all these people who wouldn't move out of his way. He lunged, digging his teeth into flesh. He bit their legs, he bit their backs; he gripped so deeply he drew blood. The victims lurched, and the others scrambled to get out of his reach, and that's how he ultimately reassembled his cards. That's also how he came to be called the Pit Viper.

As I stood in the pit, I noticed only one other woman besides myself. She was on the second step, and popped in and out of my sight as the men blocked her. She was petite and was trying to add some inches to her short frame with chunky platform sneakers. Still, she was straining and bobbing and craning her neck. While the other traders merely had to wave their arms to make a trade, she was swaying, ducking, trying to peek under, through, around, and in between armpits. The entire time I watched her, she didn't open her mouth once. My attention was diverted as a trader next to me spit right onto the pit floor—just missing my shoe—then resumed trading. I stared at the pool of saliva.

"A little too close to the action for ya?" Tom chuckled. "Don't exactly want to see people who were sweeping gymnasiums last year dictating the swing of the Market?"

Tom's first day in the pit, back in July 1998, had been during the Asian crisis, when Asia's economy went into meltdown, and the international economic unrest rippled into the S&P Futures pit. Tom had sold a small number of contracts to a trader he knew, who had bought them as a favor to the new guy, and then suddenly, with news regarding Asia, the Market shot down. Tom's nerves seemed to pulsate, and when he began buying the contracts back, his voice was cracking like a preteen kid's. "Buy-eee O-o-ne!" He ended up making $2,500 in a few minutes.

"That was it, one trade, and I left," Tom had told me. "I thought it was a gift and I didn't want to press my luck. It sounds like a joke now, but when you're brand-new and you make money like that, you don't want to get greedy." Shortly after that came the Russian Ruble crisis, keeping the Market extremely volatile. Futures traders, in actuality, love crises. Large leaps or dips in the Market provide all the more opportunity to make money. You can hop on and ride—making money as the Market shoots up, making money as the Market U-turns and barrels down. But to a new-comer, it was a terrifying time to begin trading—with such rapid, erratic swings it was easy for an inexperienced trader to get wiped out in a single day. "I was so tense and nervous that I didn't trade a whole lot," Tom said. "But when I did, I was lucky enough, and studious enough, that I ended up making money."

Tom didn't much like it in the pit, probably because he felt similar to the way I did—intimidated, out of place, and downright scared—and I didn't even have money riding on anything. In the soup, he was far away from the brokers and couldn't easily get the trades he wanted. Besides, there was such rigmarole with errors, which are called out-trades, where people renege on trades, or insist they didn't trade with you, or that your price wasn't recorded correctly, or that they actually traded with the guy next to you and, too bad about the confusion, but you're going to have to eat it, and Tom hated all the bickering. He also disliked the notion that his reward for working his way up, up, up to the point where he was in with the brokers— aside from the fact that it'd likely take years—was that he'd have to live by quid pro quo. "They'll give you some fluff trades, but they'll expect you to take some orders when it's busy, or when they're in need. You've got to scratch their backs too," Tom explained. "And then there's the gray area, and that can lead down the slippery slope where there's corruption, and I can't guarantee that I wouldn't have gone that way."

I was surprised to hear him admit this. "You really think you would have done illegal things?" I asked.

He smiled guiltily. "I know I'd be tempted. Really, really tempted."

"What about now?" I asked. "Now that you're older and you've earned your own money?"

Again, the guilty grin. "Yeah, well, all that temptation, even now."

I wasn't quite sure at that point just what the "gray area" consisted of; of course, I knew money had nefarious power, but I couldn't yet conceptualize just how possessive it could get in an arena full of die-hard capitalists. I had not yet witnessed greed embody somebody. But I figured my lesson would likely come soon enough, for so far I only knew one trader, and he had just confessed that he doubted his own moral fortitude in this environment.

Tom led me out of the pit. He knew he wasn't going to make any trades, and he was starting to get uncomfortable with the both of us standing there doing nothing, our faces familiar to no one. In many ways, it was desirable to stand out on a trading floor; in other ways, it wasn't, and Tom had warned me that people here were often edgy. He claimed it stemmed from the FBI busts—Operation Hedgeclipper and Operation Sourmash—that occurred in the late 1980s, where undercover federal agents masqueraded as traders and eventually indicted almost fifty people on charges of illegal trading here and at the Board of Trade. And even before that, in the late 1970s, a dozen people at the neighboring Chicago Board of Options Exchange were arrested for cocaine possession after Drug Enforcement Agents conducted a yearlong undercover investigation called Operation Candy.

I followed Tom across the Floor, picking out what traders *did* want noticed: their off-the-wall jackets—a red jacket with cue ball–sized polka dots; another, with twisting grapevines, the owner, it seemed, a wine connoisseur; an equestrian jacket with horses show-jumping; an all-white jacket, making the trader look like a doctor, as if he were, in a roundabout way, fulfilling his mother's dream of her son wearing a prestigious white coat.

One thing was for sure, a trader's physical appearance was not highly valued. Showering in the morning, in this profession, seemed optional. Some subscribed to the mentality that the more offensive you were—in particular reference to body odor—the less you would be bothered in the pit, the more space you might be granted, and the more likely it might be for you to get a trade just to get you to shut your mouth or move a few inches back. It was a rather disgusting philosophy, and certainly not one adhered to by all, or even most, of the traders, but there were those die-hards who consistently rolled out of bed and directly into work. Of course, there were also those who shunned this extremely casual attitude, and they would arrive with shined shoes, slicked hair, and manicured nails. But for the majority, it was khaki pants and sneakers, an outfit that had become such a force of habit that traders think it's an acceptable dress style outside the Floor, as well. It's the trader version of your father's black dress socks worn with sneakers, or of tube socks pulled to the knees—style blunders that make others, especially women, groan, but in the eyes of the wearer are perfectly fashionable.

As Tom and I headed up the winding steps, heads turned, as if these men had never seen a woman before. I'd heard they rated women with trading hand signals—only I wasn't yet conversant enough with the signals to know if they were doing it. At last, on a high tier, we found two empty seats at computer terminals. From here, I could look out over the action, taking in all that was going on below. It was oddly peaceful up here, and what had seemed a swarming mess below began to morph into something more along the lines of a symphony. Everyone had a different piece, but they all had to play to the same tune. With Tom's guidance, I traced the positions in this orchestra: the brokers on the top step of the pit, along the rim, were like the conductors. They traded large sums of other people's money and were referred to as the Paper. They typically worked for large brokerage firms and often executed orders large enough to move the Market. But these brokers only delivered the tune, they didn't write it.

The musical notes, in the form of orders, originated across the Floor, where rows of phone clerks received calls from customers. With a series of rapid-fire hand motions, the phone clerk signaled the order to another clerk standing outside the pit. That clerk would then give the order to the broker in the pit, who would trade it with the Locals—those like Tom who traded for themselves. "That's why traders standing next to brokers in the pit are in hog heaven," Tom said. "If brokers need to get rid of stuff, Locals can often buy way beneath the Market. Those Locals right next to brokers, they buy, sell, thank you, thank you. Sell it, buy it, thank you, thank you. It's all green, green, green."

I asked Tom about the numerous traders in the pit and at the computers who were wearing headsets, and he told me they were communicating with one another to buy contracts on the computer and then sell them in the pit (or vice versa) to profit from price discrepancies. Of the traders on the computers, I noticed a few women. They, along with the short men, stood on stacked phone books or reams of paper so they could see down into the pit. One trader at a computer was clipping his nails, the trimmings falling to the floor.

Back in the pit, a trader swung from the railing, shouting in beer-vendor cadence, "Anyone got anything?" Another guy in the pit was doing a little dance, shaking his bottom and strutting to a song only he could hear. Suddenly, a trader rose above the pit, as if he were levitating. He had climbed up on the pit railings, and his clerk was steadying him by grasping the back of his jacket. The trader towered above everyone's heads, suspended by a single arm jutting from the crowd. He began waving his hands like he was preaching. The other traders around me at the computer terminals paused to watch the spectacle.

"He thought he had made a trade, but no one is claiming it," Tom explained. "So now he's screaming."

"Even more than usual," the trader on the other side of Tom added. After a few more oversized gestures, the trader disappeared, as if he had been swallowed back into the mob. Tom and I watched the action for a while longer. To me, everything going on in the pit was meaningless. I had no idea what the signals translated to, and I couldn't distinguish what anyone was saying, it all blended into a collective roar. I tried to focus on specific traders and to follow them through a few trades, but the whole scene was so overwhelming and all the motions were so instantaneous that I couldn't even zero in. "Slow day," Tom said, shaking his head.

"Fucking molasses," the trader next to me said. Then he turned to me. "Sorry about the language."

I wondered how long it would take before I could appreciate that this was, in fact, a slow day. How long before I could look at all the electronic reporting boards that lined the walls and, rather than just seeing rows and rows of thousands of glowing numbers, actually glean information? How long before I could watch the pit and be able to understand what was going on? How long before this place didn't make me feel bamboozled?

A misfired trading card soared through the air and landed at my feet. People scattered unused trading cards for the hell of it—if they made a bad trade, whoosh, they whipped a card to the floor. If they made a good trade, they threw it like a Frisbee to celebrate, and at 3:15, the end of the trading day, as the series of boxing-match bells sounded, they ripped their extra cards in half, and in half again, and tossed them into the air like confetti.

$ $ $

Despite my yellow jacket and my ID card, I was not yet an official clerk. In order to become one, I had to take a test on the first Friday after I'd been signed on. If I missed the test, there'd be—surprise—a $250 fine assessed to Tom.

I had the handbook from which the test questions were supposed to be derived, and it was chock-full of everything from hand signals to all the different types of orders—a Market order, a Limit order, a Market-if-Touched order, a Fill-or-Kill order, a One-Cancels-the-Other order, a Market-on-Close order. Of course, they were all designated with acronyms, so I found myself in alphabet-soup hell: what's an MIT, FOK, OCO, MOC? It was like learning to speak a different language, especially since I had no prior experience in the Market, and couldn't quite grasp the big picture of how everything fit together. I began to wonder if there would be a fine for failing the test.

I called Tara for help, even though I knew she had the tendency to be roundabout with explanations. "What's the difference between a Buy-Stop order, a Limit order, and a Stop-Limit order?" I asked.

"Well, the first thing to keep in mind," she said, "is that you don't have to own something to sell it." This wasn't helping.

I called Tom. "You know I'm not good at explaining things," he said.

"I know. I'm desperate."

He thought it funny that I was finding all of this quite difficult to comprehend. "Didn't I notice a couple of framed degrees hanging on your wall?" he teased.

"Yes," I snapped. "From utilizing the other side of my brain."

Several years ago, a large trading firm at the Merc had participated in a study to see if specific qualities of successful traders could be pinpointed. Everyone in the trading firm was given a two-hour test that combined number questions, reasoning problems, an interpersonal skills sections, and analytical-thinking questions. The results were surprising: the top trader—the guy who consistently made the most money in the pit on an annual basis—scored the lowest of the entire firm; and, with due justice, the worst trader of the firm earned one of the top test scores.

While this outcome may have been reassuring to others cramming for the trading test, it worried me all the more, for I was the type of person who'd choose an essay question over multiple choice any day. I liked to analyze and ponder and debate. I liked problems with more than one correct answer. It was becoming clear that these were not the qualities that made one a good trader. Trading was the epitome of objectivity. It was Up or Down, Buy or Sell, Yes or No. What had I been thinking when I got myself into this? You needed to have an ease with numbers (which, admittedly, I didn't), and you needed to be okay with making a staunch decision based on very little information (I really *liked* information, and I *liked* collecting it, so much so that I was quite used to the comment "You sure do ask a lot of questions"). Certainly nothing I'd ever learned academically was relevant now, and the more I tried to memorize the manual, the more I realized that the things you needed to know for trading were things you couldn't cram for. I might as well have tossed my elaborately constructed, painstakingly pored-over master's thesis out the window, for it seemed to me that the number one most vital skill for a trader was: street smarts. Followed in a close second by: quick reflexes.

Tom offered me final words of wisdom: "The one thing you can count on at the Merc," he said, "is that there is *always* someone more stupid than you." Banking on that—and realizing that if I did fail I was out nothing more than the $100 registration fee, and several weeks of taunting from Tom—I headed, unprepared, to the Merc on Friday. I made a point to arrive early because the one thing I had learned was that the chance of getting lost on the way to the assigned room was great.

From the elevator I followed the stream of yellow jackets to a classroom on the third floor of the North Tower. Most of the clerks looked to be in their early twenties, if that. The women played with their hair, or primped in compact mirrors. The men fidgeted, or stared blankly into space. There was a lot of hairspray, piercings, and acne. Only a few—me included—had the handbook opened.

"Do you know what's going to be on this thing?" one clerk with spiky hair asked another with eyeliner out to her temples.

"It's hard. I already failed it once," the eyeliner clerk replied. Some of the attendees were falling asleep, doing the rubber-necked head bob; others had relinquished and, with their heads down on the table, were drooling away. At 3:15, the time we were to begin, a short, stocky man with no neck entered the room.

"We're going to start a little late because there was a mix-up with the classroom," he said with a heavy Chicago accent. "Apparently, people are being sent to the wrong floor. *I* was sent to the wrong floor." He pulled up behind a table at the head of the room. "If you're sleeping, I'm going to have to kick you out." Groggy heads slowly rose. More clerks trickled in, until there were around twenty total; only five, including myself, were women. A slender man in a dark suit entered and silently took a place in the front corner of the classroom.

"Listen up," the instructor said, making me feel as if I were back in high school, where barking was the most effective way to speak to the class. "$138 trillion—that's *trillion*—is traded here." After this money-laden attention grabber, he introduced himself as the vice president of a brokerage firm and said he'd started out as a clerk, too. Then he introduced the suited man, the Head Officer of Trading Force Security, and turned the class over to him. The Head Officer seemed clever and sly. He, too, mentioned the $138 trillion.

"You're going to see firsthand what money does to the human character," he said. He let the words hang in the air for us to ponder. The clerk in front of me twisted his lip ring. The Head Officer then switched to military style, drilling rules and their corresponding fines. He distributed a revised rule packet, which contained a dress code reminder that emphasized key phrases and words, such as: "Form-fitting pants for females are acceptable only when worn with tops which cover mid-thigh or lower"; and "Anyone wearing clothing that draws unusual attention (e.g. bare midriffs or revealing blouses, dresses, skirts or pants) will not be admitted to the Trading Floors or will be asked to leave until the clothing is changed."

When I was on the Floor with Tom, I had seen a clerk in skintight leather pants and a crop top, her belly button—pierced—showing. As if he read my mind, the Head Officer acknowledged that there might be discrepancies. "The Committee makes the rules, but the cotton can be woven in many different ways," he said, then paused, as if it were a point of contention that had been brewing for years. The Merc was a self-regulated business, and the Head Officer seemed to be alluding to the difficulty of trying to discipline the same people who footed his salary. It was congruent to the private-school teacher scenario, where you have to find a way to keep the kids in line, while also keeping their high-maintenance parents happy. Only, on the trading floor, the kids and the parents were one and the same. The other clerks didn't care much about any of this and they shifted restlessly. With a long, final look at the bleary-eyed faces, the Head Officer retreated to the door.

The instructor waited until the door clicked shut before he rose halfway from his chair and leaned in toward the front row. "I want to make this as painless as possible for all of you," he said. "So we're going to talk about everything before I pass out the test. Now write this down, and if you didn't bring anything to write on, remember it: False."

Confused, I wrote "False" in my notebook. "Now," he said, "this is the answer for number . . ." He touched his chin with his index finger. It was the traders' hand signal for "Buy One." On it went until he'd covered twelve "possible" test questions. "What are the hours of the Eurodollars pit? What are the hours of the Yen pit?" He motioned with hand signals: 7, 20, 2. I wrote down: 7:20–2. "The Cattle is open from—" Hand signal for 9, 5, 1 (9:05–1). "Why? Because the hours of the Market correlate with the kill cycle of the animals, the same with the grain market and the elevators of grain. Moving on, a broker is a member who executes trades. This would be similar to question number—" Hand signal for 7. I scanned back to number seven, I had written: True.

When the test was finally distributed, the twelve questions looked an awful lot like the twelve "possible" questions we had gone over. I had lucked out, and I couldn't wait to tell Tom that I passed with a perfect score. Surprisingly, several students still managed to do poorly on the test. It was a bit unsettling, like when you realize people are allowed to miss a generous number of questions on their driver's exam and still be granted a license to get behind the wheel.

$ $ $

Over the weekend, I phoned a friend of a friend, whom I'll call Calvin, who had been trading Options on the Merc Floor for several years. Calvin had graduated from the University of Chicago and went straight into the pit. I was looking for advice and perhaps to strike up a rapport so that I'd have one person among the thousands whom I knew. "If I had a wife or daughter, I wouldn't let her go down there," he said to me. "It's a dreadful place. I mean just take me, I'm swearing all the time, my language has utterly deteriorated. I know how I fucking behave, and I'm one of the nice guys. It's like one woman for every hundred men down there. And it's no secret that a lot of women come down there because there are tons of men with tons of money. Likewise, a guy who hires a chick because she's hot, well, all I have to say is good for him. Good for both of them. They've got their motives defined all right.

"I don't like to talk too much about the Floor," he continued, "because there are things that go on in the pit that shouldn't, and they need to stay in the pit. Shadiness is anywhere that money is involved. There's so much room on a trading floor for indiscretion, for improprieties. Money makes some people turn into fucking assholes. Now don't get me wrong, I love my job, and I don't break the rules, there's no point, only bad things will come of it if you do. Some people have lines they won't cross, but others don't."

I wanted to press Calvin for more, but his diffidence was clear. He had no interest in telling me any specifics, and he certainly had no interest in looking out for me or being my buddy. Why should he, I supposed, when the trading floor was the epitome of every man—and especially every woman—for himself? I needed to accept that this wasn't going to be a straightforward, starting-a-new-job scenario where people would come to me to introduce themselves and wish me luck. This was a place where, if you screwed up, someone could come at you with a raised fist. This was a place where you had to project enough confidence that you didn't get taken advantage of, but not enough that you came off as knowing anything more than anybody else. This was a place where you couldn't care who was touching you, who was screaming at you, or who just knocked you over. This was a different world, and getting in—let alone fitting in—was going to be far more complex, far more thorny, and far more hardening than I had ever anticipated.

THREE

Whipsaw

When the Market moves up and down with seeming randomness, and you get caught in it all—buying the High, selling the Low, getting pushed here, tossed there—you're whipsawed. This type of market that jumps all over the place is also referred to as a choppy market, and one thing's for sure, traders hate choppy. After a whipsaw day, you'll hear traders moaning, "I got all chopped up."

Monday morning. I announced to the cabdriver: *The Merc*. The closer we got, the more brightly colored jackets speckled the sidewalks, as traders made a quick dash for a bite to eat before the opening bell. I'd never been on the Floor alone, but now I had my ID, my jacket, and I was, by all accounts, officially a clerk. I laughed to myself at how special I felt, despite knowing that my yellow jacket placed me directly on the lowest rung of the ladder, the bottom step, beneath the soup, a peon to everyone with a trader's jacket and a badge. But still, there was no denying that I now had something most people didn't: access to one of the busiest trading floors in the world.

I was all excitement and nerves as I hopped out of the cab in front of the imposing granite towers. A ragged man begging for change stood near the entrance, and I paused to watch trader after trader drop coins and bills into his tin cup—if you were going to panhandle, this must be the most prime corner in the city.

Through the revolving doors, across the lobby, and up the escalators I went, trying hard to look like I was confident—I wasn't yet striving for confident as in "I belong here"; merely, confident as in "I think this is the way you get to the trading floor." The other two times I'd been on the Floor Tom had led me around, and I was so busy looking at everything and taking it all in that I'd paid little attention to details such as right turns, left turns, and exactly how many floors up was the clerks' coat check? There was absolutely no way I could ask for directions here—"Excuse me, where's the trading floor?" I'd be ridiculed. So I resorted to my only other option: follow the crowd. I followed them up the first escalator, up the second. A man on the down escalator, in a black-and-white trader's jacket, eyed me the way he would if we were in a bar, then mouthed "hello" as we passed. I certainly didn't know him. I didn't know anyone here.

I noticed dozens of yellow jackets riding down from the fifth floor, so I headed there, where—sigh of relief—I recognized the coat check. The woman behind the counter was halfheartedly doing a crossword puzzle, looking about as bored as one could possibly look. I told her my number and she took my jacket from the hanger and handed it to me.

Opposite the escalator was a bathroom, and I stopped there to glance in the mirror at myself in my new jacket. By objective standards, I looked ridiculous—the jacket was too long, too boxy, too yellow. But this was the Merc, and here I looked just like every other clerk.

The roar of the Floor grew louder and louder as I headed back down. At the turnstile, I hesitated, half expecting my ID card not to work—but, there it was, the green light. "Have a good day," the security guard said. I approached the archway, took a deep breath, and stepped onto the Floor.

The commotion! The colors! The noise! People dodged me as I paused in the entranceway. I felt the overwhelming rush that I'd experienced both times before. Only now I also felt a creeping panic starting at my toes and inching up—where was I supposed to head to? Where was I supposed to stand? How was I supposed to navigate this place? I had no spot, no home base, unlike everyone else who was running around, rushing here and racing there. They all had a specified task, or mission, or single goal, whether it was Buy one! Buy ten! Buy one hundred! or, Deliver this paper here, now! I was completely lost—awkwardly in the way of it all, getting sideswiped and tousled, my hair blowing into my eyes as others bolted by. Forget my naïve rationale that I could navigate this place because I had recently navigated Europe by myself—at least Europe had maps and signs and general rules of conduct, and the most challenging thing was to remember to look the opposite way when crossing the street. Here, I didn't even know where to look, people were darting from every direction. The only thing that was clear was that I needed to move the hell out of the way, and quickly.

I pressed myself up against the wall. My first instinct was to find a phone, call Tom, and beg him to come to the Floor—immediately. But he was home trading, and I knew I shouldn't bother him when the Market had just opened. Besides, I could do this. Other women had done this, and I could—*would!*—do this too. I scanned the Floor, trying to get my bearings—okay, the S&P pit was to my right, the Nasdaq pit was back and up the winding stairs, Cattle and Hogs and other Commodities were on my left, and the rows of computers were straight ahead. I scanned the price-reporting boards—still a bunch of meaningless numbers. The only thing I could decipher was the line graph above the S&P pit that traced the day's movement—the Market had been leaping all over the place, but currently it was down. Now, relax, I told myself. I focused in on the music of the pits: Twenty on five! Half on one! Seventy on two! Seventy on five! Half on ten!

Just then, a tap on my shoulder. I turned to face a security guard, his citation book and pen poised. He informed me I was violating a rule: my Capri pants, which came mid-calf, were too short. I apologized profusely. "It's only my first day, I didn't know." The guard looked at me oddly, as if he wasn't used to people being so nervous and apologetic. "I'll let you off with a warning this time," he said. "But next time you'll be written up, and fined."

As he left, I turned around to a near head-on collision with a burly trader. "Watch it!" he growled, and shoved me with his shoulder as he barreled by. I needed a quick escape, and headed to the nearest doorway—the women's bathroom, where the anonymous stalls had likely provided a sacred refuge for many women.

As the bathroom door closed behind me, the noise of the Floor dulled. There was one other woman inside, a trader in a red jacket, and she was, of all things, brushing her teeth. She finished and rushed out, hardly noticing me. Not a minute later, another woman rushed in. She gave me a fleeting half-smile, then reached into the pocket of her black trader's jacket and, to my surprise, pulled out a little travel toothbrush. She hurriedly brushed her teeth, then raced back to the Floor. How odd—it wasn't as if the pit was anything close to hygienic, most of the men didn't even comb their hair, let alone break from the trading day to brush their teeth, even though they all seemed to relish getting in people's faces.

I took my time at the mirror, trying to figure out a plan of action, where I should go, where I should stand. As I deliberated, I didn't realize that I was, at that very moment, violating yet another rule that could cost me—rather, Tom—a $100 fine: I was in the *members-only* women's bathroom. My bathroom—the clerks' and the rest of the public's—was on the fifth floor, by the jacket check. Until recently, this members-only women's bathroom hadn't even existed. For years the men had their members-only bathroom, but the women traders would have to use the fifth-floor bathroom along with the clerks; clearly, leaving the Floor and riding the escalator upstairs was quite a disadvantage if you had a position in the Market. The bathrooms had been just a single example of the hierarchy of the Floor—a throwback to the caste, a ritual of upperclassmen and lowerclassmen. It was the Greek system of this particular work world—with pledges and hazing and initiation by fire into the brotherhood. There was, I would learn, no sisterhood.

Luckily, no one caught me when I left the bathroom, and from there I made my way up the obstacle course of a staircase to the computer terminals. Guys imitated a radar signal as I walked by. I couldn't find an empty chair, so I leaned against the rail, trying to look busy, or at least engaged, or at least not completely lost and terrified. I watched the worker ants in yellow jackets scurry through the colony of paths and tunnels and turns.

There are different types of clerks: runners, desk clerks, trade-check clerks, and—the highest rank—arb clerks, who communicate via hand signals. The runners and desk clerks are mostly employed by the Merc or by trading firms, such as Merrill Lynch. These clerks are not necessarily after a job as a trader; this is a minimum-wage job that also requires minimum thought. The trade-check clerks run around the Floor, verifying trades. They carry a stack of carbon-copy trading cards, where the trader has recorded numerous trades—namely, the number of contracts bought or sold, and to whom, and the price. The clerks yell out the traders' acronyms to each other, looking to match up their bosses' trades with the record of the person he or she traded with. "You bought five at seventy from RMBO [Rambo], right?" The other trade-checker confirms, "Yep, sold you five." They each cross off the trade on their card. Occasionally, there will be an error or a mix-up—the cards will represent two different prices, or one side will have no record of the trade. A discrepancy like this is called an out-trade; if not cleared, it's prime time for a full-blown argument between the traders.

These clerking jobs are purely routine. However, if you slip up and make a mistake you'll have hell to pay. Traders have no problem reaming out clerks, screaming at them for all to hear. Tom said he'd seen it happen many times—tempers would flare and a clerk's an easy target, especially if he or she was careless. As Floor legend has it, a broker once let loose on a clerk, verbally tearing him to the ground, then firing him in front of everyone. The clerk walked off the Floor, and thereby took his revenge—he left with a stack of unfilled customer orders tucked in his jacket pocket.

The clerks who use the hand signals, called "arb," tend to be treated more like equals. They are often the sons, daughters, or younger siblings of traders, and they are here to learn. For them, clerking is more like an internship or apprenticeship, and they are most often the ones who go on to become traders themselves. They shoulder extreme responsibility—it's their job to make sure orders quickly and accurately reach the trader or broker in the pit. Often, these clerks wear headsets to communicate directly with a customer or with their firm's trading desk. Sometimes, an arb clerk will be assigned a station, a sort of lookout spot, where they can keep an eye on other brokerage firms or various pits. From there, each clerk has a direct sightline to other strategically planted clerks, and they communicate with hand signals back and forth, sending important information via the rapid-fire arb assembly line into the pit. It is all about sightlines, and weird workspaces are contortioned using odd materials—I noticed one clerk standing on seven piled-up plastic stepstools; another balanced on three carpet-covered wooden platforms, stacked one on top of the other like building blocks, so that he could reach a shelf held by brackets that doubled as his desk.

I decided to perform my clerk duty and check in with Tom. Numerous phones are stationed throughout the upper tiers, and I picked one up and dialed his number. "You still in one piece?" Tom asked.

"Barely."

"Has anyone talked to you?"

"A security guard."

"You mean no one's hit on you yet?"

"Don't you want to know about Market stuff?" I asked.

"I think I'm done trading for the day," he said. "I made some money this morning and then started working on my car." Tom's car, a silver, fully loaded Corvette, was his number-one pastime. He kept the car so shined up with a special polymer wax that it glowed; he tinted the windows; he installed a top-of-the-line stereo; he upgraded every system to bring the car to its fastest standard; and he equipped the car with a Taser security system, which, if the interior was touched, would emit 50,000 volts. "But it's at a low amperage," Tom had assured me, "so it won't kill, but it could be entertaining." He carried a pager that would alert him if the Taser went off. Although Tom liked to think of his car as a "chick magnet," what it primarily seemed to attract was cops, and in the first week that he had the car, he'd racked up two tickets in the same day.

I felt a tap on my shoulder and turned to face a man in a pale blue jacket, which I knew signified a Merc employee. "You can't use this phone," he said.

"Which phone should I use?" I asked.

"I don't know, but not this one, this phone needs to be kept free."

"Who's that?" Tom asked from the line. "Tell him you're on with your boss."

"I'm on with my boss," I reported back.

"You have to use another phone," the man snapped, then walked away.

"Tell him to go screw himself," Tom said, as if it would be fine to just say that to someone.

Nearby, an alarm sounded—a Globex emergency. The traders started screaming: "My computer just cut out!" "I've got a position on!" "Who's going to eat this? I am, that's who!" "This is bullshit!" I ducked as the Globex techs hustled down the aisle. I couldn't hear Tom above the noise, so I hung up and slipped out of the way, to the back area behind the pits where the clerks congregated.

Newspapers, magazines, unfinished crossword puzzles, and candy wrappers were scattered around the clerks' area. There were cafeteria-style tables and stools, and about a dozen clerks hanging out, occasionally calling off traders' badges to check trades. But mostly, they were joking and roughhousing. Someone had an orange, and they were whipping it at each other, the orange growing more dented and leaky with each hit. One male clerk grabbed a petite female clerk who was passing by and wrapped his arms around her. "Don't worry, I'll keep you warm," he said. "I didn't know I was cold," she quipped, and squirmed free. Another woman clerk walked past me, choking me with her perfume. She had metallic gold nails, like claws, and her neck, wrists, and fingers were covered with brassy jewelry. It was like a little clerk clique in and of itself—and I was on the outside, leaning against the rails.

Not long ago, a friend of a friend named Darcy Cook, who'd been a desk clerk for many years, had told me how she'd eventually blended into life at the Merc and how the culture had become her culture. Her work uniform became Keds, a polo shirt, and khakis. Every pair of pants would inevitably develop a weathered strip that would eventually split in two at the precise spot where she leaned against her slab of desktop to take customer calls. Darcy never brought a purse to the Floor—there was no secure place to put it—so instead, she carried the proverbial Merc wallet: a trading card bent in half over your money, driver's license, and credit card. She learned how to project her voice from the diaphragm, how to throw a trading card with the precision of a dart, how to shoot a rubber band great distances, and how to whistle loud enough to get someone's attention. She also mastered the art of ubiquitous listening, where you focus one ear on one conversation and one ear on another. This comes in handy on the Floor when you have more than one person screaming orders at you. On Fridays Darcy looked forward to running over to a dive on Washington Street whose specialty was pizza puffs. She and the other clerks would get dozens of them and sneak them onto the floor.

"Whenever you came in with the combination of pizza puffs and vanilla shakes," she said, "it meant you were hungover." And, Darcy had me know, "the trading floor is the only place where hangovers and farts are applauded." During the summers, she, along with most of the Floor, would go to as many Cubs games as they could. "You know you're from the Floor," she said, "when you can shout for the beer guy louder than anyone else in the stadium."

About the only thing it seemed I had in common with any of the other clerks was the yellow jacket, but to them it made no difference. A few of the guys had smiled in passing, but the women hardly took notice, and if they did, they gave me an up-and-down look—hmpf, newcomer, we don't need another girl around here.

It was not uncommon for male traders to date female clerks. Numerous traders met their wives this way, although they didn't like to advertise that fact, as it perpetuated the stereotype. The stereotype, I was learning, worked both ways: the female clerks were pegged as gold diggers, mining their way through the pits. The male traders were pegged—or revered—as womanizers, taking clerks to nearby apartments rented for the sole purpose of a private after-work getaway.

At lunchtime I escaped the building and headed across the street to a packed burrito place. I realized I had forgotten to check my jacket, and I felt weird walking around in public in the yellow polyester. But when I entered the restaurant, a half-a-dozen others were in their jackets, too. It was odd seeing the unfashionable jacket away from the Floor, out in the real world. But I supposed that to anyone who frequented Chicago's Loop, it must become a normal sight. Tara had told me that when Tom first started trading, he loved walking around the Loop in his red trader's jacket. Once, when she was with him, they wandered into a bath and body shop near the Merc. A salesgirl raced over and, without even acknowledging Tara, began fawning over Tom, asking him what it was like to be a trader. "We were obviously in there shopping for me," Tara said. "He was even holding my hand."

"What did Tom do?" I asked.

Tara rolled her eyes. "He ate it up."

I ordered my burrito, but there were no empty tables, so I ended up sharing one with another woman clerk. I awkwardly introduced myself like it was the first day of school. She seemed disinterested, but indulged me nonetheless, saying her name was Tanya and that she was a clerk in the Currencies. I told her I was new to the Merc, and she offered up that she'd been there for two years, since she was twenty-one. I tried to make small talk, and asked her if she had ever made a serious mistake.

"Once," she said. "I wrote an order and it must have fallen on the floor, because I couldn't find it. So I wrote it again. Well, the broker had picked up the original order off the floor, and both orders got filled. It was a $2,000 error. He started yelling at me, and I started crying. Then he got mad at me for crying, saying, 'You can't break down under pressure!' " Tanya took a bite of her burrito. "Best advice for the Merc, keep to yourself. I'm friendly, but I'm not friends with anybody." With that, she crumpled up her burrito wrapper and tossed it on the remnants of her meal. "Don't worry," she said with bored cynicism. "Someone who looks like you will do just fine here."

I found myself lingering over my burrito long after Tanya had left. How was it that I had been so excited about getting on the Floor, and now, a few hours into my first day, I didn't want to go back? I had always considered myself relatively skilled at adapting to new situations—I'd chosen to attend a college on the other side of the country, where I didn't know a soul, and had loved it. I'd worked at a top television newsroom in Washington, D.C., and had no trouble quickly fitting in with that frenetic environment. I even had a stint working on Capitol Hill and had navigated that with enthusiasm. Why should this situation be any different? I hadn't felt fear dealing with professors, reporters, or congressmen. But the trading floor abided by none of the typical rules that governed most every other institution—as dissimilar as the other places I'd been were, there was still some degree of predictability, some level of knowing what to anticipate, and some familiarity with the expected decorum. But the Floor was an amusement-park ride, the kind that jerked you in every direction, and my ears were still ringing and my head still spinning.

After my long lunch, I did return to the Merc. Only, I avoided the Floor and instead navigated my way to the viewing gallery. There, I pressed my forehead to the glass as I looked out over the entire Floor. Even from up here the shouting was still audible, only it all blended together into an oddly relaxing, dull roar that lulled and crescendoed like ocean waves. I found it mesmerizing. The Floor was my fish tank, and I watched the guppies scurrying and the piranhas lunging, and the way all the different colors, shapes, and sizes merged in the massive space.

On one side of the viewing room was the gift shop, which carried everything from silk scarves, to yo-yos, to duffel bags, to golf club sleeves—all bearing the Merc insignia. Pigs and cows were big in the gift shop—there were pig and cow beanbag toys, pig and cow pens, pig and cow hats, T-shirts, sweatshirts—all in honor of the Pork Belly and Cattle pits.

On the other side of the viewing room a guide was lecturing to a group of tourists, the majority of whom didn't speak English. They smiled and nodded politely at the guide's pauses, even though he'd said something along the lines of "It's not uncommon to see fistfights break out in the pit."

"See those clerks in yellow jackets who are running around?" the guide continued. "They earn minimum wage. But the clerks on the outside of the pit, the ones doing all the hand signals, if they are really fast and have been around for a while, they can make up to $100,000 a year. The traders who trade for themselves can make or lose any amount of money, millions, sometimes, depending on how much they are choosing to risk. The brokers get a salary and a commission for every trade they make, which can be around a dollar or two a contract, and they can trade thousands of contracts a day."

Two American students, girls in jeans and crop-top T-shirts, with backpacks slung over their shoulders, had joined the group and were the only ones who seemed to comprehend anything in the lecture. They exchanged wide-eyed glances as the guide tossed out the fact that they were looking at some of the richest people in the country. One girl raised her hand. "Okay, I know this is, like, a little off the topic, but how do you become a broker? I mean, like, what do you have to study in college?"

"There are guys who've been down there for years and are very successful and they only have a high-school diploma," the guide said.

"Well, I mean, I'm gonna go to college," the girl said, "but, like, I just wanted to make sure you didn't have to go to business school or anything."

"I guess it might help," the guide said with a shrug, "but it's not necessary." The girls, unimpressed, exchanged "whatever" looks.

"Any other questions?" the guide asked of the tourist group. They smiled and nodded. The guide stared, waiting for a hand in the air. The sudden silence caused the group to become slightly unnerved, and they began whispering to one another. Finally, the designated speaker of the group looked up and smiled.

"Uh, sir . . . we would like . . . to know"—she motioned toward the Floor—"where are . . . the women?"

$ $ $

In most other fields, a woman works her way up; in this one, it's down. At the Merc, you start at the top tiers of the Floor where you are a low-level clerk. You don the mustard-colored jacket that announces to the world you are *just* a clerk. From there, if you are one in a thousand, you move down to the top levels of clerkdom, where you are near the pit and are allowed to deliver or arb trades that someone else—most likely a man—has ordered. If you survive this, you have a shot at getting your own badge, someday.

If that day does arrive, then you've made it down to the pit itself. You pick out your very own badge acronym and jacket color. Chances are you are being financed by a trader—again, in all likelihood, a man—who bought a Treasury bill that guarantees your seat. Often, that trader, in return, will take a percentage of your earnings; however, it's not uncommon for a trader to back someone with no strings attached—maybe the trader got his start that way, or maybe he thinks you have an exceptional aptitude for trading, or maybe he's taken a strong liking to you—whatever the case, if he's willing to risk that kind of money, it means he will not miss it if it disappears.

You put your jacket on for the first time, and it makes you feel like *somebody*. But your pride instantly vanishes as you enter the pit and hear the whispers about you—"How'd *she* get in here?" "She'll never last." You wade your way into the soup. It's sink or swim now, there's not much in between. Only, you've got it worst of all—you're the only woman in the entire pit, and chances are, you're shorter than most of the other traders.

If you've got what it takes to survive this, you can finally reach your one chance to rise. Your goal is an upper step of the pit, where you have sightlines, and where you're near Paper—standing next to these top brokers is key. If you can make it there, if you can secure one of these prime spots that, even though it's illegal to mark, everyone *knows* is yours, well then, you have arrived.

Of course, if you're a woman, and you've worked your way into the pit too quickly, people will raise an eyebrow. "Who's fronting her T-bill?" or "Who's backing her?" are likely euphemistic phrases you'll hear. No one will deny that there's never been any of that going on, but regardless once you've made it to the pit, the bedfellow issue makes little difference. You, and you alone, have to know what you're doing—and if you're a woman, you *really* have to know what you're doing—or you're dead. And broke.

It wasn't until 1967 that a female was allowed to buy a seat on the New York Stock Exchange, which christened her a member who was able to trade on the Floor. Although, for Muriel "Mickie" Siebert—bestowed with the title the First Woman of Finance (note: not the First *Lady*)—buying a seat was far from easy. Although she had been a top financial analyst on Wall Street for over a decade, nine out of the ten male traders whom she asked to sponsor her seat application refused; plus, the NYSE instituted a special condition before accepting her: she had to produce proof of a bank loan for $300,000 of the $445,000 cost of a seat—something no male trader had ever been required to do.

Around the same time, the Chicago Mercantile Exchange was hemming and hawing about opening their doors to women. The Merc Board of Directors was divided, and one member complained: "How am I going to concentrate if there's a woman in a miniskirt? And besides, if they lose money, aren't they going to burst into tears?" A decision was finally reached: the Merc bylaws would be amended to allow women on the Floor, with one condition—a dress code. Women's skirts could be no shorter than two inches *below* the knee. However, five years would pass before the first woman would actually step into a pit to trade.

In 1969, N. Leonard Jarvis, a financial expert with horn-rimmed glasses and greased-back silver hair, wrote a book called *A Woman's Guide to Wall Street*. It was the front-runner in addressing the growing interest in the stock market among women. According to the book jacket, the target audience was wide-reaching: from the housewife to the widow, divorcée, or single girl. In the book, Jarvis used many analogies to shopping, such as "Stock market fashions," and "Where to shop for Wall Street bargains." He even stated: "As a woman, you actually have advantages over the male investor. You probably have more leisure time in which to read, learn and make decisions. You have your feminine intuition and your basic knowledge of shopping and bargain hunting." Have we really come a long way (baby)?

In 1972, the first woman, Carol Norton, made a trade from a pit at the Merc. She fell into the business after making a deal with a friend, who happened to be Merc chairman Leo Melamed. She—an expert bridge player—would teach Melamed how to play bridge, if he—an acclaimed trader and innovator at the Merc—would teach her how to trade. Eventually, Melamed would go on to attain Life Master status in bridge, while Norton would make enough money trading to become a part-owner of both the Chicago White Sox and the Chicago Bulls.

I, however, wasn't making much progress. I quickly realized that if I was going to have any chance at survival, I needed to learn the language of the pits, and that I could no longer view the Floor the way the rest of the world did—as a chaotic mess, all that disorderly gibberish that could be glimpsed on CNBC. So I began memorizing the hand signals, called arb, from the trading-floor orientation manual. That part was quite simple—the hand signals for the numbers one through five are the basic counting-on-your-fingers signs that you'd teach a child, only the number three is done in the way that every preschool teacher would reproach: the A-Okay sign, with the index finger and thumb making a little circle and the other three fingers, including the pinkie, waving in the air. Numbers six through nine are the same as one through five, only they're turned horizontally, so six is your right index finger pointing left. Add your middle finger for seven, the "wrong" three on its side for eight, and so on.

However, memorizing the signals and being able to use them—let alone mastering them—were two very different things. It was like learning to speak a foreign language by studying vocabulary lists in a textbook, then trying to communicate with a native speaker who invariably talked circles around you. I practiced in front of a mirror, shouting out the numbers as I formed them. Of course, this was cheating, for I was thinking up the numbers my hand should form, as opposed to instinctively reacting to what the Market dictated.

As primitive as communicating via hand signals is, arb was a relatively new technology, so to speak, on the trading floor—one that revolutionized the way business there was done. It was the mid-1970s, in the Gold Futures pit, when arb began catching on. Gold was having a wild ride and customers would call in, looking to take advantage of the frequent—yet momentary—discrepancies in the price of the cash Gold market versus the Futures. Taking these quick profits from two related markets is called arbitrage, only in the time it took for a clerk to write down the order and run it to the pit and hand it to a broker, the opportunity was often lost. There needed to be a more rapid way to deliver an order from the phone clerk to the trading pit; thus the hand signals—dubbed "arb"—were honed and began to be used by other pits as well. Arb became the high-speed conveyor belt that did away with the mass of paper and decks of orders. Arb also turned out to be a more confidential way to conduct business because there was no written order waiting around on a desk for any competitor to sneak a peek at.

Through arb, you can communicate every action involved in trading. To indicate the number of contracts you want to buy or sell, you form the numbers near your face. One through nine are made with your fingers at your chin. For ten and above, you move up to your forehead and start all over again—vertical index finger tapping your forehead is ten, add your middle finger it's twenty, then turn everything on its side for sixty through ninety. For odd lots, like twenty-five, you're going to do two fingers at your forehead for twenty, then, in a continuous motion, bring your hand to your chin and do five. For one hundred, you make a fist at your forehead. If you're somebody big and important, you may need to do an order over a hundred; for this, you start with your hand at your forehead, making the number for how many hundreds and then adding on the fist. It's a fluid motion, so for two hundred, it's the number two, then a fist, both at your forehead; for seven hundred, it's the horizontal two, then a fist.

You now have half of what you need to communicate your order— you've got quantity, the number of contracts. But you still need a price, what you're bidding or offering for those contracts. This is done with the same signals, only in the air, with your arms outstretched above your head. You communicate the price in a type of shorthand by using only the last digits of the Market price. So if the S&P Futures are at 952.70, you look at the digits behind the decimal, and since this Market moves in even ten-cent increments, you can drop the last zero and shout "Seven!" while making the seven sign in the air. If the Market's at a round number, say 1,050.00, then you make the "even" sign, which is a fist in the air, and simply shout "Even!"

Before you put it all together, there's another vital concept to keep in mind: if you are buying, your palms face toward you, then you communicate price first, followed by the number of contracts. If you are selling, your palms face away from you, then you communicate the number of contracts first, followed by price. Think of it this way: if you want something (buying), you're bringing it all toward you; if you don't want something (selling), you're pushing it all away.

It all seems rather simple, right? I thought so, too, until I had Tom drill me with pretend orders. "Don't worry," he assured me. "We'll start with a small order so you won't lose too much money if you screw it up." That is, if I didn't screw it up too badly, and if I caught my error quickly, and if I actually could figure out how to reverse it and get myself out before the Market moved too much and left me in its dust.

"Bid four for one contract," Tom said. "And don't forget to scream it at the top of your lungs as you signal it." I made the four, only it was floating somewhere near my waist . . . where were my hands supposed to be? Oh yeah, in the air . . . I think. And what about the one contract? I wagged my index finger, realizing I might as well stick it in my ear because, by this point, the Market was likely long past four—it wasn't going to wait for Novice here. Tom was trying not to laugh.

"Okay, Einstein," he said. "Remember, when you're buying, you're bringing something to you, so your hands are in the air . . . there you go, make a number four in the air . . . with your right hand . . . and, you're *buying* . . . what do you do when you're *buying*?"

"Start with the price," I said, beginning to grow frustrated.

"What else do you do when you're *buying*?" Oh yeah, I remembered, palms inward; I turned my hands toward me. "There you go, Einstein," Tom said.

"Enough with the Einstein," I snapped. "And I know what to do from here." I brought my hand down into a number one at my chin.

"It almost looks like you want six contracts," Tom said. I straightened my index finger. "Now what do you yell?"

"Um . . . *four . . . on . . . one.* Four on one!" I finally had myself one contract.

"So let's say the Market goes up," Tom said, "and you want to sell your contract at seven and take your profit." Here we go again. Sell it at seven . . .

"Why are your hands in the air?" Tom asked. Oh yeah, I was selling, so I was pushing everything away from me. Hands at my chin . . . palms facing out . . . one contract . . . finger straight, don't want to be stuck with five short contracts . . . now push your hand into the air and make a seven . . . hello, short-term memory! Seven is a lopsided two. Now what do I shout? Um . . . "One . . . at . . . seven!"

It was painful how bad I was. I knew I was overthinking everything, and I tried to reassure myself by remembering what it felt like to learn similar skills, such as typing or playing an instrument. Like arb, these required an almost Zen-like state of mind, where your fingers had to automatically assume the proper positioning—and the moment you started saying the letters or chords in your head, your momentum would be lost. When I was first learning to type, I was distraught. I remember relentlessly practicing with a computer video game, where letters would zip across the screen and you had to shoot them down by typing them. I also felt frustrated when learning to play the guitar—and still did when learning a new song. I had to dissect each song and play only a few chords at a time, over and over, so that my hand would get used to the consecutive formations. With arb you needed to get to the point where the progression flowed naturally, almost unconsciously. Only then could you expect to coordinate your hands with your mouth with the numbers on the board with the hundreds of voices shouting in your ears. Done well, arb is an art form. "It just takes practice," Tom assured me. I decided I was going to need more than that. I needed the help of professionals. I enrolled in a one-day pit trading seminar at the Merc.

The Loop was oddly empty on the Saturday morning of the seminar, and it was even more odd to be the only one riding up the escalator at the Merc. No husky voices, no shouting, no constant din that grew louder and louder the closer I came to the trading floor. Of course, I was grateful that no one was around when I had to ride the escalator right back down, because, silly me, the escalators didn't go to the floor I needed, it was only the *elevators*, and only those from the *lobby*, and I must be sure to use the proper ones for the tower I wanted.

Finally at the classroom entrance, I was handed a sample trader jacket, which I was told I must wear. It was all stiff and starchy, and much too big. I was also given a name tag and told to choose a badge acronym. It was too early on a Saturday to be creative. I picked CARI. The classroom was full of men of varying ages—although most seemed under thirty—and only one other woman. During our brief introductions, however, she said she wanted to trade on the computer, not in the pits.

The head instructor, a short, energetic former trader, launched into his monologue. "This is the pros," he said. "It's not like you're captain of your high-school football team, or even your college team for that matter. It's the top league. Nine out of ten who try don't succeed. The ones who are left standing are there for a reason."

This was not the first time I'd heard such a grave statistic. It had been presented in various ways: 80 percent of traders last less than a year; 90 percent of beginning traders lose all their capital within a year; over 90 percent of all commodity traders fail.

The instructor told us to stand up. "Now you're going to repeat after me," he said. He bellowed from his stomach: "SELL ONE!" His order reverberated across the silent room. "Now you try."

Suddenly, everyone let loose: "SELL ONE!" Everyone, that was, but me. I assumed it would be like when a teacher tries to wake the class with a peppy "Good morning!" and the class responds in a weak, singsongy way. Of course, the peppy teacher gives them a second chance. "Come on, you can do better than that, put some oomph into it!" But this wasn't the case here, everyone was raring to go the first time around—full force into it, determined, brazen, not a bit of timidity. Except for me. It felt weird to yell like that, to hear my voice ring out in an otherwise quiet room. Especially when it was a female voice, rising above the collective baritone and floating on top of it, resonating for everyone to hear how unnatural, how different, how squeaky, and so very dissimilar it was from what SELL ONE was supposed to sound like. That was the lesson, of course, to prepare us for entering the pit, but it was surprisingly awkward for me, with my quiet voice that made me sound like a ten-year-old and that tricked phone solicitors into asking to speak with my mother. Even in situations when I needed to yell—for a taxi, or to shout to someone in a crowd—I always seemed to think I was louder than I actually was. And it was about to get worse.

The head instructor, along with several other instructors—a few of whom had on real trading jackets with real badges—led the class to the lower trading floor. Two of the course instructors were women. They were also both the daughters of the head instructor, although the older had actually been a broker on the Floor for several years. She was tiny, both short and petite, but had that no-nonsense, don't-let-looks-be-deceiving air about her that I imagined the Floor had created. She was wearing her old trading jacket, with her badge, TIGR, which some were pronouncing Tiger, and others Tigger, giving off two different connotations.

Since it was Saturday, the Floor was completely empty. The time-stamp machines echoed in the eerie silence of a place that was meant to be roaring. A few scraps of paper lingered on the floor, having escaped the giant, swizzle-necked brooms of the cleanup crew. For some reason, it felt as if we should whisper, and the instructors laughed, because I guess this was the response they saw every session, but could never quite grasp the logic behind it. This was a trading floor, you were supposed to be loud, as loud as you possibly could be, and here we were—especially me—all shy and unobtrusive as we headed into the abnormal, cavernous quiet of the Nasdaq pit. The instructors planted us directly in the soup, while they took top-step broker positions. I pictured the traders who stood where I was standing, flushed-cheeked twenty-five-year-olds, shouting their brains out, eyeing a spot on the step they could one day call their own. The Nasdaq pit is a medium-sized pit, crammed on Monday through Friday with around seventy-five men—and one woman, one lone woman, a veteran, who had traded elsewhere and had come to this pit when it opened, securing herself a spot, and status. But now, we students floated around in the soup, not sure where to stand or where to look.

The instructors doled out blank trading cards and demonstrated how to hold the deck in your left hand and a pen in your right, and how to make the signals without dropping anything. Usually, trading cards are printed with a trader's acronym and clearing firm number. One side of the card says SELLER, the other side, BUYER. Each side has five columns where the trader fills in: CARS (the abbreviation for the number of contracts), MO. (month, because this is Futures, and there are various contract months you can be trading), SELLER/BUYER (you fill in the badge of the person you traded with), PRICE (what you bought or sold for), and BR (bracket, a code that changes every fifteen minutes to help prevent falsified trades from being added at a later time).

We practiced making signals in the air, then filling out the cards— Quick! Quick! Quick! Can't waste time writing!—then throwing our hands into the air again. Now, do it faster—really, *really* fast! Just for the record, I learned that when you're shouting the price, only neophytes say things such as "fifty" and "twenty-five" and "zero." Unless you rather enjoy announcing to the entire pit that you are a greenhorn, you say "half" and "quarter" and "even." I also learned never to say "Bought it! Buy 'em! Bought 'em!" or any other spin-off, unless you wanted everything—that is, every single con-tract—that was being offered.

Then it was time for a game of pretend: pretend you're a trader, pretend this was real money you were trading—*your* money—pretend the instruc-tors of the course were real brokers. Ready, set, go!

And I was left at the starting gate, choking on dust. The others were off!

"Five on one!"
"Buy one!"
"One at six!"
"Sold!"
"Six on two? Six on two? SIX ON TWO!!"
"Buy two!"
"Cari, open your mouth!"

I flipped around, it was TIGR. Hey, why was she picking on me? She should remember how it felt to be new. She gestured to me like, "What the hell are you waiting for?" Fine, then, fine, I'd just *Buy one at seven!* Oops, that wasn't right. It was, um, give me a sec, *Seven on one!* There, I did it! *Seven on one!* And my hands did it too—lopsided two in the air, index finger vertically on the chin. I did it!

"Can't hear you!" she yelled at me.

Huh? But you're standing right there, TIGR, you saw me, and come on, you had to have heard me! Ah, but this was a game of pretend, pretend the pit was jam-packed, pretend everyone was screaming and vying for the trade, and I wanted it, I wanted it so badly it was going to have to start at the tips of my toes and reverberate through me, engaging my entire body, gaining speed, gaining momentum, gaining power, and my whole self had to be thrown into it, so that the sound waves that propelled across my throat would nail you smack in between the eyes, *SEVEN ON ONE!* And TIGR wanted me to do it like that right now, like all these other students screaming like wild banshees. Well, here goes . . . only, TIGR wasn't looking at me anymore, she was trading with someone else, and after she sold to him, she turned to another wild banshee, and then another.

"Cari, one at seven?" Behind me, a dark-haired, round-faced instructor stood with a trader jacket and a badge, TURK. "One at seven?" he asked again, staring intently at me.

"Yeah, I want one at seven," I said.

"Sold!" He whipped his hand like an auctioneer.

"Thank you," I said. He chuckled, for obvious reasons, this wasn't exactly the mind-your-manners environment. Pleases, thank-yous, you're welcomes were a ridiculous waste of time, and here, more than anywhere else, time was money, ticking away, ticking away. Turk gave me a wink. I smiled bashfully. Write it, he mouthed, and motioned like he was writing.

Oh yes, I had almost forgotten. I wrote up the trade on my card: "Bought: 1, Price: 7, TURK." And within the first five minutes of my pretend trading career I had learned an invaluable trading lesson, one that could simultaneously make or break me, one that went back to the primal laws of the nature of business, of give and take, of want and have, of supply and demand: befriend the broker who thinks you're cute.

Turk, it turned out, was as suave as they come, especially considering his age, which, he informed me, was quite deceptive. All I could get out of him was that he was the youngest member at the Merc, despite the fact that he could easily pass for somewhere in his thirties. The only son of immigrants, Turk compensated for his tender age by perfecting an anachronistic air: he professed his weak spot was chivalry; he had his trading jackets custom-tailored—no ill-fitting polyester here—so that they resembled sport coats, albeit garishly colored ones, such as orange; he also took considerable pride in his precise diction, along with his lapses into haughtiness. He had a gold trading badge, which is the most expensive seat a member can own (or lease), and which allowed him to trade in any pit under the Merc roof. He tended to gravitate toward the Pork Bellies, the Russell 2000, and the Currencies.

A couple of days after the seminar, Turk and I met for lunch at Pazzo's, an Italian restaurant across the street from the Merc. He was quite mindful to hold every door and to take my coat and pull out my chair and seat me. The restaurant was crowded, although no one seemed to look twice at Turk's bright turquoise sport jacket, likely because a telltale trader's badge was pinned to the lapel. We began discussing the seminar, and I told him that the head instructor had insinuated that I probably wouldn't make a great trader.

"In what manner did he do this?" Turk asked.

"Well," I said, "he told me I needed *a lot* of work."

"Ah, it's a man's world," Turk said, "because we men are afraid of women. Women are better traders. They have their heads on. They get in, get out. We have to move the Market because we're *men*. Why are most bids even? Because men like to raise their fists high in the air. It's a pose of strength!" He shot up his fists to demonstrate, paused for effect, then gracefully lowered his arms back to the table, where he interlaced his fingers and smiled at me as if he sensed that I was quite impressed.

I smiled back politely, then looked down at my menu. He pondered his menu as if it were a scholarly text, and then, entrée decision made, abruptly slapped the menu shut and even more abruptly discarded it at the end of the table, where someone would come and remove the bothersome thing. The waiter appeared and Turk ordered a tonic water with a twist of lime; I ordered an iced tea.

He described how his interest in trading had started with an enthusiasm for gambling. "When my classmates were trading baseball cards, I was trading Soybeans," he said. He quieted a bit when I asked him about his background. Reluctantly, he admitted that he'd grown up in the Chicago suburbs, but his pep returned when he said he had finished high school early and went to Cambridge—although from his ambiguities, it seemed he never graduated. He quickly changed the subject back to trading, and surprised me when he said he subscribed to several trading philosophies, one of which was the effect of the lunar cycle on the markets.

"You really think there's a connection?" I asked, trying to sound open-minded.

He delved into exposition about the tides and historical charts and the documented cyclical nature of the stock market. Far-fetched? I thought so, but it wouldn't be long before I learned that he was far from the only trader who earnestly believed in such forces, and that some of the most widely used technical trading methods were actually derived from much more bizarre correlations.

Our drinks arrived and Turk took a sip. Suddenly, his face contorted and he shoved the glass away from him as if the liquid was vile, putrid. He called over the waiter, hand shooting up in the air—a pose of strength! "This is soda, not tonic! Tell your bartender there's a considerable difference." He waved off both the glass and the waiter, then turned back to me. "I have a very discerning palate," he said. "And I will make you a bet that they will probably forget the twist of lime." He let out an acerbic snort. The truth was that he wasn't old enough to have anything much more than a twist of lime with his tonic—or soda, for that matter.

"So what drew you to the Merc?" I asked, in an effort to change the subject.

"You have two of the most dangerous things on a trading floor," he said. "Emotion and money. And when you mix them, it's exhilarating."

He said "exhilarating" as if just thinking about it gave him chills. I had
to agree with his choice of words. Only, for me, the exhilaration stemmed
from the fact that I was still quite terrified.

An awkward silence fell over our lunch, and as much as I'd hoped that
Turk would turn out to be someone who might help me adapt to the frenetic environment of trading, I wasn't exactly eager to enlist him as a friend
on the Floor.

As I picked at my pasta, I began wondering why I was so eager to make
friends. This was business, and that should be my only concern: learn the
business. But there was far more to this business than just the mechanics of
it. There was a definite rhythm—deft traders embraced it, felt it in their
gut; not-so-adept traders were oblivious to it, or inadvertently fought it.
There was also an underlying framework of social order, and I wanted not
just to understand the intricacies of trading, but to understand the intricacies of the Floor, and for that, I needed a mentor, a friend.

After lunch, Turk and I said a hasty good-bye, and he scurried back to
the Merc. I hung back, needing to gear myself up for my return. Despite my
longing to be a part of it all, the Floor made me feel like I didn't belong, like
I was out of place, like people were staring at me, or that I was going to get
in someone's way and get yelled at or cause an error—or, perhaps worst of
all, that I was going to trip on all the debris and make a dramatic, head-
turning, spectacular fall flat on my rear end. But I forced myself to return,
step on the escalator, swipe my card, and enter the rabidness.

That afternoon, I hung around the outside of the S&P pit. Everyone in
a yellow jacket along the rim of the pit was flailing his arms like someone
had just swerved in front of him in traffic. Sell! Sell! Sell! Their hands were
lurching, rapid-fire. I maneuvered my way through the mass of bodies.
"Excuse me, please," I said, and those who did notice, shot me an amused
glance at my attempt at common courtesy. I kept forgetting that here you
didn't say things like, "Pardon me for a moment." You said, "I gotta go take
a piss."

I felt an all-too-familiar tap on my shoulder: the floor police. I was
wearing open-heeled shoes. I apologized profusely (partly because it
worked last time, but also out of simple habit). I'd be let off this time, but
next time I'd be issued a fine. I squeezed myself in between a rail and
a young clerk with a headset buried in a mass of curly black hair. The

headset microphone was flipped up, and he was taking a little break, skimming the *Chicago Sun-Times*. He stood as he read, for there was nowhere to sit and nothing to lean on, and besides, he probably couldn't stray far from the pit. We struck up a conversation. "I'm going to start trading soon, but for a firm," he told me. "There's no better way than to learn on somebody else's money." I told him that I was trying to learn how to trade and was getting frustrated with how difficult it actually was.

"The more I appreciate it and get the feel for it, the more I can't understand how women do this," he said. I suppose I should have been insulted by his comment, but for this place, his logic seemed rather pragmatic. "See, look at that woman there," he said, pointing at the pit to one of the few women among hundreds of men. "See, she's trying to get an order filled, but she's overshadowed by that tall guy next to her. He weighs over two bucks easily." We watched her dodge in and out of elbows and shoulders. A shout soared above the collective roar from the pit: "Somebody have the balls to take me out already! Goddammit!"

"We are so much like animals," the clerk said. Then a voice came over his headset, and he turned to give a thumbs-up to a guy across the Floor. Without a second's hesitation, he flipped down his mike, dropped his newspaper to the ground, stepped back up to the rim of the pit, and his hands started flying.

Without him to talk to, I stood there for a while, looking lost. Eventually, I gave up and headed to the viewing room, which was quickly becoming my haven. I leaned against the glass. The introvert in me had superceded the wannabe trader. I rationalized that I needed to step out of the whipsaw and try to make sense of it all from a comfortable, *safe* distance.

I forgot that I was still in my clerk's jacket until I heard a man stage-whisper to his wife that that girl over there has one of those coats on and does she think he should ask me a question? He tapped me on the shoulder. "Hello, I'm Big Bob and this is my wife, Evelyn," he said with a thick southern drawl. He launched into more of a running commentary than a question. "I've only seen this place on the TV. Look at them, all those hands in the air! Well, I'll be! There go the fingers, look the fingers in the air, too! Looks like mayhem! Some nice man at the restaurant we ate lunch at, right there down the street, told me this was buy and this was sell." He turned his hands toward him, then away from him. "Look! Look, that one there is buying! And there's another one!"

"Ooh!" Evelyn cooed. "He must have gotten a good deal, lots of 'em look like they're lookin' to buy."

I wanted to say that while, from up here the Floor seemed like crazy, freewheeling fun and easy money, it wasn't as amusing when you were actually down there in the middle of it, getting thrown around in the turbulence.

"Well, look at that!" Big Bob shouted. "That one just gave a raspberry! Did you see that, Evelyn? A raspberry!"

FOUR

Fill or Kill

Fill or Kill is an impatient, daredevil order that a customer will give a broker when placing a large trade. It's common for the broker to shout the order in the pit three times. Let's say his order is 150 contracts, he'll yell: "150, Fill or Kill!" . . . pause for takers . . . "150 Fill or Kill!" . . . pause . . . "150 Fill or Kill!" If no one bites, the order is dead.

n front of me, on the up escalator at the Merc, stood a woman draped in a full-length, black mink coat. I assumed she was a trader, but she didn't step off the escalator on the level of the Floor. Instead, she rode up with me, to the clerks' floor, where she approached the jacket station and traded her mink for yellow polyester. She slipped on the clerk's jacket over her baby-doll T-shirt, which emphasized her pierced belly button and obviously augmented chest. We both headed to the bathroom, where she stopped to primp at the mirror, adjusting a diamond earring with her French-manicured nails. I awkwardly tried to make conversation, feeling as if I were back in high school—I, the gawky freshman, she, the experienced and popular senior.

"Have you worked here long?" I asked.

Without looking at me, she said, "I've been a trade-checker off and on for five years." I wished I could ask how she managed this type of upkeep on a minimum-wage trade-checker salary, let alone an infrequent one. Instead, I followed her out of the bathroom. She headed to the escalators going up. I'd never been on the upstairs trading floor, but I followed her anyway. Luckily, she couldn't have cared less what pit I worked in, or who I worked for, or that I even existed. As we walked onto the Floor, heads turned to acknowledge her with stares. A couple of men gave her a nod, but no one said hello. It seemed strange, like it was understood that either you didn't talk to her or she wouldn't talk to you. I tried to catch a name on her ID—either hers or her boss's—but with a terse "bye," she was off into the mass of clerks, climbing the steps to her spot.

So, this was the upstairs trading floor, and I was standing there looking completely bewildered. The only thing I knew was that I was facing the Eurodollars pit, the busiest Futures pit in the world. The pit, which ran the entire length of the trading floor, was packed with hundreds of people; it looked like a football field, with a goalpost of Market reporters at each end. I tried to pretend I had a destination, and I lingered along the stairs that led to a smaller pit jutting off the main one. Rising above this smaller pit was a stadium-style landing, divided into rows just wide enough for dozens of clerks to stand sideways in a single-file line, chest to back, chest to back. They were arbing at a dizzying pace, with a variety of unusual signals that looked, to me, like shadow puppets on speed.

Aside from the basic arb, each pit has additional and unique signals of its own. There are signals for specific brokerage houses: for the Commodity firm Refco, you puff an imaginary cigarette—or more aptly, the reefer to which the firm's name is likened; if Paine Webber has just dropped a large order, you start rubbing your neck, like a pain. The months in which contracts expire have signals as well: for May, you flap your jacket; March is the first two fingers prancing in unison, or "marching," in the air; for August, you swipe your hand across your forehead, as if it's a sweaty brow. When the order you're working is filled, you signal a thumbs-up; if you're still working an order, you rotate your finger about your ear, like describing someone's crazy. If you slice your throat back and forth with your finger, it means Kill the Order! And then there are the fake-out signals where a trader works out a secret code with his clerk—like, if I rub my chin after a large order, it means this order is bogus, it's just for show, just to throw people. Or, if I start scratching my nose before the order, it means do the opposite—so if I'm saying *buy*, it really means *sell*. If all goes according to plan, these teasers can mean that everyone who's following the leader will push the Market exactly the way you want it to go, while you're raking in the profits. Of course, a false move, a real itch, a nervous twitch, an unconscious gesture—how many times have you, deep in thought, unknowingly rubbed your chin?—and you could be in big trouble.

In the jam-packed landing, one arb clerk in particular—a woman—

stood out. It was obvious she knew exactly what she was doing. Her arb was precise and quick, blink of an eye, like a reflex. The firm way she held herself, and the look on her face, emanated stability and confidence. There was no fear there—no lip biting, no crinkled forehead, no jittery leg bob, no teeth-clenching—none of the attributes of so many of the other arb clerks. Her agile hand flashed the constant, accelerated sign language as she simultaneously, but calmly, performed other tasks, such as talking into her headset, nodding to someone across the pit, or taking a brief second to dab a paper towel at her perspiring forehead or at the back of the neck of the guy in front of her.

I watched her until the bell rang, and then I timorously climbed the steps and approached her, catching her name on her ID badge: MICHELLE. I stammered that I was new here and was wondering if sometime I could talk to her about the workings of this pit. Guys in yellow jackets swarmed over. "I'll teach you, I'll be your very own, private tutor," they clamored. Michelle was instantly annoyed with them. She threw her arms up and boomed, "Back off!" They scattered like roaches in bright light. When they timidly looked back, she followed up with, "Hey, it's a woman thing!"

Michelle and I made plans to meet next week after work on a day that happened to be her birthday. "It doesn't matter," she told me, "I'm celebrating my birthday over the weekend. Besides, by the time you turn forty it gets to be no big deal." If I had seen Michelle chauffeuring grade-school kids to and from soccer games, it would have been more believable that she was forty, but here on the trading floor, among pimply nineteen-year-old boys and girls with glitter on their faces, forty seemed out of place for a clerk, almost unfathomable. And yet, when I began looking, I spotted a handful of older faces in yellow jackets. Professional clerks, they're called—some had attempted to trade and failed, others never possessed the desire to trade in the first place. They were addicted to the action of the Floor, but not to the risk.

I met Michelle across the street, at Pazzo's at 2 p.m., which was the time her pit closed. We headed through the empty restaurant to the back bar, which was also empty. Michelle plopped onto a bar stool and ordered a Bloody Mary. I ordered a glass of red wine. "I hardly ever do this, go out with people after work anymore," she said. "I'm too tired, and besides, who wants to after you spend all day with them, butt to butt."

Our drinks arrived and she slid an olive off the plastic spear. "I got caught up in the scene in the late eighties," she said. "You're around it and you're more susceptible to it. As the years went on, everyone kind of dropped out, one by one they disappeared. And I just kept going full blast. It's been seven years since I went cold turkey. I would be dead today if I hadn't quit. The last day I did coke, I fell in my bathroom and hit my head. I woke up and couldn't see anything, but I had left the water running, so the whole place was flooded. I was kicked out of the apartment and was in rehab in California within four days. I know if I ever touch the stuff again I'm dead."

I didn't know quite how to respond. I was taken aback by her sudden candidness, and I felt awkward that she was confiding all this to me when we had just met. In a way, I was flattered that she felt comfortable enough to do so; only, I'd learn in a matter of hours that I was the one being naïve—nothing was sacred on the trading floor. Everyone knew everyone's business and you got used to telling all in the bluntest terms possible. There was not much that was considered personal, privacy was something to scoff at, and if you thought you had a secret, you were delusional. Besides, drug abuse was all too common in this environment for anyone to be hush-hush about it. A lot of people on the Floor had been former addicts. They say you either come back healthy, or you don't come back at all.

A few traders trickled into the bar. They all knew Michelle and said hello as they passed. They settled onto bar stools, looking weary and slightly dazed. They ordered beers and seemed to wait for no one in particular.

"There was a lot of crash and burn," Michelle continued. "A lot of traders would go down in a bad spiral. You'd see them one day just throw their cards and walk off the Floor. Then, the next time you'd see them, they'd be wearing the yellow jacket. I mean it's not that hard to blow your whole career—it's a rough day and some clerk makes an error and there goes $500,000, and you don't have the money to pay it back." She took the last cigarette from a pack and let it dangle from her mouth while she dug in her pockets for matches. "It takes a lot of restraint," she said, as one of the men leaned over with a lighter to help her out, "to make money in there."

Michelle had been an arb clerk in the Eurodollar Futures for sixteen years. She was six feet tall and had a raucous laugh that could be heard across a room. A childhood friend, Terry, had brought Michelle to the Merc. Terry's boyfriend was a broker in Eurodollars, and then Terry became one, and then she convinced Michelle to come clerk for her. "Terry and I grew up together since we were ten years old. We were best friends," Michelle told me, then half-smiled. "But it's a whole different world on the trading floor, and everyone can be really rough. Terry could just be this bitch! We used to fight. She'd say, 'You don't like it, you fucking leave!' I'd say, 'Fine. Bye.' And she'd grab me by the leg. 'Get back here now!' "

After several years, Terry began cutting back her hours, and Michelle started to look for new opportunities. Terry encouraged her to trade. "Terry had done very well and she said she'd back me, that I would make a great trader," Michelle said nonchalantly. "But I never wanted to trade. I still don't. I really like what I do. I make good money, even though I never went to college. I don't need those kind of headaches of trading, I didn't need those pressures." So Michelle moved up the ranks of arb clerk, plucked from one firm by another firm, each more prestigious than the last, and each upping her salary. She now worked for a group of brokers, in an off-shoot of the Eurodollar pit that deals with what's called the "back months" of the Futures contract. She was in charge of the firm's two largest accounts, and it was her responsibility to instantaneously arb the correct orders to the broker in the pit. She often wore a dual headset with individual micro-phones so that she could communicate with both of her customers at the same time, although each conversation was private. To me, it sounded nearly impossible.

"The talking thing in the headsets drives me bananas," Michelle said. "I was so nervous at first. You have one guy barking in one ear and one guy in the other, and you're flipping the microphones up and down. And then, on top of the voices in your head, you're arbing to all these people, too, and, well, sometimes you just look at your hand and it's doing something dif-ferent than what you're mouthing and you're just like, whoa, what's going on here? But the worst is when I got all this going on and this clerk on the step below me turns around and hits me in the shins, and goes, 'Gee, Michelle, you're shaking, and it's not even that busy. You better watch it or you're going to lose your Lee Press-On nails.' I hate when he does that. I tell him to back off, but he still keeps doing it."

"Does he think he can get away with it because you're a woman?" I asked.

She laughed heartily. "I never feel like a woman at work. People would come to the Floor and see all the pushing and shoving and go, 'But there's a girl in there!' And the guys would say, 'There's no girl, that's just Michelle.' " She grinned. "When I got this new position, one of the customers told my boss, 'Oh, you're going to have to watch your language now that you've got a woman working for you.' And my boss goes, 'Who? Oh, Michelle? Nah, she's been down here longer than anyone, she's heard it all.' "

For as funny as Michelle found it, you'd think she'd hardly seem feminine, but that wasn't the case, for she possessed the stereotypical feminine traits of manicured nails (real, not press-ons), and she ranted that she was going to be working until she dropped because she spent way too much money on clothes ever to retire. She also insisted that she wasn't bothered by the men's perception of her. "It makes me feel like one of the guys. And I am," she said. "Except for when they grab my butt—I can tell whose hand is whose, they do it so much. Believe me, if I was going to claim sexual harassment, I've got a pile about this high." She held her hand a few feet in the air. "But they're not doing it to be disrespectful, they're playing, it's friends that I know. And the truth is, if I ever need help, they're right there. There are guys that I bicker with all the time, but if anyone else comes in and says something offensive to me, they're right behind me. 'You don't talk to her that way!' " She smiled proudly. She clearly enjoyed the fact that the guys looked out for her, but what she seemed to enjoy even more was that she didn't *need* them to look out for her.

"Once, a new clerk came into our pit," she said. "He was this big football player, and he stood in my spot. I said, 'Excuse me, you're in my spot, you're going to have to move up.' And he said, 'Fuck you.' This other clerk looks over and says, 'I wouldn't talk to her that way.' The big guy says, 'Who the hell does she think she is? She's a goddam female!' And the other clerk looks at him, then says, 'Let me tell you something, don't fuck with her, because you're not going to win.' So the big guy goes, 'Yeah, right,' and he shoves me. Another clerk comes over—and these are guys I've worked with for years—and they're like, 'We're telling you, you better watch it.' So he goes, 'Yeah, right,' again, and he does this butt-shove thing to me. Well, I grabbed him by the back of the neck and threw him over the rail, his head down. And I said, 'I'm telling you, step up and get out of my spot now, or you're going the rest of the way over.' And the other guys are laughing and saying, 'We told ya!' Well, he moved himself up and I didn't have any trouble with him after that."

"Would you really have thrown him over?" I asked.

Michelle smiled. "I've been down there too long to be pushed and slammed around anymore," she said. "I've had a split lip, a black eye—a lot of that was guys just talking and telling stories and their arms were swinging and I got bopped in the mouth. Once, I got whiplash. Another time I got thrown out of the pit. People were pushing and shoving, and I went down four stairs and almost hit my head. But then the pit started getting really crowded. It was crammed so tight no one was going to get thrown anywhere—I could pick my feet up and not drop. I did it many times, I'd lift up my legs and I'd never drop."

She plucked another olive from her drink. "The guys play all tough and rough," she said, "but then you get to know 'em. There was this one clerk, Big Mike. He's six feet four, rides a Harley, wears these big biker boots, has the tattoos, the earrings, all that. One day I went on break and I see Mike with an older lady. Anyway, I go, 'Mike, what the hell are you doing? Get your butt back in there and get to work, it's my turn to go on break!' And he goes, 'Mom, that's her.' His mom stands up. She gets in my face and says, 'You lay off of my baby boy!' I started laughing so hard, I couldn't help it. All those guys are a lot of talk. But they're actually good deep down—which is really quite surprising. There are still those pigs, believe me. Oh God, if I slept with half the guys I've heard I did, I'd be one happy woman—a quarter of 'em even!"

I automatically assumed that Michelle had always possessed a brash persona. I pictured her a tomboy from the start, perhaps the only girl in a house full of older brothers who forced her to learn at an early age how to stand her ground. But she insisted otherwise. "Oh, I didn't start out this way," she said. "There I was in the beginning, panicked and sobbing. They were all yelling at me and I didn't get how to do anything, I just didn't get it!" I was shocked, for it was difficult to picture Michelle ever being anything close to vulnerable, but she sounded, well, like me. She claimed that she owed her transformation to one man, Romey Bracey, her mentor of sorts, and a former veteran clerk who had taught the definitive class on arb. His outright claim was that he took whiny suburban girls who came to the Floor and turned them into ferocious tigers.

"Romey would say to me, 'You have more than most people I've seen, so just suck it up, woman! Quit your cryin' and do it!' " Michelle said. "He gave me the confidence I needed." I asked if Romey was still teaching his arb class, and admitted that I could surely use it, but Michelle shook her head. Romey had left the Merc a few years ago, after having been a clerk there for two decades, and Michelle wasn't sure where he was now. It wasn't uncommon on the Floor for people just to disappear. There was a saying: "No one leaves the Floor voluntarily." Everyone would chalk it up to a blowout— from trading, from stress, from drugs, from all three. You got used to the fact that you could stand next to someone in the pit for years and then, one day, never see him again. You didn't keep tabs on people, and you didn't ask too many questions—because in this field there was a chance that someday it might be you.

The bartender cleared Michelle's empty glass and asked if she'd like another. "Yeah, why not?" she said, then turned to me. "This is only the third time in the last couple of years I've stayed down here after work, because I know where it will lead. I don't know how many nights I'd be out with Romey and a bunch of others and I'd go, 'I've got to catch the 12:25 train! If I miss it I'm stuck down here all night.' And suddenly, it's like, 'Oh shit, it's a quarter to one!' " Michelle dunked the olives in her drink, then, with her fingers, pulled them off the swizzle stick, one by one, biting them as if they were candy.

Those who did leave the Merc often didn't stray too far—the Loop was their stomping ground and the Merc culture was all they knew. Because of this, Chicago could often feel like a small town where everyone seemed to know one another. This was one of those curious moments, for a man strolled into the bar, and as soon as Michelle saw him, her face lit up. "Where have you been?" she demanded. As if on cue, the man was none other than Mr. Romey Bracey.

"Aw," Romey said bashfully, "I quit that shit."

Romey was tall and lean with a chiseled face and an unwavering smile. He was wearing a cable-knit V-neck sweater and penny loafers. "You're Mr. Preppy now," Michelle teased. The others at the bar called out hello to Romey, and offered similar comments on the outfit, such as, "What's with the Izod?" and "Since when did you go back to parochial school?" Romey pulled up a bar stool. Michelle introduced me and said that we were just talking about how I could use his arb class. He wasted no time in letting me know that he was the Best Arb Clerk *and* the Highest-Paid Arb Clerk in the history of the Merc. He listed these distinctions as if they were just tidbits of info, rather than bragging gestures—but no one at the bar so much as raised an eyebrow to dispute his claims. Romey had been, in fact, profiled in a front-page *Wall Street Journal* article, the tongue-twisting title of which—"Fickle Fingers Flash: The Signs of Cash in the Trading Pits—Fast-Moving Digits Translate into Big Bucks in Chicago," and the exact date of publication, Tuesday, May 16, 1995—he rattled off from memory. "Once I started doing arb," he told me, "I was like, this is what I was made for."

A short-lived clerk from the Gold pit had first showed Romey how to arb. When Romey moved to the Eurodollar Futures pit at the time of its birth, in 1981, he took it upon himself to start teaching the new clerks there how to arb. When one of them presented him with an envelope with cash as compensation for his time, Romey realized he was onto something. He wrote up a curriculum and spread the word; soon he had so many students that the Merc gave Romey an official class in the educational department.

Romey's teaching method involved more than just demonstrating the hand signals, it was a whole philosophy. He espoused the importance of mental attitude, of that place your brain had to be so that you could *really* arb, so that you could have five people screaming and arbing to you and you could process it and arb back to each one, and then add it up and pass the order to the pit—and so that you could do that a hundred times a day, five days a week.

Romey took extra care with the women in his class, for he felt, in a way, like a kindred spirit—just as there were very few women on the Floor, there were likely fewer African Americans like himself. I found it surprising that Romey's most lasting initial impression of the Merc wasn't of the action or the chaos or the money; rather, it was of the way the men interacted with the handful of women on the Floor. "We're in the pit and these cats are calling these girls bitch, and . . . well, cunt," he said. "It just amazed me how disrespectful these white boys were to their women. It's stuff that a brother would *never* do. Ne-ver! Because Grandmama would slap the taste out of your mouth! That was the thing that caught me the most off guard—it's an environment where people can express whatever they're thinking, and it just flowed out of them. It's no wonder a lot of women came and left. I think it's mainly because they had no one to believe in them. Or, they came in there for the wrong reasons. A lot of women just wanted to hook up with a man or be around all that money. They didn't come for the real deal, they came for the bullshit, and that's what they got. But they have different characteristics than the women who make it."

Michelle agreed wholeheartedly and launched into a story to prove it. "There was this girl I brought into the business," she said. "I've known her since I was four years old. Well, she was married, but she met a trader, Rocket—his badge was ROKT—and started seeing him. One day, her husband finds a credit card in her purse with Rocket's name on it. So now she's married to Rocket, and all she talks about is all the money, and the house they're building, and how much they spend on everything. She was never like that until she came to the Merc."

Romey shook his head. "You bring a woman into that environment without the right sage, without a sensei, so to speak, to direct her, and she'll get flattened," he said. "A lot of chicks come in naïve and men just take advantage of them like fuckin' vultures. I've seen guys taking chicks out on boats with magnums of champagne. But those girls, they knew what was up, they knew what time it was."

Even though I didn't personally know any other women on the Floor, I could identify with what Romey and Michelle were describing. When I was on the Floor with Tom, I didn't feel vulnerable—but I certainly did when I was there by myself. It was easy to see how young women could fall prey— take into account that the average clerk was fresh out of high school—or, at most, college—and, just like anyone on their first job, she was eager to please, not to mention starry-eyed because of all the wealth. Even I was impressed by the monetary figures.

Romey had channeled his frustration with the gender inequities by teaching the women in his arb class how to stand on their own. " 'You're going to be the baddest bitch in the force,' that's what I would tell all my girls," he said. "They would all cry, and I'd say, 'One day, the men will all tremble when you talk!' I wanted to make it a point. I wanted to make it so that the men would feel what it's like to be humiliated. And, sure enough, every single one of my girls—I'd see my chicks in the pit come out on cats! Man! They'd grab them. 'You fucking asshole! You better get me my fill!' And I'd look over and be like, yeah, that's what I'm talking about, the baddest bitch on the force." He turned to Michelle. "I always knew you were different," he said. "Most women never experience or reach what you have." He gave her a sentimental nudge. "You were the highest-paid clerk on the Floor—besides me. We did good."

"Another?" the bartender asked. Romey nodded.

"Eh, what the hell," Michelle said, then turned to me, as if I were her conscience, the angel on one shoulder, while the traders on the other side of her were the devil. "The last time I went out after work, it was months ago," she said. "I can't even remember when."

Romey first came to the Merc on the urging of a childhood friend, Ted, who was a clerk, and, as Romey described, a swashbuckling young guy like himself. The year was 1979, and Romey put on his best suit and headed to the Floor with Ted. "I was looking very sharp," Romey reminisced. "But I get down there and not only is nobody dressed in a suit, but it was very unusual for a young black man to come down there, especially projecting that kind of corporate image. I stepped up into the pit and looked around because I wanted to see what was going on. And all of a sudden this guy yells, 'What the fuck do you think you're doing stepping into the *pit*? Who does this guy think he is?' I stepped down and all I could think was: 'I want to do this.' "

Romey hounded the human resources department on a daily basis until he landed a position as a pit reporter, a thankless job where he wore a pale blue Merc employee jacket and stood at a podium with a microphone, calling out where the Market was at. The only feedback he and the other reporters would receive was a stream of insults when they were lagging, or when the traders—or even just a single trader who was stuck—*thought* they were lagging. The pit reporters were often the scapegoats for traders who were disgruntled with a confusing or fast-moving Market. But, in fact, it was one of these traders and one fortuitous day that changed Romey's entire career, if not his life.

"See, these guys would make trades but they wouldn't call them out," Romey described. "So if I didn't record it, they'd go, 'Hey, asshole! Don't you know I traded sevens? Get the trade in!' They were humiliating, even though *they're* the ones sitting there making trades and not even telling you. So one time, I see this guy doin' it! He makes a trade, he doesn't call it in. And it was this real cool dude too. But I saw him with my own eyes, so I shouted, 'Hey, punk, did you just make that trade? Now how'm I going to get that trade in if you don't call it in? Call your trade in, asshole!' So here I was, doing what they do. All the cats were just looking at me, amazed—but I had learned from them how to be like that! So the cool dude, he looks at me, then goes, 'Hey, I like that in you.' He came over and gave me five—and that's a big thing in the pit. He said, 'I like your style, man.' After I got with him like that, people would go, 'I better call out my trade because I don't want this young black boy to embarrass me.' So I got this kind of status thing and got to know everybody and they were all like, 'Yeah, that's our boy!' "

One day, a broker from Merrill Lynch walked up to Romey and said he liked the way he handled himself in the pit. He asked Romey what his salary was, then said: "I'll double that. You start with me as an arb clerk on Monday."

"The bottom line on being a good clerk," Romey told me, "is to do volume without making mistakes. If I can do fifty orders and not make any errors, while this guy can only do twenty, well then, I'm the baddest dude in town. Everything is mental, it's focused, and it's direct. Every word, every gesture is to get something done effectively and quickly. We're not wasting thoughts, we're not wasting words, we're not wasting gestures. That's the way my mind worked, and that's the way I taught my clerks to work. And that's why we kicked ass."

It so happened that while Romey was gaining popularity and prestige, his boyhood friend, Ted, was experiencing the opposite. Ted had started trading, and the money started flowing in. One day a news crew came to the Floor and Ted, fresh off a great trading day, was quoted as saying something along the lines of, "Trading is like taking candy from a baby!" When the story aired, Merc officials and other traders blanched, for Ted had made trading seem not only easy, but also—gasp!—immoral. Ted was swiftly ostracized, and when no one will trade with you, when no one will let you even *see* the candy, it's impossible to take it. One sentence, said on a whim, and Ted's trading career was over.

Romey, however, claimed that his own personality was custom-made for the trading floor. It's true in the sense that he's quite savvy; *he'd* never have been caught telling a reporter how the Floor *really* was—especially in those untamed, intoxicated 1980s. However, if anyone knew how it really was, it'd be Romey. Just sitting with him now at Pazzo's made me sense that back in the day, to hang out with Romey was to feel like you were in the center of everything. Romey had that magnetic kind of personality, and his vivacity earned him quite a following on the Floor, from fellow clerks right on up to top-echelon Merc management. He was *the* guy, and he was well aware of it. But he deserved the distinction, for he knew how to maneuver, how to *work* that type of environment.

"I mean, I came off the block, for one thing," he explained. "So I'm not intimidated by a confrontation—but I am not Machiavellian, I am more philosophical. I want to take confrontation and turn it into camaraderie." Romey's boasting was mitigated by his apparent sense of compassion, and through our conversation he cited numerous references to the works of Shakespeare, the theories of Taoism, and the teachings of Confucius; he said he studied guides by positive-attitude gurus; and, what was most impressive to me, was that the final lesson in his arb class went something like this: "I tell them, 'Listen, now that I've got you all good and all, you are going to become an asshole at one point and that's the only thing I don't want you to do.' I've seen it happen," Romey said. "I've taken some cat who was shakin' in his boots and whose mother came down to thank me for helping her little boy, and six months later I see this guy treating some new clerk who's scared to death, like, 'Hey, you fucking asshole!' So I called him on it and said, 'Hey, don't you remember me?' And he was like, 'Yeah, sure I do, Rom.' And I said, 'You help *him* like I helped *you*. You nurture him.' "

A top-step arb clerk has the highest level of responsibility next to a trader or broker. These are the clerks who work for the big houses or the big firms, processing the big orders, dealing with the Paper. From afar, their jobs look cushy—they can be pulling close to six-figure salaries; they get off work, at the latest, at quarter after three; they never have to take work home with them and weekends are all theirs; and they don't have to shoulder risk or assume any payment for errors or discrepancies. So why aren't people lining up in droves to become arb clerks? Well, there's this one thing: pressure. Deadly pressure. I had felt the pressure just watching the arb clerks on the Floor, their hands constantly lurching.

Michelle and Romey not-so-fondly reminisced about the busiest day every month—Unemployment Day, more commonly referred to as Unenjoyment Day—when the Market hinged on the release of the updated unemployment rate. "I'd have orders in my hands, orders in both pockets, and orders under my chin, like this," Romey said, pinning his chin to his chest. "And, *and*, people were flashing orders at me. So I'd add up all the orders and tell my guy in the pit, 'Sell five hundred!' He'd go: '50, 100,18,75,32,15,8,9,20,8,8,8! What's my total?' and shove me this card where he jotted everything down, and I'd have to go in my head 18+75+32+15+8+9. . . . I had to spit out 'You've got 149 left!' and hand him back the card. There's no time to take a pen and do this shit. And I'm like, *please* let that count be right."

When Romey talked of orders and numbers, his cadence took on that of a staccato military drill. It was yet another unique characteristic of the trading floor—everything said was several beats faster and several octaves louder than normal speech. Romey demonstrated this to me by speeding through numbers at a pace that would make an auctioneer dizzy: "Selltwentyfiveeighteenfiftyahundredwhatareyoudoingnow?" To me, it seemed that every movement on the Floor was accelerated, too, so that the whole place appeared stuck in fast-forward motion. A sentence was condensed to a single hand signal; a huge contract was a fist at your forehead—you weren't scratching your head, rubbing your temple, or pushing hair out of your face—no, you were communicating a hefty order, completing a business transaction, in a single second.

Romey explained that he held true to a personal philosophy: nothing counts but results. Every day before he'd walk into the pit, he'd pause with his foot on the first step and say out loud, "Strictly business, no mistakes." Then he'd get to work. "I became a little cocky, but I never turned into an asshole," he said. "Life was good, you're getting the best of everything. I mean *everything*. But you know, I had a million-dollar error once." He'd slipped this in so matter-of-factly that I had to repeat his words in my head to make sure I'd heard correctly: a *million-dollar* error. He'd also said it with more of a tinge of bragging than of embarrassment. I wanted to hear the story, but Michelle's Bloody Marys had taken effect, and, while she normally had a strong voice, it was now bulldozing, and she was off onto a story of her own.

"This one guy, IRON, he used to put in five hundred-lots that were always two ticks off the Market," she said. "Well, the orders were fake, and he did them so he could call them out and look like a hotshot. See, he'd cancel them as soon as they got close to the Market. Well, one time he got busy and forgot to pull the order out, and this five hundred-lot got filled. He was screwed because the order didn't belong to anybody, it was bogus. He started going nuts, trying to make up excuses. It cost him an absolute fortune. This is what these guys will do to impress people, to look big."

Romey and Michelle continued going back and forth, their stories building one on top of the other, each spurred by some loose thread mentioned in the previous story, each about real-life people who seemed more like characters straight out of a Hollywood casting agency than just their co-workers. I sat there, sipping my glass of wine, feeling as if I had a front-row seat to a strange two-person play that was entertaining and repulsive at the same time. It was amusing to me how traders knew little shame—no information was too disparaging or too embarrassing or too self-implicating. Crazy characters and crazy times were part of trading floor life, and the stories about this craziness became legendary. Besides, what other field had so many people with vastly disparate qualities housed under one roof? Traders were former attorneys, former truck drivers, former dentists, gamblers, mathematicians, kids right out of high school, the list went on and on, and they were all shoved together, shoulder to shoulder. It was an absurd scenario, when you really thought about it—no wonder it all melded in bizarre ways across 70,000 square feet of trading floor.

"Oooh, ooh!" Michelle squealed—she had thought of another story: "There was this one trader, WAGS—and this was years ago—he went to a two-hour lunch once and came back drunk." Michelle laughed. "You could always tell when he'd been drinking because his lips would turn ruby red, I don't know why, but they would. Anyway, somebody else's clerk was pissing him off, so he marched up to this clerk and started yelling at him." Apparently, Michelle reported, the clerk was drunk, too, and in true Bugs Bunny–Elmer Fudd fashion, the clerk grabbed Wags's face mid-tirade, and kissed him! "They both started laughing hysterically," Michelle recalled. "A little later, the clerk started pissing Wags off again, and this time Wags grabbed the kid by the throat and yelled, 'That's it, you're done, mister! Get out of here!' Everyone else started yelling, 'Have another drink, Wags!'"

Romey sighed, as if he were too old and wise to find much of this amusing anymore. "Having to deal with the mental pressure of the Floor every day will fuck you up," he said. "I'm telling you I had nightmares, everybody does—I'd dream that I couldn't fill this trade and it was driving me fucking crazy and this big dude kept screaming at me, 'What about my fill! What about my fill!' And I'd wake up pouring sweat and panting. And I just remember how happy I was that it was just a dream. I mean, just think about if you make a real error and it's ten grand, and it's only nine a.m. You get shell-shocked, and you're working scared, so now you have another error, you lose five more grand. And now you're creeped out. But you got to make it through. Fear is running through your body. You are scared to death. You finally get off work, what are you going to do? You going to go home and sleep? No. You hit the bar, that's what you do. You drink it off, smoke it off, because you made it. And everybody's in there celebrating that they made it through that day. That's what it boils down to. Then by six o'clock, you're fucked up. You gonna go home and go to sleep now? I don't think so. It's a fucked-up world. The next thing you know, you're waking up in somebody's office at the Merc and it's the next morning. You lose patience too, because your mind is used to working so fast. How can I have patience with you when I'm thinking eight times faster than you are? Nobody can keep up. So now you speed things up because sitting still ain't fast enough for you. You need to be around people who are moving as fast as you are. Well, I started living a little too fast. I started getting too pleasure-oriented. Now, c'mon, how long can you do that shit?"

I almost felt sorry for them; it was like they had gotten sucked in and by the time they realized it, they couldn't get out. The life that seemed so glamorous had almost destroyed them. Trading, I was learning, produced very strong-willed individuals, who, as unlikely as it may outwardly appear, were also easy victims. As my time on the Floor would go on, I'd be reminded of Romey's words again and again, for they would provide something of an explanation for the personalities and actions of the traders I would meet and befriend—people who were as crazy as they were likeable.

"It's been seven years that I've been clean," Michelle volunteered. "After about two years, this guy came up to me after work, and he was practically foaming at the mouth. He was slurring his words and saying, 'Why'd you quit?' I'm like, 'Probably because I looked like you.' And he goes, 'Let's get some, I'll make a phone call.' I walked away but he kept following me, saying, 'Come on, I'll buy it.' Then some guys from my pit came over and they're like, 'We know what she went through to get off that stuff, and you get away from her and stay the hell away from her!' "

Romey didn't share with us any specifics about his former habits, but in recent years—perhaps in an effort to compensate for prior damage—he said he'd adopted a new-age lifestyle. He was presently on a strict cleansing fast, consuming only liquids and vitamin and herb supplements, no solid food. He claimed he hadn't eaten in three weeks. Acceptable on the restricted diet, however, appeared to be Budweiser and cigarettes. Old habits die hard.

"You know, I never miss the Merc," Romey said. His wide smile had long since disappeared, and his face was drawn. "You'd think you would, but you leave that place and it's like the world comes off your shoulders, you are a human being again. People who've left, it's like they gained five years. The stress melts, their eyes look different. You never have a day of peace there. Every day is pressure. You never know what's going to happen." Michelle nodded as she twirled the swizzle stick in her drink. "Just fasten your seat belts," she said.

"When I think about the things I've seen and the things I've done," Romey mused. "I made an error once, it was like forty or fifty grand, a big error—but it was a *winner*." He told us that the previous time he'd had a winning error he'd taken it to his broker, thinking they'd split it, but the broker had kept it all. So this time, Romey took the trading card to a desk clerk he knew, a sweet woman who was a librarian before she came to the Merc. Her eyes popped wide when she looked at the card. "Let's split this three ways," Romey whispered to her. "Thirty-three percent to you, thirty-three percent to me, and thirty-three percent to taxes." She didn't say anything else about it all week. Right before the closing bell on Friday she handed Romey an envelope. It was packed with $100 bills. "That was the biggest take I ever took," Romey said.

He stared at his empty beer bottle as if needing to focus on something while thoughts, long since forgotten, bubbled to the surface. "I still think about the Floor a lot," he said. "See the thing is, we top clerks worked too hard. We never realized what was going on behind the scenes, all the guys who were making the real money are just sitting upstairs, and all they do is place orders for people and they don't care if they win or lose. And there we are down on the Floor, sweating and killing ourselves. It's like the owner of

a team up there in the VIP box while the football player is out there gettin'
his head broken in. I don't care who it is, the nicest guy down on the Floor,
it's taking a toll on him, even if after work he goes right home to his family, it's *still* wearing him down because he has to be in an environment
where you have to be under so much stress to perform, to produce. And it's
coming at you from every different angle, and there's a chance—a fact—
that you might lose it all tomorrow, or that you might make a mistake to
cost somebody else a million. It's just a fact. I do not miss those days.

"See, everybody has an Othello, a fatal flaw. My Othello was that I was
naïve. I should have taken that environment and squeezed it and made it
work for me, but I made it work for everybody around me. I could have
demanded things, I could have demanded my seat, I could have demanded
a quarter on every contract. Every Alexander the Great needs an Aristotle.
There should always be a mentor on the cuff, watching your back, pulling
you to the side, saying that's cool, but do it like this now, and putting you
back. Otherwise, you either get lost in yourself or lost outside of yourself. I
never had the tutor that I needed, and it hurt me. I could have taken what
I had and, at this point, I could have had my own company, my own online service, had my own classes on the Internet." He sighed. "But, you
know, life is still good. There's a divine motion, it keeps everything in place,
it's all about me not interfering with that. I used to tell my students, 'Don't
think. Just let me program you and you just respond to the program. Once
you start thinking, you're going to fuck up everything.' " Romey motioned
for another beer.

"Another?" the bartender asked Michelle; he had long since stopped
asking me.

"These are really going down easy," she said.

Romey had hit on so many of the things I'd been feeling—the need for
a guide, the downfall of overthinking, the pressure of the fill-or-get-killed
environment, and, oddly enough, in an arena of thousands of people, the
loneliness. I had started thinking that maybe it was just me, that I wasn't
cut out for this, that I was a writer and should go back to doing just that.
But Romey's words were reassuring. He—the best arb clerk in history—
had felt these things too.

There was one story I still needed to hear. "Romey," I said, "will you tell
me about your million-dollar error?"

Romey grinned. "Well," he began, "I was legging the spread. This one broker, he and I had done about five thousand spreads, and then all of a sudden he decides to get fancy. See, when you leg it, you buy one over here, then sell another one over there, both at a certain price. Sometimes, you leg it so that you buy one and then work the other side, which is called 'legged up.' But if it goes the wrong way, you're screwed. So anyway, this broker gives me five hundred, but only gives me one leg. I'm thinking he's going to be legged up and he'll give me the other side when he's ready, but *he's* thinking I would just automatically do the other side." Romey shook his head.

I marveled to myself, for errors on the Floor seemed nothing more than just a little misunderstanding, a simple omission, everyone's fault, and no one's fault. And yet, this error had caused $1 million to disappear. "My guy had to eat the money because he didn't want to lose that customer's business," Romey said. He shook his head again, but his eyes were all starry, like the error was a play in a basketball game that should have, could have, been beautiful. But the effort alone still seemed to fascinate him. He, just one person, one clerk, was able to have a million-dollar impact. In the oddness of the trading world, this made him proud.

FIVE

Limit Up

Limit Up is the point of maximum bullishness allowed in a Futures market. Each market has different criteria for how much of an upward move can take place in a single day. Once the top price has been reached, trading is halted until a sell order at or below the limit is made. In the past—especially in Commodities—trading has been stalled for weeks, months even, at Limit Up. Limit Up didn't always exist, but was instituted as protection against a fast-moving market. The opposite is Limit Down, which is when the Market hits its maximum point of bearishness.

t came as a complete surprise to me to learn that one of the largest and most successful Futures traders was a woman. Bev Gelman—badge BEV—traded Eurodollar Futures at the Merc and stood in the back-months pit, directly under the landing where Michelle was perched.

Eurodollar Futures was currently the most actively traded Futures market in the world. In this pit, you traded the interest rate of U.S. dollars deposited in offshore banks, and each contract was standardized to represent the interest rate of a three-month deposit of $1 million. The Eurodollar pit was the largest in size on the Merc Floor, and it was no coincidence that many of the Eurodollar traders were extremely tall. Height is an amazing advantage in a pit as big as this, and many firms purposefully recruit traders from college basketball teams. One such recruitment ad stated: Must be at least 6 feet 3 inches. Rumor had it that some traders of smaller frame would hire big, burly guys just to save a spot for them in the pit, although that practice violates Merc rules. It's reasons such as this that make some pits tougher for women to break into; from what I'd gathered, this one was the toughest.

The back-months pit, a subsidiary of the main pit, handled the Eurodollar contracts that spanned up to ten years into the future. Traders bracketed these contracts into ten categories designated with color names, each of which has a different hand signal; for example: holding up your pinkie was for Pinks; touching your thumb against your ring finger was for Golds (not to be confused with rubbing your thumb against your fingers like the symbol for "money," which was the signal that Goldman Sachs just came in with a large order); and a twisting motion, like you're juicing fruit, was for Oranges. Because of all the different years and months and colors and other contract groupings, called bundles and packages, it was common for traders here to make complex trades and elaborate spreads. With under one hundred people, the back-months pit was much more intimate, although just as—if not more—violent. It was here that Bev Gelman was a Local, and here that she was queen—*and* king.

Because the Eurodollar Futures market is based on the price of money, it got crazy in the pit whenever the Federal Reserve held a meeting. It just so happened that this month, when Alan Greenspan and his cronies gathered in Washington, it was predicted that they would change the interest rate. I decided to visit the Eurodollar pit that day and be present at the precise hour of 1:15 p.m. central standard time, when the new rate would be announced. I made my way up the steps of the back-months pit, to the third row of clerks, where I found a foot of space and wedged myself against the railing. Michelle was on the step below me, in a full-body-contact line of clerks, signaling back and forth to the rows of brokers at the phone terminals that stretched like bleacher seats along both walls of the Floor.

I leaned far over the rail and tapped Michelle; she turned to say hello. "See Bev?" she asked. She pointed to the opposite of what I imagined the hugely successful, legendary Bev would look like: a petite, fair-skinned woman with short blond hair, wearing a lime green trader's jacket. Bev seemed hyperalert, scanning all boards on all walls. Her eyes were wide and darting back and forth, up and down, robotlike—gather data, process data, repeat.

Tom and I had agreed that I could take some time to watch the best player—besides, Tom reasoned, new pit, new gossip. Tom, like practically every person on the Floor—everyone in the industry, for that matter, from Chicago to Wall Street—knew of Bev Gelman. While most traders had something ugly to say about most other traders, you'd be hard-pressed to find one who didn't revere Bev. They viewed her as an artistic trader who came in and leveled the playing field. They said she had the guts of a man and the brains of a woman. They described her as unbelievable, a complete dynamo, the maximum Bull or the maximum Bear. Wall Street loved her because she took on their largest orders and would give them the best prices. But an acquaintance's husband, a retired trader who used to trade with Bev, offered up this: "Bev's a genius, but don't try to get to know her. I mean, don't go asking her questions about trading, or questions about anything for that matter. Really, I have two words for you: stay away." Admonishments like this were usually in reference to a big, bulky man with a face unnaturally crooked from frequent encounters in dark alleys; or to an über-corporate woman in the ultimate power suit, with a stare as icy as her tone, and a belief that the spikier the stiletto heel, the better with which to step on you. People didn't typically talk this way of a rail-thin, thirty-nine-year-old, unadorned woman who, by all accounts, was pretty regular-looking, and whom I probably would have glossed right over if I hadn't known the reputation that preceded her.

For over a decade, Bev had stood in this pit for the entire trading day—7:20 a.m. to 2 p.m.—without ever leaving to go to the bathroom, or to sit for a moment, or to get a sip of water for an undoubtedly dry, raw throat. Even when she was pregnant, she stood in the pit, among the pushing and shoving, almost right up to her due date. And then one day she realized that she *could* leave, because when she did, trading would virtually stop. Big institutions would preface their orders with the question "Is Bev in the pit?" And if she wasn't, they'd call back later. In recent years, when Bev allowed herself time off for vacations, the guys in the pit took to playing darts—why not, without her, business dried up. I'd heard that Bev had been offered positions at firms for locked-in salaries of a couple of million dollars a year, but she wouldn't take them. Besides, during a typical year for her as a Local, she brought in double-digit millions.

"I stare at her and I lose myself sometimes," Michelle said to me. "It gets my boss pissed off, but I'm in awe. I just wonder, how does somebody's mind work that quick? I've been here for sixteen years and I've never seen anything like it—the things she absorbs and the way she calculates it all. She has her eyes always so wide open and she never blinks. It's like, if she blinks she'll miss too much. You can always count on her, no matter how busy she is. And she'll give you a trade that's a half-tick better than anybody else because then she knows she'll get the trade that she wants. She's smart—why hang with everybody else when there's too many people in the same price you are? Pay up a little and you're going to get everything. She loves what she's doing, that's for damn sure. Nobody does the size of Bev. She's top dog back here. The guys respect her, they really do. Once in a while, if everyone's attacking her for a market, she'll yell, 'Will everyone get the fuck away from me!' and then you know she's reached her breaking point—but that's rare. But when Bev does take a hit, she takes a *big* hit."

Michelle pointed to a clean-cut trader in his late twenties, standing next to Bev in the pit. "She's training her boy real well too," Michelle said. "He's adorable, although just a *wee* bit younger than she is. Hey, women go for the loaded men, why not the other way around? His name is Sean, for a while he would do whatever she would do, follow-the-leader kind of thing. But now, he's starting to do his own thing. He really caught on and is doing very well. He's like one of those child prodigy kids. He used to work for a firm that handled customers in Japan, and I heard he speaks fluent Japanese and lived there for quite a while. He was making a lot of money, but when Bev gave him an offer like, 'Here you go, I'll buy you a seat,' how can you turn that down? She had a $100,000 car, 'Here, why don't you drive it, I don't use it much.' " Michelle shot me a must-be-nice look. "But don't get me wrong," she said. "Bev can be really rough on the Floor." Michelle was intermittently arbing as she talked, but now, with the announcement fast approaching, something came over her headset and all small talk was over. She flipped around—back to breakneck speed.

The clerk next to me shuddered. "I'm getting nervous," he said. "I always get nervous on these days." Three other clerks seemed to share a different sentiment and were horsing around, shouting, "Hold him down, I'll spank his ass!"

Another clerk said, "It's going to get hot in here!" Going to? I was hardly moving, and yet sweat beads covered my forehead. No air was circulating and it was a close, sweltering day. The electronic boards that lined the wall glowed with a zillion red and green digital lights. I followed down the column: FRONT REDS, GREEN, BLUE, EDU1, EDZ1, EDH2, EDM2 (in trader shorthand, the ED stands for Eurodollars, and the other letters designate months, U is September, Z is for December, H is March, M is June). I had no clue what this all translated to, and just staring at the rows and rows of illuminated numbers made me dizzy. The smell of lit matches permeated the space, a common practice—just like in fraternity houses—to neutralize foul odors. News photographers were on the Floor, perched up near the computers, positioning their massive zoom-lens cameras, waiting to capture a still-frame of chaos.

The large digital clock on the wall flashed 1:12 p.m.; three minutes until the Fed announcement. Traders called out Bev's name. She bounced from foot to foot, hand fluttering to her mouth. "Seven bid" "Eight bid" "Eight bid two" "Nine bid" "A hundred steady Red. Are you filled?"

1:13 p.m.: Bev's clerk—a young woman—motioned to her from outside the pit with a nod and a thumbs-up.

1:14:55 p.m.: As close to silence as you could get on a jam-packed trading floor. "Get ready!" a market reporter yelled. Suddenly, there was a rumble, then a roar—all arms were up. I looked to the boards for the rate-cut announcement to flash in yellow, like Tom had taught me to do for the S&P and Nasdaq pits. Only, here, no yellow. I flipped around to face the other boards. No yellow. This pit, unlike most others, had a television, and, by default, I looked at the screen where CNBC had the number flashing—it was a quarter-point cut. I would have just lost all my money on being a flake.

The pit looked like an octopus gone crazy with all the arms flailing like tentacles. The traders were screaming, some with such hoarse throats that I almost expected to see their larynxes fly out of their mouths along with the trade. Bev shouted directly into the ear of the guy next to her. Her eyes were wide, as though they could pop right out, and she haphazardly nipped at her nails with nervous energy. Her face registered a mix of extreme concentration, and a keen awareness of every single thing that was going on around her. Michelle was right: Bev didn't blink.

To the far left, pushing and shoving broke out. No one even turned their head as they got clobbered from behind. A guy could keel over on top of you—you just kept on trading. The fight dissolved in the swelling mass. The frenetic pace held steady. Because there were so many contract months and years and colors, this pit traded with an arsenal of funny little hand signals that looked to the untrained eye—such as mine—like bizarre tremors. A clerk near me was hopping up and down, waving two fingers, switching between the hand sign for one and four and some other sign where his middle finger was bent, like he was playing an invisible string instrument and running through a rapid chord progression. Another clerk gave a hand signal that looked like he was waving. Another had his first two fingers bent and flitting in the air, like he was tickling an invisible person. Traders clapped their hands—which signaled they needed a market spread—and yelled "Green Deece" for the December green bundle of contracts. The traders on the phones against the far wall plugged their ears to hear the calls—some held a receiver up to each ear. It had been only fifteen minutes since the announcement, but to me, it felt like hours. Already I was sweaty and my head was ringing from the yelling—and I hadn't even done any-thing, nor was I in the middle of it, but a safe distance above, where I had—by Floor standards—ample footing and no fear of getting smashed. But I was beat just watching those below me. For them, there was probably no concept of passing time. It had been a blip—a blip plus or minus several thousand dollars, or, if you were Bev Gelman, millions.

A trader with the apropos badge of FAST jittered like he'd had fifty cups of caffeine. He was wearing earplugs—or maybe it was a hearing aid?—and he was angry about something. He gave a guy a shove, and like dominoes, the guy rammed into the two guys in front of him. A trade later, and FAST was appeased; everything seemed to have been worked out. Two-second bygones.

Another fight broke out and Bev got knocked in the head by a trader's elbow. She didn't even pause. "Threes!" she shouted. "Sixes! Threes! Threes! Threes!" Her hands were in the air. Her watch, slender antique silver, was open and sliding down her wrist. There was not a second to fix it. The trader in front of her took her offer, and as she was dealing with him, she instantaneously flipped around to buy from someone behind her. Bev was the master of ubiquitous hearing.

Suddenly, a hefty, swollen guy in a navy jacket, with the badge LION, jumped from his spot on the top step and pushed his way through the pit. His face was rubicund, and he reminded me of a cartoon figure where you could see the steam shooting from his ears. With thundering steps, he waded through the soup to a broker half his size, and gave him a good shove. The broker held his footing and continued trading, pretending that Lion wasn't towering over him. Lion shoved him again, then for good measure, screamed in his face, bellowing one long, ferocious *Arrrgghhh!* like a foghorn, directly in the guy's ear. The victim, through a stoic test of wills, hardly flinched. No one else seemed to care, all they knew was that

Lion was taking up too much room and blocking sightlines, so everyone started a concerted effort of shoving him back to his spot.

Finally, Lion, his face now a purplish-red, retreated to his step, screaming, "Fucking shit!" There, he took out the rest of his frustration by hollering at a clerk dangling over the rails behind him. This was, I believed, the fifth fight so far, in around a half hour—although it was possible I'd lost track.

At last, at ten minutes until the Close, there was a lull—for about sixty seconds. Michelle lifted up the headset earphone of the clerk in front of her and fanned his face. He kept right on arbing. A clerk just outside of the pit entrance took advantage of the momentary breather and opened his pants' zipper. He stuffed his hand in, made some adjustments, then zipped back up with a motion like he was starting a lawn mower. He rocked from his heels to the balls of his feet; a man satisfied, for all to see, only I doubted anyone but me even noticed.

Back in the pit, a little gray-haired man with the badge JOG, who looked much too old and frail to still be playing this game, trudged through the soup. Two bodies away from him were the beginnings of yet another fistfight, clenched hands lingered in the air, threatening. The fight, like the others, was absorbed into the sway of the pit. Suddenly, a collective moan rippled through the crowd, and everyone's face turned sour as they started fanning at the air. A clerk entering the pit took note and pulled his jacket, Dracula-style, over his nose. Still another shoving match erupted—jackets were grabbed this time. It was near where Bev stood, and I watched the corpulent Lion lunge toward her. As if Sean were a knight defending his princess, he swiped back at Lion, who was twice his size. Lion ducked out of the way.

1:55 p.m.: Traders started hopping, like they were jumping rope. The pit grew more agitated. The gong sounded to signal one minute left before the Close. Now, everyone on the entire Floor was hopping. Except for me, I was clenching the rails in case things got violently out of control.

The fifteen-second gong. Madness. The pit was no longer just hopping, it was jumping. The Market reporter behind me said, "It's all fun and games until someone gets bloody."

Or sticky. I lifted up my foot. I'd just stepped in a wad of gum. Then, *ding, ding, ding, ding!* The trading day was finally over.

The shouting immediately ceased, and like actors breaking from character the second the curtain fell, the traders instantaneously shifted gears, their arms dropped, their jaws unclenched.

Lion, however, was not happy. He was still crimson. Sweat stains encircled his neck, and his eyebrows met in a V.

"He's got a temper, doesn't he?" I asked the clerk next to me.

"Lion?" the clerk said. "You should see my boss. He's a mean motherfucker. He stands on the top step right under us, so you can't see him going nuts. I just try to stay back. Otherwise, something's bound to be my fault."

"Does he yell at you?" I asked.

"Once in a while, but mostly he just makes me feel really guilty. 'You let me down,' that kind of guilt."

After the pit had cleared out, around six traders remained, looking disgruntled—Bev and Lion among them. I couldn't hear all of what was going on, but it seemed she was trying to settle a dispute. Lion started up with her, she challenged him, and they wagged their fingers in each other's faces—Bev, so frail and pale-looking; Lion, a splotchy red, stocky block. For as petite as Bev was, she somehow came across as amazingly intimidating. Perhaps it was just this environment, for I knew how much clout she carried here; I wondered if I'd have the same impression had I met her at, say, a party without knowing any background information.

A clerk next to me filled me in on what the problem in the pit was: "A new broker, who's only been in the pit for a few weeks, sold through the Market."

"What does that mean?" I asked.

"He sold at a price lower than the range, which you're not supposed to do. The broker claimed he was just following the order he was given, but he should have known better. It was this complicated spread, and Bev was on one side of the trade. She bought twenty thousand contracts from him and made $2 million."

"Two million? On one trade?" I asked incredulously.

"Yeah," he said with a sarcastic lilt that implied *Wake up!* This is a trading floor, happens all the time. "Lion and some others were on the other side," he continued. "They lost money. And now the brokerage house wants Bev to settle at a better number for them, which means she'd have to give away some of her profits."

The traders in the pit went back and forth, stating their cases, disputing numbers, shaking their heads. Words were flying: "Violation!" "He called it in wrong!" "Buy-down!" "Sell-down!" "We'll have a lawsuit on our hands!" The men argued with no voices, just a hoarse, raspy scratchiness. Bev spoke quickly, with terse snippets of sentences. The broker who had erred, a short, harmless-looking, balding guy—the one from the soup whom Lion had been hollering at—appeared shell-shocked and said nothing at all. At some point, he silently wandered out of the pit. When he eventually returned, he looked slightly more calm. Had he gone in the bathroom and vomited? Cried? Popped a Valium?

Everyone in the general vicinity of the pit was conferring in their own little circles—the Market reporters, the clerks, the phone brokers, all whispering. The clerks around me came to the consensus that Bev was not going to—and should not—settle.

A man in a suit arrived on the Floor and entered the pit. In a voice too soft for me to hear, he discussed the situation. "I absolutely understand your point," Bev said, "but I verified with him, and he said, 'Yes. Yes.' That's what he said."

The new broker, needing to defend himself, finally spoke up: "That was the Market they gave me, that was the spread."

The others shook their heads. Lion whipped his pen to the ground.

"So the greatest fucking trade is the thirty-second loser?" Bev said. "Remember the last time we were all here? Do you know how much it cost me the last time the Fed cut rates? Three million. I sold 350 of 'em, and got 200 back. Three million the last time! Do you guys remember?"

Three million? And I had thought the two million they were currently arguing about was a ridiculously large sum. I laughed to myself at my own naïveté. If I was lucky, I'd see half that in my lifetime, and here they were, making that and losing that in one day, on a single trade, over the span of a few minutes. And, of course, Bev had made many other trades today, too. How many of those were winners? Million-dollar winners? I rested my chin on my arms as I leaned against the rail. So why didn't Bev just save herself a lot of aggravation and give some of her trade back? When you had that much money was it worth your time to argue over more? Here, at least, it was. You couldn't just give in on the Floor; it's not about the money, or even about being right or wrong, it's about being tough, and, probably most of all, being feared.

Sean was among the group still in the pit, and he weighed in, "Reality is that after the Fed eases, and it's that loud and fast in here, even I don't know where anyone is."

"It's true," Bev said. "Even the boards are printing behind."

Lion had plopped down on a pit step, and now that he'd had a chance to calm down, some of the viciousness had melted from his face. I had decided that I detested him from the moment I saw him shoving his way through the pit, but now, his on-fire rage had been replaced by a flushed-cheek boyish quality that made him seem like a chubby housecat. I'd come to recognize a normalcy in transformations such as this; traders' steel exteriors would fade with a short respite after the closing bell. Terminators in the pit would return to their regular selves, and would often, surprisingly, be decent, nice, easygoing people.

The group in the pit started tossing out numbers, ways to compromise, in terms that were nothing more than gibberish to me: "Five-hundred-fifty last five-year bundles." "Two-year bundle L5 was the spread." "Two-year versus last five." "Tens."

Bev snapped, "Are you out of your fucking minds? I am not doing that trade for anything less than five." The man in the suit pulled Bev aside. The new broker at the center of it all waited silently, his hands plunged in his pockets. I wondered how he was going to show his face in this pit tomorrow?

At some point, a decision was reached. Because I was still working on mastering the language, I didn't understand what the outcome was. I searched for some hint of emotion, but they were all poker-faced. In this game, you win some and you lose some, and they all knew that you better not pout or gloat because one day you're bound to be on the opposite side—and it's the sore loser or the exultant winner whom everyone remembers and makes a point of getting back at. The place cleared out immediately; no one dawdled or hung around to chat. I tried to find another clerk who could tell me if Bev had won or lost, but I was suddenly the only one in yellow.

When I returned home, I had an urgent need to scrub off what felt like a layer of sweat and grime from the Floor. After showering, it was my habit to flip on the radio or the television, but instead all I craved was silence. I called Tom that evening to share the open-ended gossip of the day. Curious, he made some calls along the trader grapevine and got back to me later with the verdict: he wasn't sure of the outcome of the dispute, but either way, Bev walked off the Floor having made $4 million.

"Today?" I said, needing to verify that we weren't talking about something a little more comprehensible—yet still remarkable—like $4 million for an *annual* take.

"Yep," he said. "A $4 million day."

SIX

Reverse Crush

This is a rare spread that's unique to the Soybean pits at the Chicago Board of Trade. In a reverse crush, you sell contracts in Soybean Futures while simultaneously buying contracts in Soybean Oil and Meal Futures. Normally, prices in the various pits of the Soybean market move together, but occasionally the prices become unaligned—maybe there's an oversupply of Oil and Meal and an undersupply of Soybeans, or maybe the price of processing the Oil and Meal went up. Whatever the case, if the pits are temporarily out of sync, you can sneak in a quick profit.

While the Merc is the world's busiest Futures Exchange, the neighboring Chicago Board of Trade is the world's oldest. Established in 1848, the Board started with only agricultural Commodities; today, over 3,600 members trade forty-eight different Futures and Options products. The Board is also the original Old Boys' Club. For 121 years, no women members were allowed. While in recent years the Merc has surpassed the Board in terms of volume and revenue, the Board has managed to maintain the reigning Old Boys' crown, and hangs on to it with white knuckles.

The Board of Trade building on Jackson and LaSalle streets was erected in 1885—the tallest building in the city at the time and the first to have electrical lighting. In the late 1920s, it was rebuilt into the block-long, Art Deco limestone structure of today, jutting out from the orderly grid of the Chicago Loop to dead-end LaSalle Street. From blocks away, you can scan down LaSalle, past the tidy row of skyscrapers, to the perpendicular behemoth at the end, where, at its peak, towers the thirty-one-foot, cast-aluminum statue of Ceres, the Goddess of Grain and Harvest. She wields a sheaf of wheat in one hand and a bag of corn in the other, and guards the square that's become known as the Financial Canyon.

On the ground floor of the Board of Trade building is every amenity a trader could want: a travel agency, a cigar shop, a hair salon, and a bar, aptly named Ceres. Before it became Ceres, however, it was called Sign of the

Trader, and they moved more alcohol during the 1980s than any other bar in the state. Its logo was the different hand signals, and traders endearingly nicknamed the bar Sign of the Finger; they also gave it a catchphrase: "Walk in, crawl out." Even the Board of Trade's lobby gained notoriety, for it was popularly considered to be the best pickup spot in the city.

My source for some of these dubious distinctions was an after-work gathering of eight veteran Board of Trade traders. My connection to them was a trader named Bob, a friend of a friend whom I had recently met at a Cubs game. He was the first contact I'd made at the Board of Trade, so when he invited me to hang out there, I took him up on the offer, eager to see if the Board differed at all from the Merc. Their happy hour began at around 3 p.m. on a summer Thursday at the outside terrace of Ceres. It seemed that male traders were always up for including a woman—even if no one really knew her—in their happy hours, but, as it turned out, I was the only female there. Most of the traders at the table were second-, even third-generation, and they all considered themselves Big Old Boys. One thing about the Board Big Boys was immediately clear: they shared a collective dislike of the Merc. They seized on every chance to put in a jab regarding the Merc, the Merc jerks, the trust-fund boys there, the lazy boys there, the silver-spoon this, and the white-collar that. I ordered a Corona, and they shook their heads, lamenting, "Oh, poor girl, you've been hanging out with the Merc people too long." One trader informed me of the distinction: "The Merc is Jews and Italians. The Board is Anglo."

"We're Irish!" another trader proudly proclaimed, and then there was a round of slams on everyone who was not Irish. The steady put-downs were surpassed only by the even steadier round of shots, each glass filled well past the white line. In between the shots were rounds of Guinness beer, and a parade of food that was Ceres signature—homemade potato chips, still hot and dripping grease, nachos, popcorn. The men devoured it all, stacking the empty plates next to those that held the remnants of BBQ wings, which they'd polished off before I had arrived.

Bob was miserable over what he described as a "very, very bad day." After the alcohol began to take effect, he went into more detail: "Europe cut interest rates, so I thought that would be good for the U.S., and I went long. But instead, the Market tanked. Straight fuckin' down." He tossed back another shot.

The disproportionate ratio of empty glasses to full was aggravating another trader, Eddie. "Who's our waitress? Where's Kathy? Where's Betty? Why hasn't anyone seen them?" A unison of shrugs.

"Don't you miss Sign of the Trader?" Chucky, a pink-faced trader, offered up. "You know how bartenders, when they're pouring, they do a count of three? Well, these guys, they counted to twelve. No lie. Times were great then. I mean I had done a full day's work and was ready to play by one-thirty in the freakin' afternoon. We'd all go out, get some beer, make it home in time to sleep for a few hours, then go out to eat. But then, you know, they started changing things. Pits started opening at 8:30 a.m., which is early, but okay, you're still out at 1:15 p.m. Then they moved the open in the Bonds to 7:20 a.m. Then they started the Dow pit, which trades until 3:15 p.m. Now they've got all-night trading. It's round the clock! The good old days are long over."

The others joined in on the reminiscing. "Yeah, remember the Quaalude stress clinics?" one trader said. "They sprang up all over. Doctors used to be able to write unlimited prescriptions."

"Yeah," Chucky said, "and remember how the big guys would hire strippers all the time? There would be strip clubs in offices upstairs at the Board. It was eighties excess. Tons of money, tons of blow, tons of alcohol, tons of sex. Back then, bosses could say 'nice tits' to a woman. The women at the Board back then were cookies. But there were only a very few who proved themselves, and they were seen as brains, not bods. My little sister worked on a computer at the Board for a short time. I guess she liked it. She wasn't a hottie or nothin', so she wasn't bothered by any of the guys."

The waitress appeared and Eddie, a row of empty bottles in front of him, said playfully, "Where have you been? I'm absolutely parched!" For a couple more hours, there was no shortage of drink or disparaging commentary. But as it neared dinnertime, the ages of the Big Old Boys and the other requirements of their lives—like wives and families—began to take precedence, and the group thinned. One guy had ridden his bicycle in and debated if he was too drunk to ride it home. He wisely decided to lock up the bike and ride it back tomorrow.

Eddie, after taking care of the entire tab, got up to leave for the train station. "Don't sleep through your stop," everyone called after him. "The wife's not going to be happy if you call her from Joliet." Joliet is the last stop on the line, and the way Eddie nodded indicated it had happened before, more than once.

I hadn't said too much during the happy hour. I had been afraid that if I opened my mouth I would've been too tempted to fire back every time they made a derogatory comment—which was about every two minutes. Under any other circumstances, I would have just up and left early on, but I was eager to learn about the Board, and I knew the only way I was going to do that was if I just kept quiet. I had heard there were fewer women at the Board of Trade than at the Merc, and I now understood why—if the prevailing attitude toward women at the Merc seemed provincial, then the attitude at the Board seemed downright primitive. There was one woman, however, whom the Big Boys had mentioned, and whose name I'd heard before as someone who was a staple at the Board: Virginia McGathey.

Virginia was a broker in the Wheat Options pit who not only owned her own firm—which is a rarity for a woman in this field—but who employed primarily women. A nearly all-female brokerage firm in this environment was something I had to see. It took some asking around, but, once again, Chicago could operate like a small town, so it wasn't long before I came across someone—an acupuncturist, of all people—who knew Virginia and gave me her phone number. Virginia, otherwise known as Ginni, was bois-terously warm and immediately invited me down to the Floor to watch her and "the girls."

Brokers trade other people's money, unlike Locals, who trade their own money. A broker earns a commission on each contract he or she trades, regardless of whether the trade was a winner or loser. Brokers have a very different existence from Locals. In the food chain of the trading floor, bro-kers are at the top. They typically carry the largest orders, since their cus-tomers are big institutions and firms. These sizable trades often dictate the swing of a market—the broker drops a huge order and the Locals react.

For brokers, the job mentality is bell-to-bell. Once the Market closes, there's no work to take home, no pressure to keep you up at night checking your positions, no reason to break into a cold sweat watching your account plunge. Your job is solely to execute trades for your customers' accounts, fol-lowing their specific orders (unless your customer grants you personal dis-cretion, and then you're allowed to make the decisions on what actions to take). Your skill as a broker enters in when you are trying to get your customer the best price in the pit; if you don't, you're not out money, but could be out a customer—official contracts rarely exist between customers and brokers, most often a relationship is solidified by a handshake agreement. This is why lavish schmooze-fests between brokers and customers occur at regular intervals. The broker lures the customer with entertainment—full-out dinners at Chicago's priciest steakhouses, private shows at strip clubs, trips to Vegas— and then consistently works on keeping the customer happy. For Christmas gifts: high-end DVD players, crates of fine wine, or, in greatly profitable years, vacations for the whole family, even a car; and then the seasonal perks: Cubs tickets, Bulls games, more strip clubs, more trips to Vegas. Loyalty tends to have a steep price tag on the trading floor. Of course, the happy customer is often apt to reciprocate just as generously.

While the broker doesn't take on the risk that a Local does, the broker— unlike the Local—does not have unlimited profit potential. To pare it down, the broker is like a store manager. Both have low risk, but both can only handle up to a certain amount of business. For the store manager, that's determined by the amount of inventory; for a broker, it's how many orders he or she is physically able to fill in a day. The store manager can increase income by charging more for the merchandise or by selling more expensive merchandise; likewise, the broker can earn more by upping commissions or by handling larger trades—it's the same effort to say "Sold!" for a one-lot as it is for a one hundred-lot. Still, there is a cap at some point. The store manager must turn people away when it's closing time, and if the lines are too long, business will start going elsewhere. Same with the broker; if he's inundated, he's not going to be able to get good fills for all his customers, and, when that bell rings—and not a second later—the day is over.

Locals, on the other hand, are like entrepreneurs. They have unlimited risk and unlimited profit potential, and they take home both their wins and their losses. Some Locals do amazingly well; others blow themselves out in the blink of an eye. But even those who do amazingly well live with the possibility of getting blown out. Brokers, likewise, can do extremely well—in the millions-upon-millions-of-dollars-a-year well if they are filling large contracts—but without the threat of going belly-up.

Brokers also have prestige. They're the Paper, and the Locals want Paper. As much as brokers need the Locals to provide liquidity, the Locals need the brokers *more*. The better acquainted a Local is with a broker—and the closer the Local can stand to a broker in the pit—the more likely that the Local will get the trades he or she wants when she wants them. The top step of the pit is reserved for the top brokers, and in the caste of the Floor, there is no better spot.

Ginni McGathey, I'd learn, was a different type of broker in every aspect; most notably, she took on huge risks—not risks in the Market, but risks on the Floor. She'd persevered despite all odds stacked against her, and she continued to risk her own standing by speaking up for the rights of others on the Floor—especially women. Ginni was the ammunition behind numerous causes that most other traders would helplessly shrug off. She often found herself in the center of controversy, and, more often than not, it was her versus the governing powers of the Board of Trade.

Ginni sent a clerk, her twenty-one-year-old niece Autumn, to escort me onto the Floor of the Board of Trade. The trading floor is a 92,000-square-foot expanse, making it the world's largest continuous trading hall. Unlike the Merc, the Board is older and not as technologically advanced; this Floor has no tiers, no winding staircases, it's no jungle gym, but that doesn't diminish the gritty magnitude. The pits are crowded and deafening and crude, and the expansive space can be quite disorienting, as evidenced by the placards taped to the wall, designating that I was facing the "South Wall." The Floor is divided in two; one side is the Financials, the other Commodities—Soybeans, Soybean Oil, Soybean Meal, Corn, Wheat. The hours in the Grain Commodities are unbeatable—9:30 a.m. to 1:15 p.m. Although I imagined that if you were losing, even a four-hour workday could seem endless.

As we approached the Grains, the opening bell sounded—*ding, ding, ding!*—like the start of a boxing match, and everyone came out fighting. Ginni stood like a maestro at the base of the half-circle Wheat Options pit. Her chorus was the Options traders, a compendium of young and old, scruffy and pressed. They looked to her as she and her brokerage group, McGathey Commodities, called out their orders. The group consisted mostly of Ginni's relatives: her two brothers; two nieces, Melinda and Autumn; and Melinda's former college roommate, Nicole. They all wore the McGathey Commodities jacket, khaki with navy accent. The badges here weren't as obvious as those at the Merc, and it was difficult to determine who was a clerk since, instead of the uniform mustard-colored eyesore, clerks wore the same color jacket as the trader or firm for which they worked. Here, the men were still required to wear ties—though they all seemed to make do with golf shirts ringed with ties loose enough to be slipped over the head. Of course, nothing matched and several glaringly bad cases were enough to make me wince.

Being here was a different experience than being at the Merc, for I wasn't a clerk, but a *guest*—and a guest of someone whom everyone knew. In my street clothes—black slacks and a light-blue cardigan—I stood out from the jackets in a way that attracted just enough attention to, I'm embarrassed to admit, give me a little ego rush. Autumn then took me on a grand tour of the Floor. We crossed through the underpass to the Financial side. While the Commodities used to be the shining glory of the Board, the Bonds have long since surpassed them. A CNBC correspondent has a regular post just outside the Bond pit, which resembles the Eurodollar pit at the Merc—wide, huge, and crazy. A couple of retired Chicago Bears had traded in this pit, one of whom—a six-feet-three, 270-pound line-man—lasted only a month before switching to a less vicious Grain pit. Like the S&P's "Pit Viper," the Bond pit had a "Pit Bull," a trader who'd earned this nickname after biting another trader's nose and drawing blood.

As we walked by, a trader shouted at me, "Someone give that girl a job!" Laughter erupted. "I'll hire her!" someone yelled in response. It was impossible to tell who was spewing the taunts. Autumn rolled her eyes. "Just ignore them," she said.

We passed the Dow Jones pit, which has had its ups and downs since it opened in 1997. Next door was the Dow Options pit, which had experienced an even worse time. Guys hung along the railings, kicking around the paper strewn about the ground. Others were sitting on the pit steps, waiting, waiting, waiting for something to happen so they could snap into action. One trader was sucking on a candy cane, decided he didn't want the rest, and, without a care, tossed it to the floor. Another trader was yelling at someone: " '*I'm sorry*' doesn't get the money back!" This was the pit in which Tara had purchased a seat a few years ago for $30,000. The seat itself is a Commodity, and a volatile one at that. Not long after Tara made her "investment," she watched it diminish to a worth of $5,000. The seat value scaled abysmal depths for over a year, and Tara couldn't even think about her holding without getting her jaw all clenched in knots. Then, miraculously, the seat made a gallant rebound, and now was all the way back to

$20,000. Tara's was one of the lowest-frills seats available; other seats that enable one to trade numerous high-volume products fluctuate in price into the upper six or even seven figures. Many traders, and nontraders alike, buy, sell, and hold seats much as they do stock shares.

We headed back to the Commodity side, where the numbers weren't flipping like they were in the Bonds. In fact, the reporting boards lining the walls were relatively static today. This side also didn't function like the arb-laden conveyor belt of the Merc, it was more antiquated: this order goes in this bucket, run this card to that person, take this order to that pit. The majority of traders here seemed older and grayer and heavier, and I felt that the general attitude was that if you were not a veteran or second-generation trader, it was as if you didn't exist.

Ginni was first generation, which made her achievements all the more impressive. At this moment, however, her position did not appear that enviable. An irate trader named Mike was jabbing a stubby finger in Ginni's face. "You know what I'd like to do?" he shouted at her. Ginni stood there, taking it, restraining herself from doing what *she'd* like to do. The trader's face was boiling, beads of sweat bubbled on his upper lip. It was not yet 10 a.m. Autumn explained to me what the situation was: just a few minutes earlier, Ginni had doled out trades to three traders, but had passed by the one now confronting her. It wasn't something she had done on purpose, it was just how the game worked—she was the broker and it was, "Ten to you," "Five to you," "Two to you," and as for the rest, nothing personal, catch you next time—unless, that is, you throw a tantrum every time I dole out a large contract.

Mike looked ready to explode, and everyone in the pit was watching. Ginni tapped her foot like, fine, I'll just let him throw his little fit, yeah, yeah, I'm waiting, what is it you'd like to do? He sucked in his breath until his chest puffed up. "I'd like . . . I'd like . . ," he scowled. The pit leaned in, as if everyone wanted to tell him to just spit it out already! Finally, he shouted: "I'd like to take all the McGatheys and get 'em all together, and BLOW THEM UP!"

Whoa, even Ginni seemed taken aback, for that wasn't your typical trading-floor threat of Screw you! or Go to hell! Everybody stared. *What was this crazy man talking about?*—and, more important, *What was Ginni going to say to him?* A hush fell over the Wheat Options pit as everyone waited for Ginni. It was almost as if the Floor had gone dark and a lone spotlight was flipped directly on this five-feet-five, brown-haired woman. Would she back down and apologize, swallowing her pride for the sake of keeping peace? Or would she scream right back at him and turn this into a shouting match? To me, these seemed to be her only two options: either slice off a chunk of her clout and hand it to him—spoon-feed it to him!— or stoop to his level, which was like slicing off a chunk of her dignity and passing it around the pit for all to sample.

Unless, that is, you are Virginia McGathey. Then, perhaps you're savvy enough to have some other plan of action. Of course, Ginni's face gave no indication of this, and she eyed the trader as if he were calmly making small talk about the weather and not bouncing around, gesticulating wildly to further emphasize his ballistic fantasy.

"Mike," Ginni said casually, "are you trying to flirt with me again?"

The pit roared! Ginni pivoted on her heels and returned to her stack of orders. The trader was bursting—his face, explosive burgundy—but the words? There were none! What could he say to *that*?

As beautiful and perfect a comeback as this was, that wasn't why Ginni did it. She later told me she'd done it to salvage the relationship, so that she and Mike didn't end up in a drawn-out fight, with daily mudslinging that would eventually heighten to the point where it would be difficult ever to recover from it all. Ginni had seen many simple feuds turn high-school-girl-catfight nasty, where even the deepest, decrepit skeletons in your closet were dredged up and tossed into the center of the pit. I had never imagined that this male bastion could be more gossipy and petty than a sorority house, but Ginni described to me the stages in which it happened: first, it would seem like an annoying midmorning game of Telephone, where the dirt on you would zip around the circle, gaining embellishment with every whisper. But then, just when you thought they'd had their fun, you'd be blindsided by the details that were surfacing—details you'd thought were private, things that even your spouse or your best friends didn't know. And now it was all common knowledge here. You would start to feel sick—it would have been better *not* knowing that people on the Floor were privy to your every indiscretion. And worse, you had to stand next to them every day, knowing they *knew*. But there was still one more punch waiting for you: eventually, if the war raged on, everyone in the pit would be forced to take sides. It would become a spiraling mess, and suddenly, your pit, where you used to joke and laugh and belch and sing and do a little dance if you'd wanted to, would be transformed into what Ginni called "The Haters."

"So, I saved Mike from all that," Ginni told me offhandedly, "because I don't need him."

Ginni had declared to me right up front: "I don't give a shit at this point about what I say. If I say something disparaging, well, many of these people here are assholes and they can fuck themselves and the horse they rode in on. The men will say right in front of you, 'She's so stupid!' So the next time he wants a trade, who in their right mind wouldn't say"—she jabbed the air with emphasis—" '*You*, zero!' " As she enacted this, a trader passing by shook his head with mock awe and declared, "No one can point a finger like Virginia."

Ostensibly, Ginni had everything it takes to be successful on a trading floor: she was extremely quick with numbers and calculations; likewise, she was extremely quick with words in the way traders and brokers need to be—effortlessly flinging applause-worthy comebacks, put-downs, and slams. But for all her tough-headedness, she also possessed the seemingly contradictory quality of open-mindedness. To hear her, you'd think you'd feel intimidated by her, but—and maybe too bad for her—you don't.

Perhaps this was why Ginni seemed the bon enfant—although a reluctant one—of the Board of Trade. She had no real desire to be the consummate do-gooder—certainly no one else on the Floor gave much value to altruism—and yet, for two decades, all the injustices, charity cases, and causes had managed to find her, showing up with pleading eyes at the base of the Wheat Options pit. Becoming involved in situations like these was a huge risk for Ginni, and she was often anguished by the almighty forces she referred to as Downstairs, the governing body of the self-regulated Board of Trade, which did not much appreciate her interference. Over the years, Downstairs and Ginni had become well acquainted due to Ginni's attempts to—in her eyes—right the wrongs and—in their eyes—meddle. She was the feisty broker, not afraid of being the loudmouth that Downstairs would like to muzzle.

"They're all screwed up down there," Ginni told me. "They pick on who they want to pick on. Blowing like reeds in the wind." For effect, she raised her hands above her head and swayed. "Oooh, we're over here . . ." she said, making her voice high and airy. She swayed her arms to the other side. "Oooh, now we're over there." She whistled to simulate a breeze.

Ginni readily admitted she'd made enemies along the way, and Downstairs reminded her of this fact by fining her every several years for various charges. She talked of the fines with a wit-tinged bitterness; these were wounds she'd long since stopped worrying about, although they'd likely never heal. I didn't understand why Ginni invited so much controversy—she seemed all-around likeable to me. But then she volunteered a tidbit that I figured could make all the difference in the world—at least in a world such as this: She was a lesbian.

For a woman to speak as gruffly and crudely as Ginni was capable, especially when she was riled up—which was often—you'd think she might have stubble on her face. Rather, she had lipstick, perfectly applied, complementing her perfectly straight bob of chestnut hair. She was, undisputedly, an attractive woman. It was no secret that many of the men on the Floor were put off by the fact that someone as pretty as Ginni took no interest in them. Ginni had never advertised that she was a lesbian, but somehow the Floor—always the breeding ground for juicy confabulation—had managed to discover it.

"Her girlfriends are better-looking than mine," one male trader—who didn't personally know Ginni but knew *of* her—informed me. It was constantly perplexing to Ginni and her firm how vital this token piece of information about her sexual orientation had become. It had been used against Ginni on many occasions, especially when she was vying with other brokers for new business. Customers had apprized Ginni, after the fact, that the competing broker had felt it necessary to bring up the issue of Ginni's lesbianism, as if it might somehow affect her performance in the pit. I found the brokers' method for trying to crush Ginni quite interesting, for it was the complete reverse of the tactics I'd previously witnessed—usually, a woman on the Floor was debased with stories linking her to numerous men or to the man responsible for putting her in the pit; but here, they tried to discredit Ginni with how many men she *hadn't* been with, or needed, or used.

Ginni simply brushed it all off as provincial ignorance. "This whole place is full of dinosaurs," she said.

In 1975, when she was seventeen years old, Ginni went looking for a job as a runner at the Chicago Board of Options Exchange, a subsidiary of the Board of Trade that was a smaller, slightly gentler arena. No one would hire her. She loved the feel of the trading floor and didn't want just to walk away, so she persisted, and struck a deal with a trader: if he would sign her up as his runner, she would work for free to gain the necessary experience.

After one week, the trader was so impressed with Ginni that he officially hired her and gave her back pay for all the time she'd put in.

Four years later, when Ginni turned twenty-one years old, she received her badge, VM, and started trading for a company. That lasted for several years, but the Options Exchange was slow then, and Ginni longed for more action. On the Exchange steps one day, she serendipitously ran into a childhood friend and told him how she wanted to move on. He wrote a phone number on a matchbook and handed it to her. "These guys I know are looking for Options people to start up a trading group at the Board," he said. "They may have something for you." Ginni called the number, and with that, she found herself an opening at the Board of Trade. To save up money, she moved home with her mom and took a second job in the afternoon, and soon she'd socked away enough to buy herself a seat in the Corn Options pit.

While there had been a handful of women at the Options Exchange, the Board of Trade was a different story altogether. Even women clerks were sparse. Ginni can remember only four other women traders on the entire Floor at that time, all fighting to stay above water in a sea of thousands of men. She also discovered that, even though she'd been trading at the Options Exchange, she couldn't just walk into the Board and be accepted— nope, she had to start over completely. She instinctively felt more inclined toward the clerks, as if they were her peers; after all, she was used to starting at the bottom rung and working up. Only, the clerks had their own circle, and the significant distinction of Ginni's *badge* exempted her from them. "All the desk people, all the clerks, immediately looked at me differently," Ginni said. "I didn't have a lot of money, but to them, when you have a badge it's like the whole aura around you changes." The flip-side caveat was that she wasn't going to fit in with most of the traders either. It didn't seem to matter to them that she knew Options forward and backward—the VM pinned to her trading jacket was completely diminished by the fact that VM was a woman.

The argument could be made that recent lawsuits brought by women against large Wall Street firms for unequal compensation or for creating an impermeable glass ceiling actually prove our society has evolved; for at the time Ginni began at the Board, in the mid-1980s, a vociferous male trader was met with a round of cheers from the pit when he summed up the overwhelming mentality of the Floor: "You," he said to Ginni, "belong on your back at home."

The original Options pits at the Board of Trade were Corn and Beans, and around the time that Ginni started, the higher-ups had been discussing the possibility of a Wheat Options pit. They wanted to assemble a group of eager and diligent traders who would help set this idea in motion. Someone mentioned VM, that she'd come from the Options Exchange, and, after all, how could a newcomer—and a young woman, no less—say no? While Ginni's name was being tossed around in a conference room in the upper echelons of the Board, back down on the trading floor, Ginni was being met with constant resistance. "I was first and you know it, and I deserve that trade!" she would scream to coercive traders who thought it all right to bully her. She'd fight for her positions day after day—until one morning, she felt a tap on her shoulder. It was a man Ginni had never before seen and he'd come to ask if she'd help put together the specs for a Wheat Options pit. "I must have just been approachable or something," Ginni told me, in her unassuming manner.

As it turned out, no better decision could have been made than choosing Ginni as a member of the founding group—and the move also changed Ginni's life. She was smart and hungry, and she took to the task as her sole way of getting an *in* at this place that discounted her before she even opened her mouth. "There I was, I had absolutely no money, I came from a blue-collar background and never went to college, I had a $1,000-a-month seat payment that I could barely afford, and on top of it I was trying to build up capital to trade with," Ginni remembered. "So when I started to put this new pit together, I finally felt like I was somebody."

It was difficult for me to believe that someone like Ginni could have any insecurities left after spending so many years on the trading floor, yet, while talking with her, I sensed one: Ginni often mentioned that she only had a high-school education. Shortly after I'd met her, she'd offered it up in an I-don't-want-to-misrepresent-myself way, although a second later, she was inadvertently negating her own disclaimer by effortlessly intermingling SAT-caliber prose with her healthy string of four-letter words. Initially, when assembly of the Wheat Options pit began, Ginni had never felt more intimidated by her lack of higher education—but that soon passed. "I found out very quickly that nobody at the Board of Trade knew their ass from first base about Options," Ginni said. "I was flabbergasted! When the Board of Options Exchange is only twenty paces away, how can this be Neanderthal Options here? But that's what really helped me out—I knew all about Options, so if anyone ever talked strategies, I could talk to them about it." Ginni took her position developing the Wheat Options pit seriously: she consulted with the Wheat Growers Association and with the chairman of the Board, and she fought—and won—to have the pit set up stadium-style and in a half-circle so the traders would have direct sightlines and open communication with the Wheat Futures pit.

And then, when the pit was near completion, someone asked Ginni a simple, yet pivotal, question: "Will you be filling orders?" Ginni hadn't ever thought about it, she had just assumed she wasn't smart enough, wasn't educated enough, wasn't well connected enough, wasn't rich enough—the list went on—to become a broker. And yet, here was a legitimate trader, asking her, with all sincerity, "Will *you* be filling orders?"

Maybe it was just that simple—maybe if she made up her mind to do it, she could become a broker. She Xeroxed a stack of résumés and handed them like flyers around the Floor. She got the looks she expected. "Who's this little girl coming around trying to get business in the new pit?" She just smiled, pretending these men—these *potential customers*—weren't complete strangers, but people she'd known for years. A trader she had worked with in the Corn Options pit had given her some daunting advice: "Go after the big commercial houses. That way, you get the big orders and you don't have to dick around with the small stuff." So there was Ginni, pitching the Big Boys, her cheery smile never wavering, even though their faces conveyed it loud and clear, *We're not going to give you anything*! But Ginni kept going, her mantra: just smile and hand them the résumé, and don't flinch—don't flinch! When a floor manager for one of the big companies told her, "I would never give any of our orders to a woman, even if you were the only broker in the pit!" Ginni, all pearly whites, replied, "You're missing the point," and walked on to the next group. Don't look back, don't look back, don't look back. And then, she finally got her turn: a firm manager looked her résumé up and down, and said: "Absolutely."

Ginni's life became the trading floor. She'd arrive at 8 a.m., spend the day trying to build her business, then at 2 p.m., after the Market closed, she'd trade-check to earn some extra money. She'd work until 10 at night, then spend an hour on the train back to her mom's house in the suburbs, and start it all over again the next morning. "I had nothing else but the Board of Trade," she said. "But it was a great thing." She managed to secure a few other accounts, it wasn't a lot, and business was going to be slow but, still, she was going to be in the pit, as a broker.

The day finally arrived when the Wheat Options pit ceremoniously opened. But for all the planning, all the hype, and all the hope, nothing much happened. There was hardly any business—and it would take time before any came. Every day, Ginni stood there, for the four-hour stretch, waiting. "I probably read every single newspaper every day of that first year," Ginni said of the awful boredom. She was one of five brokers in the fledgling Options pit, and one of the only ones who was first generation. Most of the others had fathers in Wheat Futures, and they wanted to hoard the new product. When an order did come through, it didn't matter that Ginni had helped establish this pit, no, she still had to fight for her survival. Her mantra became a steady, defensive shout to the nepotistic crowd: "This is my deck and you're not going to tell me how to fill it!"

But then a curious thing happened: business picked up, and with that, there was a surprising shift in power. "As orders started coming in, the sophistication of Options hindered the other brokers because they didn't know what the hell they were doing!" Ginni said. "When their customers started calling, they would come up to me and say, 'Now, how do I fill this order? What does it mean when my customer's saying this or that?' " Ginni felt violated that everyone just expected to feed off her expertise—she'd fought and scrimped—and moved in with her mother for goodness sake!—to be able to stand in this pit. And here were these men—her competitors—who'd been handed a seat, and on top of that, they now expected her to help them? How unfair could this get? But it was her mother's advice that stuck with Ginni: "You reap what you sow. These kind of people will die by their own hand. You don't have to deny them when they come to you—it will all happen on its own."

And, ultimately, it did.

Ginni gave me one of her favorite examples of how it played out. Early on, she'd been elated when a large trading firm promised to give her their business. Only their idea of business was tossing Ginni the chump change while giving the prime orders to two other brokers in her pit. "There was no way I could go up to them and say, 'Hey, I thought you were going to give the business to me.' It just sounds so whiny," Ginni said. "I wanted to stay away from the stereotype of 'Oh there's this girl going around and complaining.' It was difficult, but it made me learn that I had to become really centered with myself." Ginni took the small business the firm gave her and was grateful for it—after all, they were one of the few firms keeping her afloat during those first couple of years. Still, it was painful to watch large orders funneled past her and handed to others who didn't know half as much about Options as she did. But Ginni went on, with bulletproof grin, just smile and trade, trade and smile.

One day, a few managers from the firm came to the pit with an issue that was perplexing them. They went through multitudes of number mumbo-jumbo with the broker who handled their large orders. Ginni couldn't help but overhear, and it was immediately clear to her that the problem was a simple conversion mix-up. Ginni watched the comedy of errors as the broker would verify an incorrect number and send a runner to deliver it to the desk manager. The runner would return, saying the number wasn't working, but no one knew why. So the broker would calculate it again, incorrectly, and send the runner back to the desk, and it would continue back and forth, back and forth, the poor runner, caught in between a bunch of befuddled egos. Finally, Ginni could stand it no longer and tapped the firm manager on the shoulder. "Is your customer having a problem?" she asked.

"Yeah," he said, exasperated. "No one can figure out what's going on!" Ginni explained the problem in a few sentences. The firm manager was amazed.

Immediately, the firm diverted all prime orders to Ginni—it was no more small lots for her! In fact, the firm was so impressed by Ginni that what they doled out to her were the large, complex, time-consuming, nail-biting orders—and this was great, except that the easy, quick-buck stuff was now handed off to the two other, relatively incompetent, brokers. Ginni knew she had some clout now, and that compelled her to stand up for herself. As diplomatically as possible, she said, "Look, guys, I'm working my ass off for you and then you get the gravy coming in and you give it to someone else." Miraculously, they saw her point, and from then on out, all business went to Ginni.

Ginni also walked away with a valuable lesson: her job as a broker wasn't just to trade, but to sell a service—*her* service, her knowledge, her agility in the pit. "I got scabs on my knees," she said, "but I have to be a salesperson. I talk to customers and tell them: 'I will guarantee that if you had your own badge you wouldn't be able to trade your account any better than I will.' "

In the tiered structure of the Floor, the broker may exert power over the Local, but it's the almighty Customer who has the power over the broker—the broker works for *them*, the large institution, the wealthy individual. The Customer is Chief, aloft in some corporate stronghold, sending the lone soldier into the pit to fight and scream for the best fill. And that's where the broker's stress comes in—for he or she is often the Customer's puppet. Pull the string one way, the arms go up in Sell, raise the other string, the puppet does Buy. And if the reactions aren't fast enough, deride and threaten and belittle the puppet as only the one holding the strings can.

The Chief's effrontery can sting, and while I was visiting the Floor, Ginni and two young brokers from her group, Melinda and Nicole, enacted a typical phone conversation with one of their larger, and more vocal, customers. Ginni dropped her voice for the imitation: " 'You idiot! Get off the phone! I want someone on the phone who knows what they're talking about! Go get someone, but not Melinda, I don't ever want to talk to Melinda on the phone!' "

Nicole took the stage: " 'Nicole, you stupid idiot! Where's Melinda? Get me Melinda! I need someone who knows what the hell is going on!' "

Melinda:" 'You dumb asshole! Oh, now you're crying, here we go!' "

Ginni shook her head. "We have no choice but to take it," she said. "I work my ass off but he'll bitch at me because he's out an eighth on a ten-lot when I just filled ten thousand of his shit better than anyone! But I've gotten to the point now where I tell him, 'You don't give me enough business for this bullshit, it's not worth it!' " She defiantly waved her hand. "Even if he did give me enough business, it still isn't worth it. I'll make less."

Ah, but when the customer was pleasant and treated the group with respect, that bon enfant in Ginni didn't hesitate to surface. In one such instance, a customer whom all the McGatheys described as "a really nice guy" happened to have his own badge along with dreamy visions of coming into the pit and trading his order all by himself. Ginni indulged him, and Melinda described the scene to me: "We know which traders make better markets because that's our job, but he's not here every day so he doesn't know this. So he comes into the pit and he's trying to fill the order and everyone's yelling so many things at him and he's looking, but he's not really seeing. So he overfills his order—he had a hundred contracts, and he's like: '25, 25, 25, 25, 25.' Then he turns to Ginni and says, 'Can you help me? I think I need to get out of some stuff.' "

"He says he wants to learn," Ginni sighed. "So sometimes I let him stand next to me and I teach him, and yeah, we lose a little money, but he's happy."

As my day visiting Ginni wore on, the Market continued to be uneventful. Business in the Grains tended to come in spurts—it was either crazy or sluggish, and when it was slow, it was often excruciatingly slow. That's when Locals would start daydreaming about natural disasters. They would get starry-eyed with visions of droughts, floods, fires, tornadoes—anything that would affect a crop, and it didn't matter if it was negatively or positively. Futures traders want feast or famine in those wheat fields or corn fields or soybean fields; after all, you can make money on the Up *and* money on the Down. Ginni had experienced her first real brush with the Commodity market's best friend, good old Mother Nature, early on in her career. She enthusiastically recalled the Drought of '88, infamous for hordes of traders shouting, "Beans in the teens! Beans in the teens!"

"I was filling up a storm then," Ginni said. "Granted, I took a bath a couple of times. But still, when things are that good, you think they can never be bad again. And it's kind of ironic because right before the drought I really thought about throwing in the towel." I was taken aback by Ginni's admission, and even more surprised that she grew quiet and contemplative when I asked about it. The seconds of silence and the awkward shift of someone brash suddenly turning emotional made me want to squirm.

"Before I had my own firm, I had started trading and I knew exactly what to do—I just could not pull the trigger myself," she began. "I think it was my own personal demons, my own questioning of myself. I'd hesitate and then the trade would be gone—but I'd still go for it anyway, only I'd get in too late and it would go against me and then I'd scramble to get out. I basically marked up a $25,000 loss and then I tried to get it back, and milked it to a $60,000 loss. I hated coming to work. I would have preferred being home in the fetal position all day. But every morning I'd come in on the train, only instead of going straight to the Board, I'd go into old St. Mary's Church and I would sit there and cry. One day a priest came over, Father Dennis. It was a little miracle that day. I had felt like I wasn't going to go back to work, but I had invested so much time and energy and besides, I was only a high-school graduate, what else was I going to do? I was $60,000 in debt and paying that off would take a lifetime if you're making $15,000 to $20,000 a year. But the priest told me, 'Go back to work, the right thing is going to happen.' "

That very day, Ginni was summoned upstairs to her clearing firm. "The head guy just couldn't figure out why I couldn't trade," Ginni remembered. "What could I say? That I zigged when I should have zagged? That I wasn't used to having so much capital behind me and trading such big size? That I felt so on my own? That women didn't network, and guys wouldn't network with women, so I had to learn everything by myself and figure out all the strategies on my own? And that once you're down, it's so hard, it's this weight you have to lug around your neck?"

The firm informed Ginni that they were letting her go, but as a courtesy, they were willing to eat her losses, that is, after they claimed her seat and sold it. Ginni's seat had appreciated around $6,000 since she'd bought it, so the firm would collect that.

"As I was sitting there," Ginni told me, "it was literally just two hours after I had talked to Father Dennis and it came to me that my seat was my only ticket to be able to do *anything*, and that if I lost my seat, I'd have to work my way up again, and I'd never have any independence. So I said, 'If you sell my seat it will take at least thirty days to get that $6,000. What if I were to get a loan and give you your $6,000? I know I'd have to find another firm to take me, but I'd at least have my seat.' " To her surprise, they agreed—and gave her one week.

"I didn't know who would loan me that kind of money when I didn't have shit," Ginni said. She went to a friend who she knew could afford it, but he said no. She begged him, and finally he said, "I don't want to do this, but I will." He wrote her a check for $6,000, and she drew up a plan that she'd pay him back $400 or $500 dollars a month, including interest. She missed a couple of months, but paid him back within the set time. On the last month, he gave Ginni her check back. "Friends don't charge friends interest," he said.

Ginni had also been able to talk her way into a new clearing firm. "I had literally $200 in my account," she remembered, "and if I had just one single error, I was busted. I lived with that pressure for a number of months. But the rest is history—it was my miracle. I took a chance, and it panned out."

And then the Drought of '88 hit. Ginni went from struggling to make $20,000 a year, to making $20,000 in a single day. "It was unbelievable," she told me. "I really didn't even know how to handle it at first. Oh, but it was great."

Ginni's next encounter with a major drought was not until 1996, but it was far from the fantastic ride she'd previously experienced. She was in the middle of the Caribbean, on the first vacation she'd taken in years, when she received a frantic call from the Floor—"Come back, a drought's hit!" Ginni tried to charter a helicopter, but even then she wouldn't have made it back until Friday. So she helplessly waited out the cruise while tens of thousands of dollars disappeared on positions she'd been holding and on lost business. The losses continued to mount even after she returned home because she had a tough time adjusting to the swing of the Market. When it finally was all over, she'd lost a total of half a million.

After that, she relegated her travel to weekends only, but in an odd way she was okay with that. "There's a stimulus factor here," she said. "I got addicted to control—to knowing what's going on all over the world. You've got your finger on the pulse of everything, and when I'm not here, I miss it." I knew what she was saying, for when I was on the Floor, I always felt smack dab in the nerve center. It wasn't like sitting in an isolated cubicle and watching from the window as the world went by.

Melinda echoed the sentiment. "I love it here because there isn't a single thing that goes on that you don't hear about or talk about." Melinda was a cute, blond, twenty-five-year-old spitfire; petite and barely five feet two inches, she flitted around the Floor, not shy in the least about speaking her mind. She described herself as emotional and sensitive, and Ginni had initially worried that Melinda would have a tough time as a broker because she tended to take things too personally. Melinda admitted to me that she'd cried a lot in the beginning—but that was over, she didn't cry anymore. Instead, she got pissed off. She described to me a time that stood out in her memory where she was particularly furious: "There's this guy, Pete—" she began.

"Oh, he's a caveman," Ginni interjected.

Melinda ignored her aunt and continued. "He was checking trades and I had just gotten my badge and—this *still* pisses me off—he was talking to me, only he was talking to my *chest*, just STARING!"

Ginni laughed as she added commentary, "He's a big fat guy."

"So I called him on it in front of all his friends," Melinda continued. "I said, 'Pete, from now on, you'll talk to me from the neck up and that's all that's available to you whatsoever!' " From the degree Melinda was fuming I had expected some egregious tale, but, I must admit, a man eyeing a woman's chest seemed relatively mundane. Ginni thought so too, for she waved it off as a bunch of nonsense, and said, "Whenever they get into that conversation about who has big tits, I go, 'You guys, you know the only reason that the male population is infatuated with women's breasts is because it makes them feel closer to Mommy.' " She howled at her own comeback.

Melinda was not having any of it, and shook her head. "You go into a *bar* and you know to expect it. But when they do it at *work*, it's ridiculous."

"The thing is," Ginni said, "it's just something that happens here, and you can do with it as you will. You can take it as something difficult or as something that you can manage and say, look I'm onto that whole game."

Nicole nodded. "Once they realize that you're not down here to find a husband or to take advantage of the men," she said, "then you do earn some sort of respect—if that's what you can call it."

Melinda reluctantly agreed. Then a devious smile crept across her face. "But you can use it to your advantage sometimes," she said. "The power we have as girls is that we know how to handle a guy. We know how to be flirty and then get rid of him. We know how to manipulate—as bad as it sounds, we know how." I couldn't help but smile, for Melinda's philosophy did sound scheming, but, I was realizing, you had to use whatever strategy you could to get ahead here. Barring illegal tactics, any approach was perfectly fair—and some calculated flirting seemed to me far less distasteful than shouting obscenities in someone's face. Ginni, however, just sighed. "Women can be cunning," she said, then returned to her stack of orders.

When Melinda was sixteen years old, she began clerking for her aunt Ginni during summers. However, she had other long-term goals far removed from the trading floor, and off she went to college at the University of Illinois, where her major was premedicine. But after her junior year, things started unraveling, and she decided to take a break from school. She sought refuge with Aunt Ginni, who said, "Sure, you can stay at my house, but come Monday morning, you're starting work." At 9 a.m., Melinda was back on the trading floor, in her old clerk jacket. Only this time, Ginni began teaching her about trading. Melinda had always thought Options were too intricate for her, but it seemed the more she learned, the more she began to like it. She developed a good relationship with one of Ginni's biggest customers, and he told her that if she got a badge, he would send her orders in the pit. But Ginni shook her maternal head. "Not yet," she said, and made Melinda clerk in different pits—first, Corn Options, where they traded more spreads, and then the Bond Options pit, where Melinda was one of three girls in the entire pit of hundreds. "In the Grains, it's families," Melinda explained, "but in the Bonds, it's all these MBAs from the University of Chicago. I learned a lot there."

At around this time, Melinda's former college roommate, Nicole, was looking for a summer job. Nicole, tall and thin, with a girl-next-door attractiveness, came across as soft-spoken and serious—not exactly advantageous qualities for a trading floor—but since Nicole was approaching her senior year as a Finance major, Melinda suggested she come down to the Board. This was not the first of Melinda's friends to be presented to Aunt Ginni with the plea of "Please hire me." Ginni hadn't expected to be so impressed by Nicole, and in the end, she agreed to take her on as a clerk.

After the summer, Nicole returned to school and began interviewing for corporate jobs. She attended a job fair, where the Board of Trade had a booth; however, one professor made a comment along the lines of, "Girls, you shouldn't even bother going to the Board of Trade table."

Nicole received job offers from banks and investment companies, and debated over which to accept. And then it hit her: she didn't *want* to do any of these. "I couldn't see myself at a desk all day," she said. "I wanted to be down at the Board of Trade where every day was *new*." Nicole rejected the jobs and, with fingers crossed, called Ginni to ask if she needed any more help over the summer. Ginni sighed and said, "Come on down, we'll see what we got."

Melinda was clerking in Bonds, so Ginni took Nicole on as her primary clerk. With all these people on the payroll, Ginni began to have visions of expanding McGathey Commodities—she'd train the girls, they'd get badges, and then the firm would branch into other pits. The Dow Futures pit was the popular new kid on the block, and a Dow Options pit was soon to follow—Ginni could take the whole group there and stake a prime spot. She sent Nicole and Melinda to clerk in Dow Futures so they could learn and get used to the energy and the movement. "The pit was crazy!" Melinda said. "There were three-hundred-point swings, each day, every day!" Because of this, everyone was eagerly anticipating the opening of the Dow Options pit, and when the day finally arrived, the brand-new pit was packed.

"We had to stand sideways," Ginni remembered. "We were sure we had a hands-down winner, and that this would be *it*, that this would be a major feather in the cap of McGathey Commodities and that we were going to be *rich!*" There they were, all crammed in, waiting for the opening bell to ring, waiting for their trading careers to be off and running. The countdown was on . . . and then, the much anticipated *ding, ding, ding!*

And . . . silence. Dead silence.

There wasn't a single order. A few minutes passed, and then two Locals, just for the hell of it, just to fill the emptiness, traded with each other. Everyone started cheering because *someone* had made a trade. "We all realized that it still takes time to develop a product, no matter how good or how promising it seems," Ginni said. "Oh, my delusions of grandeur!"

Ginni continued to dabble in the Dow, and, during a lull in Wheat, she and I walked over to the Dow Options pit. It was still practically empty, and she said it was okay for me to sit next to her on the pit steps. Normally, someone without a badge isn't allowed in a pit—but it was so dead, no one was around to care. After a few minutes of zero action, we headed back to Wheat.

Despite the Dow Options disappointment, Ginni had enrolled Melinda and Nicole in a pit-trading course—an expanded version of the one-day trading seminar I'd taken—to prepare them for getting their badges. The girls found a little apartment and became roommates again. At night, they'd face each other and practice making the hand signals while yelling at the top of their lungs. When their neighbors started to look at them like they were crazy, they began practicing in the car so no one would hear them. They'd drive around the city and yell to each other until they lost their voices.

Melinda received her badge and brokerage license first. She and Nicole had decided they'd use their first names, so Melinda chose MLN as her acronym, which, she joked, also doubled for "million." Nicole quickly followed, and chose NIK.

"People always think that we must have slept with somebody to get a badge," Melinda said. "They think that any girl down there that's attractive, either (a) doesn't know shit, (b) is a golddigger, or (c) some guy gave you a badge because he felt like he had to. And people will say that!"

"But you know what," Nicole added quietly, "maybe seventy-five percent of the time it's true." I appreciated their struggle, and to me they sounded a lot like successful actresses who wanted to make it clear that they'd rejected the proverbial "casting couch" and had worked their way up on their own merits.

Ginni told me she had laid down one rule for the girls: they were not allowed to date anyone from the Board of Trade. "I was worried," Ginni said, "because women here have to be wary of falling prey to men." We were sitting outside the Wheat pit as Ginni said this, and as I looked across the Floor I glimpsed, taped above a desk, a barely clad centerfold. "There was a little mix-up, though," Ginni continued with a sarcastic toss of her head. "They must have thought I said, 'Only date men from the Board of Trade.'" Both Melinda and Nicole showed me the diamond rings on their fingers—given to them by traders.

When Melinda first got her badge, she decided to go into the Corn Options pit, for she had clerked there and knew the faces. Ginni's customer who'd originally suggested that Melinda start brokering, kept his end of the deal and bestowed on Melinda her first order—a five-hundred-lot! "If you want to talk about baptism by fire," Melinda said. "My badge was still temporary—it was written in marker—and new brokers have to go into the middle of the pit, plus, I'm essentially taking business from the other brokers who've been in that pit forever. So I stepped into the middle to drop this huge order, and my hands were shaking. They teach you to hold your pen in one hand and your cards in the other, but if you start shaking, grab onto your coat." She grabbed, she listened, she took it all in, then she screamed as loud as she could, and filled the entire order.

When Nicole received her badge, Ginni sent her into the Soybean Oil and Meal Options pit. It didn't take long before Ginni and her group bestowed a special award on this pit: The Most Dickheads Per Capita. "It's a pit with Haters," Ginni told me. "They spend all day trying to screw each other. See, each pit is its own little community, some are uplifting, some pull each other down. A pit is a collective of all the people within the confine. Some neighborhoods are fun and it's because they all decide to share with one another. In others, everyone's afraid of one another and they're all locked in. Nicole's pit needs a neighborhood watch." As I peered across the Floor, I never would have guessed by the looks of the Soybean Oil and Meal Options pit that it could be so vicious, although I suppose that's what's often said about serial killers. Still, it appeared much like every other pit, a mix of the veteran guys, most balding and stocky, and young second- or third-generation guys. There was even a woman, part of a mother-son team, both of whom were Orthodox Jews—he wore a yarmulke and she wore a wig, a long-sleeved blouse, and an ankle-length skirt.

Ginni and the girls, it seemed, could rant for hours about the Haters: "They are all blustery; they are all so full of themselves; all they talk about is whose Corvette is better than whose Porsche; there's nobody in that pit who's over five feet eight, so they have a collective Napoleon's problem!"

"Sometimes people are jerks in the pit, but outside, they really are good, nice people," Ginni said. "But the Haters, they have a sense that everyone's out to get them, everybody's trying to steal from them, so they instantly have an adversarial feeling about anyone who trades with them. They yell and yell, then they get the bid and they suddenly shut up—like sticking a bottle in a screaming baby's mouth."

Melinda said there was another girl who recently tried to trade in that pit and was ridiculed out. "That's when you go, 'Fuck them!'" Ginni said. "Sometimes they try to get me going, and I'm like, 'You want to start something, come on, what d'ya got?' There's no way that they know more than me. And there's no way they can ream me to the ground like I could ream them. So if they want me to ream them in front of all their friends, I will. This happened to me in Corn Options in the very beginning. It was even before they knew about the lesbian thing and started using that against me. It was always 'You stupid bitch!' I even went home and cried to my mom a couple of times. But then one day some guy in the pit called me a cunt. I turned right around and I said, 'Oh, call me a cunt. Does that make your dick hard? Does that make you feel like a man? I bet you go home and fuck your wife with that!' Those guys were stopped cold. Eventually, they started coming back to me with things like, 'You should be flat on your back with your legs in the air!' or 'You're a big stupid dyke!' So I'd say, 'Well, tell your wife to stop calling me then!' " She slapped her thigh. "Ow-ooo!!" she howled. "I've said it all, and it embarrassed them, and eventually it stopped them from trying to challenge me."

Ginni took pains to make sure Haters didn't surface in the Wheat Options pit. She encouraged the pit to socialize, and she'd organize outings, like golf games and picnics. She even got together with a competing broker to throw a Christmas party for the pit. I'd heard about Ginni's Christmas parties from a retired Local who used to trade Wheat Options. Ginni and the girls would arrange a gift exchange and would even bring gifts and sweets for other pits. It was described to me as a bizarre, yet extraordinary, event—a holiday party for a bunch of people who couldn't stand one another. "Imagine having just been called every name in the book by the person next to you, and then turning to him with a little wrapped gift," the retired trader had said. "That's what Ginni and her group do, and it really is something."

As I was fast learning, you'd be hard-pressed to find a trading pit that isn't ruled by braggadocio—humility, modesty, and aw shucks will not get you too far around here. Yet, Melinda told me it could get worse. There was a difference between an arrogant, pushy loudmouth in the pit—a Hater—and someone who became a Frankenstein-like creation, whereby the mix of elevated ego, superior status, a free-for-all environment, and, of course, tons of money, manifested a monster. One such monster could be found a few feet away in the Corn Options pit, and the story that the girls described was shocking.

When Melinda traded Corn Options, she'd stood next to a woman clerk whom I'll call Julie, who was a cute twenty-five-year-old, but who had the misfortune of being the object of interest of a particular broker twenty years her senior. Julie had obliged him with a date, but then ended up getting back together with her old boyfriend, who was her age and whom she eventually married. The broker himself ended up marrying—another twenty-five-year-old woman, whom he subsequently brought into the pit to be his clerk. Often, his new wife would have to stand next to Julie, and would relentlessly complain about it. So, in a junior high school attempt at consoling his wife, the broker began picking on Julie—only with the viciousness of a bitter stalker.

"I can smell you getting fatter and fatter," he'd say to her. Julie would stand there, trying to ignore it. He'd push further. "I can smell your crotch," he'd say. "You're a fat whore." Every day it happened, and every day Julie would take it until she couldn't help the tears from streaming down her cheeks. The broker made no attempt at whispering his comments—they were said so that everyone could hear, only no one did anything. One day, Julie's mother came to visit the Floor, but even that didn't deter the broker. "I can smell swine here," he said. "I just want to take a pin and pop that fat whore."

On it went, and day after day Melinda heard him and fumed. "He'd be standing right next to Julie and me, laughing about all this to his wife," Melinda told me. "And, not that it matters, but Julie's not even fat! Growing up with Ginni—and my mom is the same way—I was raised not to put up with that crap." Melinda would report everything to Ginni. At first Ginni waved it off, saying, "That broker's a cadaver, and all those other guys are fucking pussies. I can't force this girl to stand up for herself. I'm not going to be the sacrificial lamb here."

Melinda ended up following business into another pit, but returned to the Corn Options pit six months later. Even after that length of time, the dynamic and the events were the same. "Can't you just smell her? Maybe she should cross her legs," the broker taunted. Melinda made daily reports and pleas to Ginni, and finally Ginni—already in the middle of a bad day—threw her arms up. "I'm sick of this shit!" she snapped, and marched into the Corn Options pit. She stepped up to another broker she knew. "What the fuck are you doing about this?" she demanded.

"Ginni, what can I do?" he said helplessly.

"I'll tell you what you can do," Ginni said. The broker who'd been harassing Julie had his back to them and Ginni tapped him on the shoulder. He turned around and Ginni said, "You motherfucker! If you don't fucking stop this, I'll beat the fuck out of you myself!" He snapped back, "It's none of your business."

"I'm making it my business!" Ginni said, and then she turned to the rest of the pit. "It's all of you here!" she said. She pointed to the chairman of the pit, and questioned, "You! Why does this go on?" Everyone was silent. With that, she marched back to the Wheat pit.

Later that afternoon, the Corn pit chairman sheepishly went to talk with Ginni. "We-ell . . . uh . . . some of the guys think we should fine you," he said.

"Who?" Ginni asked.

"We-ell . . . I don't really want to get in the mid—"

"Who?" Ginni demanded. "I'm entitled to know my accusers!"

"We-ell . . . you did kind of interrupt trading in Corn Options . . ."

"Go ahead!" Ginni said. "Go ahead and sign a fine! But I want a meeting with the pit committee at the end of the day!" A fine for $250 for using profanity in the pit was written up, and at the end of the day a meeting was called. "We're all in there," Ginni recalled, "and they go, 'We-ell . . . we think that you came in the pit, and, we-ell . . . did anyone hear Virginia swearing?' There were eight guys there and seven of them said, 'I heard some yelling, but I'm not really sure what it was.' I go, 'You idiots! If you heard me yelling, you heard me swearing! Yes, I *did* swear! And I'm telling you, in light of the extenuating circumstances, I had to do it, because *you* wouldn't! I think you should dismiss this charge against me and leave it as a job well enough done and over.' " But the charges weren't erased.

"They are all spineless jellyfish!" Ginni blasted.

Shortly after, another committee meeting was called to address the situation between Julie and the broker. Melinda pressed Julie to get a lawyer, but she shied away. At the meeting, the broker appeared with a high-priced attorney at his side. Half-a-dozen people from the pit testified to hearing the broker's verbal abuse toward Julie. Julie also reported that the broker had been circling her house at night. In the end, Ginni's fine for $250 was overturned, and the broker reportedly received a minor suspension and a slap-on-the-wrist fine of a few thousand dollars, although no regulatory actions regarding this situation appear on his public record.

But now, looking back, Ginni believed the whole incident did change the blind-eye attitude in the Corn Options pit—and maybe in other pits as well. "That kind of thing isn't happening anymore," Ginni said. "Well, if it is, it's much more covert." Julie is still a clerk in the Corn Options pit, standing next to the broker and his wife every day.

"Most girls on the Floor don't have someone like Ginni who will teach you not to be intimidated by all these people and to be confident about yourself," Melinda said.

"I don't know how I would have done it without Ginni," Nicole agreed.

"There are no other role models down here," Melinda continued. "We do this thing with the Visitor's Center, where groups like high schools come through and Ginni will give a talk. It boggles my mind when they ask questions like, 'Are the guys mean to you?' That kind of stuff wouldn't come out if they didn't automatically think that the guys were dominating the women. To me, this is all I've ever known. My aunt Ginni started on the Floor in 1975, the year I was born."

"You're lucky, you grew up thinking that the possibilities for women are innately there," Ginni said to Melinda, then sighed. "I had all the difficulties, but I always had true intentions, and I thought that on some level other people did, too. But, no. A lot of people inherently cannot be true to themselves—or be truthful in the world. They give you lines of crap, they lie. But I held true to my own personal philosophy that I was not going to compromise my integrity for the almighty dollar, as much as that dollar was my goal. I don't have seven digits in the bank like a number of people who've been here as long as me. Part of that is disheartening; I feel like, ahh, maybe I should, maybe I've made all these mistakes. I know the managers of the Board think I'm a bitch." She caught herself starting to get riled up and let out another one of her sighs. "I just want to sit down here and fill orders, but I have been dragged into more political frays time after time. But those damn dinosaurs don't want anything to change! I think it comes down to the fact that being a woman, you really are alone and independent here. If you have no one to talk to, it's this very, very heavy load to be carrying around. I wanted these girls to be able to bypass the trials and tribulations I went through. This business, like no other, offers you the opportunity to really challenge yourself and to say, Who am I? What can I do? How far can I succeed? If you take advantage of it, you have such freedom. And freedom is what this job is all about."

As it neared the Close, Ginni's niece Autumn escorted me off the trading floor. She told me she was almost finished with college, and I asked if she wanted to follow in her aunt's footsteps.

"No," she said, without a second's hesitation. She crinkled up her nose. "It's not worth it to stress like this over wheat."

SEVEN

A Sustained Trend

A sustained trend is a consistent pattern to the Market, where there's either an *uptrend*—that is, the Market is making higher highs and higher lows— or a *downtrend*—the Market is making lower highs and lower lows. Traders lie in wait of a sustained trend so that they can just hop on and ride it all the way up, or all the way down.

The baby had arrived at Tara's little studio apartment on Wells Street; only, it was quite a large thing, and was far from cute with its Medusa-like head of wires and cables and connectors and cords.

Tara's new plan was to jump on the growing trend and trade Futures from home on the computerized system, like Tom. This way, she could still trade but wouldn't have to feel intimidated by the raucous pits, or her petite size, or the fact that she was a woman. Tom had agreed to be her mentor, which meant she could call him whenever she needed, and he'd help her. Tom had inspired the stars in Tara's eyes—much like he had for me—for when he spoke of his job, he made it sound like the ultimate career: lucrative and fun, with fantastic hours, just watch some numbers, press some buttons, and BAM! it was just that easy to make several hundred bucks in a few seconds. "A monkey could do what I do," Tom once told me, as if that was yet another job perk about which to brag. When Tom surprised Tara by showing up one night in a silver Corvette that he'd just driven off the lot—the car he had dreamed about owning since he was a boy—her mind started whirring. Maybe *she* should trade on the computer, and then she would have enough money to pursue *her* passion: a career as a singer-songwriter—*her* childhood dream, which she had attempted full force at numerous points, only to stall for lack of time and money.

It took all afternoon for the Globex installation man to set up Tara's new arrival. Tara tried not to hover as he plugged a blue cable here and a black one there and strung a red one over here, and around there, and then the phone wire, or was it the cable modem, and, jeez, wouldn't all this electrical stuff blow a fuse? Four hours later, the setup was near complete, and the baby resembled a fully functional trading machine. I came straight to Tara's from the Merc to see the new setup. It was impressive, with dual monitors and a mouse that could leap from one screen to the next. The installation man hesitantly asked if Tara wanted him to stick the code strip on her keyboard, which would detail the function of the keys. "Sure," she said.

He gave her a relieved smile. "A lot of the guys have it all memorized and get offended when I ask," he said. " 'I don't need *that!*' that's what they say, like I'm suggesting they don't know what they're doing. And, you know, it doesn't take too long before they go and hit the wrong button and then they're stuck in some trade that they had no intention of doing."

But the next day, despite the keyboard code strip, one of Tara's first trades was an accident. She quickly learned what every new Globex trader quickly learned: trading by accident was near effortless. It happened—people's cats, cleaning ladies, and toddlers have traded for them. "The cat made me money," a trader once confessed to me. It's ridiculously easy to place a trade, you hit just one button—which has been a source of debate, since some would prefer a fail-safe, an Are you sure? notice, or two buttons that you have to hit in sequence. But the majority of traders feel that anything more than one button would take away their edge, that all-important hair of a second that could cost them a trade.

So, after numerous hours of setup and anticipation, and thousands of dollars spent on the equipment and start-up costs, Tara, straight out of the starting gate, accidentally hit the hot button and instantly found herself owning one contract—which she didn't want. Her stomach leaped to her throat. Frantically, she called Tom. "Help! Help!" she cried, but Tom's luck had taken a wrong turn and he snapped, "I'm losing money! I can't help you when I'm down!" and hung up on her. So much for Tom as mentor.

Tara desperately hit some more buttons and sold her one contract to get out of the trade. By sheer luck, the accidental trade ended up being a winner—she made one tick, the smallest amount the Market can move, and earned herself $12.50. When her heart finally stopped fluttering, she looked over the trade report. Out of all the thousands of people on Globex with whom she could have traded at that very moment, she had traded with a familiar acronym: TPW. It was Tom.

On the technical side, the Globex machine, among other brands, allows a trader to trade what's called the e-mini, which is a smaller-sized version of contracts such as the S&P 500 and Nasdaq Futures. An e-mini contract is one-fifth the size of a regular Futures contract, and the ticks—the smallest incremental movement of the Market—are less money as well. For example, in the S&P 500 Futures pit, ticks move in .10 increments, and each movement is worth $25. So, if the Futures market is at 1147.20 and it moves up to 1147.70—and you've got a long position—you just made five ticks, which is $125. On the computer, with the e-mini, each tick moves in quarter increments and is worth $12.50. So, if the e-mini market is at 1147.25 and it moves up to 1147.75, you've made two ticks, or $25. The other major difference is that the e-mini market is not bell-to-bell, but is open for trading around the clock, five days a week, worldwide. You can trade in the wee hours of the morning—with someone from Singapore, or London, or Berlin—and surprisingly, many people do.

On the computer, it's the same ball game as in the pit, only a completely different field. Computerized trading has spawned a whole new wave of traders who are, in the comfort of their own homes, upending the old powers and changing the way Futures trading has been done for more than 150 years. Some see this as a boon; others do not. The Merc sees computerized trading as the trend of the future, and in recent years, out of a mix of prescience and necessity, the Merc revamped the Floor to include rows of computer terminals. The Merc has also taken to full-force promotion of e-mini trading, complete with an advertising campaign with billboards in major cities that read: "E-MINI FUTURES. Like SPDRs and QQQs. But Insomniac Friendly."

Other trading forums, like the Chicago Board of Trade, have not taken as active a role in embracing technology—and, many feel, to their detriment. Tom jokes about what the Board of Trade might become one day soon: a soundstage? An ice-skating rink? Maybe an airport hangar? Others, however, insist this will never be the case, and that pit trading—with the hand signals and nods, each trade recorded in ink on cards—will endure.

"In one hundred fifty years, open outcry will still be here," one highly successful veteran trader said, then added in true trader fashion, "and the chance that I am wrong is zero."

Despite the fact that Tom made his living—and, he'd note, a nice one at that—trading on the computer, he still felt that pit trading was superior. "Open outcry is the true test of the Market finding fair value," Tom told me. "With open outcry, you have all these opinions coming together, you have people who think the Market is overvalued, people who think it's undervalued, the sentiment, the psychology. On the Floor, you know who thinks what, and who's who, you can see all the big orders come in, you know what Merrill Lynch is doing, what Goldman Sachs is doing, what the big Locals are doing, and by seeing it happen, by having those orders tossed into the pit and getting the reactions, that's the only real way the Market can find a true balance. The computer can't handle this depth the way open outcry can. The computer is anonymous, you don't know where trades are coming from, who's making them, or why. Computer trades happen, then they're gone. They're just a blip."

"So, do you think being in the pit would make it easier in some ways for you to trade?" I asked.

"You learn to read faces in the pit," he said. "The brokers look harried when they have a big order. In the pit, you're playing against people, playing against the Market, playing against your own weakness. Here, at home on my computer, I can't really care what anyone else is doing."

On the flip side, some traders feel that computerized trading levels the playing field. On the computer, it's about the first trade, the best trade; it's not about who you know or whose brother-in-law you are. Of course, on the computer there's also no way to know who's male or who's female, who's six feet six inches tall and intimidating, who's five feet three inches tall and baby-faced, who's loud, who's reticent. Terms have sprung up for these advantages of computer trading, such as "price transparency," which means that anyone around the world can see the current price, whether you're a $50 billion institution, or a one-lot trader in sweatpants; and FIFO, which stands for "first in, first out," meaning, if you're faster and your bid is better, you've got the trade. Computer trading is also touted in Declaration of Independence–like terms: "Open access, equal access, and fair access for all."

Traders like Tom do have the advantage at times, too—he has CNBC and CNN on all day while he's trading, so in the event of breaking news that could cause a major jolt in the Market, he has that all-important sliver-of-a-second head start over the traders on the Floor. Most Futures pit traders don't have access to a TV and can only react to the large orders that the brokers deliver. So by the time the broker shoots up his hands and shouts the order, two steps have already occurred: (1) the customer or firm has already heard the breaking news and, based on it, made a fast decision to buy or sell; and (2) the order has been called to the Floor and clerks have arbed it to the broker in the pit. It's only after these steps that traders on the Floor realize something BIG just happened—although often, they won't know what. But *what* doesn't matter to them; all they care about is how the Market is going to *react* to what has happened—and that they get on the winning side of the surge or stampede to follow. Tom, however, can be right on top of it, eking out a position (or getting out of one) a blink of an eye before the havoc—and sometimes it's that one or two seconds that can make all the difference.

A prime example was in December 2000, when the Florida Supreme Court announced a recount of presidential-election votes—and the Market threw a tantrum. Because Tom was watching CNBC, he had a three-second advantage over the traders in the pit. For those in the pit, days like this are extremely dangerous—there's no warning, no newscaster abruptly pausing from the talking-head mode and staring confusedly at the camera as a frantic announcement is pumped into the wire in her ear; no two-second signal of, "This just in: We have results from Florida. . . ." No, in the pit, the only warning is a *feel*—the Market may pause, or sputter . . . and then, when large customer orders surge in, the Market will launch into the leap or the dive, the skyrocket or the plummet, the ride it or weep. In the pit, you have no time to speculate *why* the Market does what it does. You got used to not knowing Why, the pit traders told me, you didn't *care* about Why, all you cared about was Up or Down.

But in Tom's little apartment, with CNBC guiding him, "This just in . . ." he knew the Why, and he knew the Market was going to react and he knew he had to move, move, move! It was all in the skill of how fast he could hit the buttons—his career had momentarily been reduced to a video game. He only did a one-lot and sold it, he pounded the keyboard—lightning speed, his fingers tingling from the surge of adrenaline. The Market bottomed out. He made $1,200 in 20 seconds on the smallest contract possible. All that Tetris in college when he should have been studying had paid off.

Back on the Merc Floor, word was that two traders got caught on the wrong side—with large positions—when the announcement came and the Market reared its head like a sleeping dragon suddenly and rudely awakened. Both traders went broke, completely wiped out. I saw a lot of somber faces that day, and I wondered who the two were who had to go home to their wives and say, "It's gone, everything's gone."

$ $ $

On one of the first trades Tara made—intentionally, that is—she lost $100, just like that! She panicked, even her knees felt tingly, but she stuck it out. She glued her eyes to the Market, she calculated what she was going to do, and then, when the timing was right, she nervously pressed the button and made a trade. She waited, with terror, then pressed the button again. She had the $100 back—plus a little extra to boot!

Elated, she called Tom, but as she breathlessly detailed her day, she realized that all this energy—the panic, the relief, the fear of more panic, the fear of less relief, bouncing from one to the other, an emotional Ping-Pong match for hours—was over a lousy $100!

She hung up the phone and turned back to the screen. Whenever you enter a trading order on the Globex machine, it makes a specific noise, a *bawnk!* to indicate you've bought or sold contracts. It's similar to the error noise on a word-processing program, where a message pops up and, *bawnk!* no matter what key you hit, *bawnk!*, until you close the message window. Tara hit a key, which was not the key she'd hit if she wanted to enter an order. But that didn't seem to matter. . . . *BAWNK!* She jumped in her seat, what had happened? Had she bought? Had she sold? And, oh my God, how much? How much?

She grabbed the phone. "Tom! I don't know what happened, it just went *bawnk!* Get me out of this!" Tom, who had made money earlier and was hardly trading at the moment, walked her through a series of steps, check this screen, press this button. And then a message popped up: the trade had been rejected. Tara sank into her chair. She was shaking.

Perhaps this was all foreshadowing, for some days later, an even greater Globex emergency: it was 8:29 a.m. on the Floor. I was standing in my newfound spot at the top of a staircase, near the computer terminals. This spot was ideal—I could look down over the entire S&P pit; I could look over my right shoulder to the Commodities; I could turn left and look out over the

Globex traders; plus, an additional bonus, I had a railing upon which I could lean.

Little by little, I'd found myself catching on—portions of the digital reporting boards now made sense and I could follow along with the general action of the pit. Hands started going up with palms out, sell was everywhere. The opening gong, and the shouting began.

And then, Globex blipped. The computers of hundreds of traders started slowing, sort of like when the Internet takes unusually long to boot. Some traders knew what was coming and flipped around to yell to the Globex techs. The techs transferred some servers, but it didn't help, the system was crashing . . . and within a few seconds the screens of hundreds of traders froze.

The Globex techs, usually bored out of their minds and offering Market speculation and small talk to anyone who would listen, were now scrambling, kicked into action—this was what all traders dreaded and what the techs waited for. The traders were screaming. "I'm keeping track!" GOLF yelled. "Do you know how much fucking money this machine has cost me!" He shoved every unoccupied chair near him, then slammed his fist onto the desk.

Twenty minutes passed—still a frozen screen. Some traders threatened that if it was off for an hour, they were going to open outcry. It happened once last year—all the Globex traders had to arb with one another to get out of their positions, proving that despite all of modern technology, the only surefire, reliable method on the Floor was an archaic bunch of hand signals. "Pmfff! Computerize the whole Floor!" a trader muttered. "This is bullshit!"

In the meantime, back in Tara's studio apartment, instinct had told her to step away from her computer. She had been so frustrated about wanting to trade but not knowing if she should pull the trigger, and something compelled her to listen to that little voice in her head and step away. So she did—two feet, to her bed, where she curled up under the covers. She fell asleep and dreamed that Globex was buying a bunch of stock for her and she couldn't stop it, it was buying and buying and she was pressing every button, but it just kept on buying. She popped awake, as if from a nightmare. She was all sweaty. She looked over at her computer screen just to be sure it was only a dream after all. But the screen looked weird, half was in code and when she hit the buttons, it produced no response. She called

Globex. The system's been down for forty-five minutes, they informed her. It will be up and running in another few. Oh, the relief! What if she hadn't listened to the scared voice telling her to step away? What if she *had* pulled the trigger, she would be stuck, she would have bought a contract and the machine would have frozen and she would have sat there helpless, in agony, with absolutely no way out! At least on the Floor, the guys could arb with one another to get out of their positions. They had a pit they could run to. But she was all alone in a silent studio apartment with a frozen machine that was no more use to her than a bag of bricks sitting in the middle of her desk. Oh, thank goodness she hadn't made a trade!

And then she realized what she was doing, and it hit her in the pit of her stomach. The relief? The thankfulness? The elation? She was a trader, and traders *trade*. Really now, was she *ever* going to be able to do this?

Back on the Floor, the screens sputtered and blinked and then clicked back into motion. The traders' grumbling lasted another few seconds— "Well, it's about fucking time!"—and then their eyes glazed over and their fingers began instinctively hitting the buttons, and they were, once again, lost in the numbers. Out of coincidence, while the computers were down, the Market had done some loops and had arrived back at pretty much the same spot it was at when Globex had frozen. For all the cursing, no one was out much money. But there was no denying it could have been disastrous, and the techs, as they recuperated, wiping the sweat from their foreheads, didn't even want to fathom what that would have looked like—someone could quite possibly get strangled. Some trader with a large position in a crazy market could just crack, and his fingers would be wrapped around a tech's throat. The techs leaned back in their chairs and fanned themselves; it would take a little while before the color returned to their faces.

$ $ $

What everyone who trades off the computer knows is that technological glitches are terrifying, and that the culprits—if ever discovered—must plead for salvation. A year ago, on a busy last trading day of a quarter, Nasdaq halted for about two hours. Millions of dollars were lost as traders sat and waited for the system to restart. The guilty party: an unfortunate computer technician at Nasdaq's home-base Connecticut office, who, while testing a new trading system, had accidentally hit a wrong command key.

According to the *Wall Street Journal*: "Though the technician attempted to abort the command . . . his screen simply minimized itself and vanished."

This incident brought back memories of perhaps the most ignominious of screw-ups: back in 1994, a squirrel chewed up power lines at the Nasdaq base, halting trading for half an hour. The Floor went into convulsions, the amount of money lost—money that simply vanished—was enormous. And there was even one fatality: the squirrel, electrocuted at the scene of the crime.

$ $ $

In 1986, market speculator Ivan Boesky delivered a commencement speech at the University of California at Berkeley's School of Business Administration, where he, in what seemed an impromptu gesture, added the now infamous lines: "Greed is all right, by the way. I want you to know that. I think greed is healthy. You can be greedy and still feel good about yourself." Of course, this was given great attention when soon after he was indicted on insider-trading charges, hugely fined, and jailed. But what seemed to bother astute reporters and commentators the most was not the lines themselves, but how the audience of sparkling-new MBAs had responded that May graduation day: immediately following Boesky's comment, they laughed and applauded.

A year later, the lines were resurrected in the movie *Wall Street*. To my surprise, it still resonated with traders on the Floor, and many would recite the monologue as if it was their personal mission statement: "Greed, for lack of a better word, is good. Greed is right. Greed works. Greed clarifies, cuts through and captures the essence of the evolutionary spirit. Greed, in all of its forms, greed for life, for money, for love, for knowledge, has marked the upward surge of mankind." I, too, had seen the movie, only I'd been under the impression that Gordon Gekko was the bad guy, that there was a reason he'd been named after a lizard.

Given the almighty spectrum of Greed and Fear, which governed every trader, Tom was at the far end, working on perfecting his level of Greed. He decided he wanted to make more money every day. He had rather consistently been making around $1,000 a day. Now that was no longer enough. "Enough," to him, had nothing to do with his cost of living expenses—he rarely spent much money anyway, except when it came to his car. "Enough" meant what he felt he *should* be making. If he was truly a good trader, he decided, then he should be making double what he was. He upped his self-imposed daily quota to $2,000. After all, what bachelor with no financial responsibility to anyone but himself couldn't use an extra $20,000 a month?

Tom's strategy for doubling his intake was to beef up his trading size—so instead of trading two contracts at a time, he'd trade ten. It seems logical that if a trader can trade one-lots and make $1,000 every day, then he should have no problem moving up to ten-lots and making $10,000 a day. While the reasoning is sound, the reality is quite different—mostly because of a single factor: emotion. For most people, the psychology of trading a one-lot is much different than that of trading a ten-lot. It's only the very best traders who have the ability to block out any distinction—their fear level does not fluctuate, so a ten-lot feels the same as a hundred-lot, and they both might as well be one-lots, because they just roll off the expert trader's tongue. The traders who can perfect this state of complete, consistent insouciance become legendary. One such master at the Board of Trade had worked his way up to become the largest Bond trader in the world. At the height of his career, he was larger than the Bank of Japan. But, of course, his success came at a personal cost, and a close friend of his described him this way: "He has ice water running through his veins."

Tom quickly discovered that he did not possess this unique talent of erasing the value of money while trading. For him, this new strategy of trading larger contracts presented a huge downside, and therein he came to understand that in addition to balancing Greed and Fear, there was one other element to be reckoned with: Risk. It was painfully evident—every second of his trading day—that the more he risked, the more he stood to lose. Indeed, on the days Tom made money he made more, but trading tends to have an odd way of keeping an equilibrium, so on his losing days, he lost more. Tara began to worry about him. "He'll have $1,900," she told me, "and then he'll give half of it back trying to make a hundred bucks." Her observation was supported by the fact that during Tom's trading day, he had taken to throwing punches at the wall. "There are so many holes that you can almost see right through," Tara complained. Tom didn't deny it, and when I next saw him, he kept shaking his hand, clenching and unclenching his fist.

"I've got to stop hitting that wall," he said. Sure enough, the small calendar that hung by his computer had been conspicuously replaced by a large bulletin board—with nothing but the calendar pinned to it.

Tom's trading style is what's called "scalping." He was quickly in and out of the Market, trying to shave a little here, trim a little there. He didn't hold a trade; rather, he took advantage of small moves of the Market. Sometimes he had a trade on for a second; at most, he would hold a trade for a few minutes. "I'm all over the place when I trade, just in and out," Tom said. "I'm a trading slut."

I thought of Tom when I heard a CNBC commentator remark, "This is the kind of Market that leads scalpers to an early grave." After meeting the drywall with his fist for several more days, Tom finally decided to cut back on his contract size—no more getting crazy with trading twenty-lots. He was going back to twos and fives, and occasionally tens, the way he used to trade. In his mind, it was hardly as glamorous, but then again, neither was having a stream of losing days.

Tara, on the other hand, had mastered Greed's counterpoint: Fear. It wasn't that she didn't know how to trade—she called the Market right with decent consistency—it was just that she was afraid to put on trades and afraid to hold the ones she did manage to make. It was the equivalent of sitting at a $5 blackjack table, betting the minimum, and after a few winning hands, getting up and leaving. Tara would ride a trade for a few ticks and then, out of fear, get out. Then she'd be mad at herself because the Market would do exactly as she had predicted, and she would have made . . . oh, what did it matter anyway, she was a baby and now it was too late. She devised a new plan to trade until 11 a.m.—two and a half hours—then walk away. That way, she wouldn't be sitting there all day stewing, feeling the stress rise, feeling her jaw clench, feeling her back tense as she followed the Market until the Close, thinking, *I should do this, and I should do that, I should, I should, I should.* But Tara quickly learned she wasn't that good at the walkaway either, and her new plan soon amounted to just another feckless attempt at some sort of method. She wasn't good at the walkaway, she wasn't good at pulling the trigger, and she wasn't good at holding a trade—this didn't exactly make for a profitable trading career.

Tom decided that he needed a change of scenery—a day away from staring at the crater in his wall in his *rented* apartment. So, he picked me up in his silver Corvette and we headed to the Merc together. What a world of difference to once again have him on the Floor with me. No butterflies in my stomach, no need to navigate, no worries that someone was going to yell at me for standing somewhere I shouldn't or for being in someone's way. I could feed off the clout of Tom's badge, and, with him here, I felt as I did that very first time—that maybe, just maybe, I could give trading a shot. We headed up the stairs and Tom found an open Globex machine and logged on. He made a couple of trades. "Gathering some spare change," he said. "Just made sixty . . ."—he pressed a button—"make that, seventy-five bucks." It almost seemed unfair that I was standing right next to him making zero. "So," he said. "Do you want to try?"

I gave him a questioning stare. "To trade?"

He stepped aside and motioned for me to sit at the Globex machine.

"On your account?" I asked.

"Yeah, I'll give you $100 to play with, and you can keep whatever you make." I realized he was serious. I suppose I should have been excited, for he was giving me the opportunity to do what I'd come here to learn about. But instead, I felt nervous and unprepared. I'd been learning so much, but could I apply it to the real thing? I sat down in front of the Globex machine and stared at the screen. The Market was going down.

"What if I lose it all?"

"Then lunch is on you."

My fingers hovered over the buttons. Although I'd never bungee-jumped, I imagined this was how it felt to be standing on the edge, talking yourself into taking the plunge. I felt the need to have a plan and to verify it with Tom: "Okay, I'm going to sell it at two and a half, and get out at one and a half." He nodded.

3.25 . . . 3 . . . 2.75. . . . My hand was shaky. I now understood Tara's apprehension. 2.50. Uh-oh. 2.50! Push the button. Push it! *Bawnk!*

I had done it, I had made a trade . . . well, half a trade . . . keep your eyes on the Market, you have to buy it back. I waited, holding my breath, for 1.50.

2.25 . . . 2 . . . 1.75 . . . 3.25 . . . 2.75 . . . Uh-oh, what was happening? The ticks went from heading steadily downward to jumping all over the place. I panicked.

"Tom!"

Tom was on it, waiting to step in. I quickly backed away and he took over. I watched the boards—the Dow was dropping, sell-offs were happening in London, Tokyo, and Hong Kong. The S&P market lurched in sharp, sudden moves. Tom was pounding buttons like he was playing a high-speed video game. I had just witnessed how easy it was to get caught—to find yourself suddenly stuck behind a jettisoning trade.

Tom, along with most traders, loved volatile days—the ups, the downs, the all-over-the-places; it was times like these that Tom saw great opportunities to scalp some money—*I'll take some here, and I'll take a little more there, and thank you very much, sorry to take my cash and run, but that's the way I play the game!* Tara viewed volatility as potential traps, quicksand lurking around every corner, and with just the slightest dip of the toe, it could grab her and pull her under until she suffocated. She couldn't trade like Tom, she couldn't get in and out of the Market quick enough. I had traded for all of two minutes, and I felt her anxiety. I'd had to talk my fingers into moving. Now Tom was hammering the keyboard like it was a manual typewriter. Tom's face was flushed, his eyes didn't leave the screen. I could have started choking right there next to him and I doubt he would have noticed. He ended up making several hundred dollars—although he said it had been scary there for a while. "Was the trade I put on a winner?" I asked.

"Yeah, it was." He paused. "But don't go thinking that entitles you to half!"

Tara eventually decided that the Market was getting too crazy for a beginner like her to trade. Yet, she still sat and watched every day, following the Market from her cramped apartment, with the music equipment—the sound board, mixers, keyboard, mikes, and a hundred wires—lining one wall, and the trading equipment—the two computers, three monitors, Globex machine, and a hundred wires—lining the other; each side a constant reminder of dreams yet unrealized.

One day I spoke with her and she said she was contemplating getting the Globex machine ripped out of her apartment. The monthly fees were making it so that she couldn't view this all as a learning experience for very much longer. She was actively spending hundreds of dollars a month on the machine and the clearing firm dues and the data feed and the charting programs. Plus, she could actively lose money if and when she did decide to trade, so the odds of an overall downward trajectory of the bank account were great. But then again, that was trading. Nine out of ten people fail—and there was only one way to fail in this game: belly-up.

But Tara ended up sticking with it. She began taking technical trading classes at the Merc, where she learned about charting and how to recognize patterns that could predict the Market. Soon, she was plotting out her own charts. She saw trading signals and trends and patterns and said in her mind, "This is a triangle formation and the Market is going to go up, and I would buy one contract here and then sell it when the Market hits this point, and I'd push the button now." But she wouldn't push the button. Instead, she pretended that she did, and then calculated that she would have made $300 in eight minutes. At some point in the afternoon, she'd decide to call it a day, and then she'd go for acupuncture or to yoga class to ease her nerves.

One morning, she woke up and decided that today was the day she would finally push the button. She watched the charts for patterns. She was jittery, and absentmindedly munched on baby-leaf spinach right out of the plastic "Salad-to-Go" bag. When she allowed her eyes to roam from the computer screen for just a second, she noticed that she had nearly polished off the entire bag.

Finally, after a couple of hours searching the screens, she saw a pattern: a head-and-shoulders formation. She knew she needed to sell it when the Market hit 20 even—the apex—and likewise she knew where she should set her point—15 even—to buy it back. Now all she had to do was push the button. This was the part that tended to paralyze her.

Twenty, the sell number, was fast approaching. Her finger wavered over the button. 22 . . . 21 . . . 21.25 . . . 21.50 . . . *You are going to push it*, she told herself.

20. Push it. 20. Push the thing. You see it, trust in yourself. Push the damn button!

She pushed it. She sold one contract. She was sweating, her heart was racing.

The Market moved down, 19.50 . . . 19.25 . . . exactly as she predicted. She was going to liquidate at 15. The Market was moving—18.50 . . . 18. . . . She didn't think she could get any more nervous, but her heart was picking up speed, she could feel the pounding in her feet, could feel the shakiness rising up into her knees, her stomach—uhhh, spinach, a whole freakin' bag of spinach!—she needed the Market to move just three more ticks, and it was headed there, the pattern was panning out, moving toward 15, and then—she pushed the button.

She was out, at 17.75. The fear had consumed her. She watched with dread as the Market continued to drop—she almost wanted it to rise, to prove her initial calculation wrong, to validate her decision to bail. But it didn't. It hit her stop point, and moved down even further. Why couldn't she have ridden it? Her heart was still pounding. She felt like she was either going to pass out or throw up roughage.

A few days later, Tara and I met for lunch at a little Asian restaurant in Bucktown, where she used to waitress. Over Tom Yum soup, she told me that she was thinking about dropping everything and going back to waiting tables. "The stress I used to think was bad was nothing," she said. "So what's the worst that could happen? Someone has a special order? At least you're not losing money."

I wanted to sympathize with her—but still, I couldn't help but wonder if all this fear she had was really just the normal aches and pains of starting a trading career, or if perhaps she did need to reevaluate why she was choosing to pursue this path. At some point, a trader's primal fear should begin to dull and typically be replaced by adrenaline. I saw it in Tom—even if he was down, he had a rush, bursting with energy to try to make his money back. The fear was still there in the sense of "I better turn this around and quick!" But it wasn't the constant choking Tara felt, that fatalistic sense of "Help, something really terrible is going to happen!"

Sure, I had felt fear when I had executed one side of a measly trade—I was scared! But I was also using someone else's money, and I was the type of person for whom even borrowing someone else's car tended to make me a little edgy. It was also my first time ever trying to trade, so nervousness was normal—but I couldn't imagine feeling that same shakiness, that same insecurity *every* time I tried to trade. What was Tara putting herself through?

I tried imagining what I'd be like if I were in Tara's position, sitting in my apartment with a community of monitors and live feeds and numbers streaming, making my own decisions about my own money and, most important, not having Tom standing next to me to bail me out. Would I be like Tara, or would I become like all the other Globex traders, in that zone where your eyes glazed over and your fingers synced with the keys and the numbers clicked with a sort of rhythm?

I wanted to get a better sense of how I'd react, so I found a brokerage firm that was offering a trial period with a simulated trading program that mimicked the S&P e-mini market—the same one that Tom and Tara traded. I put $500—fake dollars, that is—in my trading account. It was the closest I could get, at this point, to trading on my own.

With CNBC in the background, various charts in minimized boxes on my computer screen, and the cursor hovering over the Enter button, I prepared to make my first trade. I had told myself that I would accurately report my day's earnings or losses to Tom, in an effort to try as much as possible to feel like I was playing with real money. *My* money.

I decided—based on what the cash market and the Futures market were doing—that I would go short. I took a deep breath and clicked to sell one contract. Instantly, I was in the Market! Numbers were flipping! The screen reported to me exactly how much money I was making or losing with every tick: +$12.50, +$25, +$12.50, +$25, +$37.50, +$50. Oooh! Press one button and make fifty bucks. This was fun!

And then it became not so fun: +$37.50, +$12.50, +$25, +$12.50, -$12.50. -$25. . . . The Market will go back down, I reasoned, and watched. -$37.50, -$24, -$37.50. . . . It was hovering, but it would turn around: -$50, -$62.50. . . . Uh-oh.

Maybe I should cut my losses and reverse my position? Everything was moving so fast that I didn't have time to listen to CNBC, or to look at a chart, or to see what the other Futures index markets were doing. In fact, I wasn't really even watching the Market at all—I was watching my balance, and I was guessing, plain and simple, what the Market would do. I decided to guess that the Market was headed up. I bought back my one contract at a loss of $50, and then bought another contract.

+$12.50, +$25, +$50. I had made my loss back—that didn't seem too hard. +$62.50, +$84. . . . And I had a profit on top of that! Only, when should I take the profit? I'd be happy making $84. +$62.50—oops, I should have taken it at $84. Still, I'd be happy making $62.50 on one trade. I took it; sold my contract and reaped my profit. My account balance: $512.50.

With no position on, I decided I needed to review the markets and the charts and make an informed decision before I jumped in again. What exactly I was basing this informed decision on, I was still not quite sure. The charts did me little good since I wasn't familiar with all the various ways of reading them and deciphering what many traders feel are typical patterns that signify what's coming next. All I could make out was that the Market was jumping around in every direction with no obvious order. The cash market headed down, so I decided, once again, to sell. With the tap of a key, I was back in.

+$12.50, +$25, +$37.50, +$62.50. . . . I was riding it down. Buy it! I took my profit of $75. The Market continued dropping—a downward trend, I decided, and got back in. Sell two! Now I was being daring, doubling my trading size, which was quite easy to do when you weren't risking real money.

+$25, +$50, +$75. . . . In three seconds I had made what would, in many other jobs, have been a daily wage. I glanced at the television to catch a report on CNBC, but by the time I turned my eyes back to my computer, the doubling had completely backfired—

-$90? How did that just happen? -$115? -$140? Oh no.

An hour later, after whittling my account down to $100, then making it back to $450, I gave up. I had lost all sense of what I was doing—if it had been bordering on a guessing game to begin with, by the end it had turned into a situation of odds: the Market had to go up/down again sometime, so I'd just wait. Had this been real life, I would have received a margin call for letting my balance drop so low. Had this been real money, I would have been trying to rationalize every step of the way how it was okay to lose $400 in less than an hour. And if anyone on the Floor had known what was going on in my head, they would have laughed me out the turnstiles—two contracts was a minuscule amount to trade, and if one tick on two contracts felt like a lot of money to me, well then, what was I doing trading Futures anyway?

I called Tom and told him of my $50 loss.

"Not bad," he said.

"You're kidding, right?"

"They say if you break even your first year, you've done well."

"That's a lot of stress for just breaking even," I said. I supposed one could compare it to starting a business and anticipating not seeing any cash flow for some time. Only, with a business once you started making money, the anticipated trend—if the business was sound—was to continue making money, and each year, make more money. Not so with trading. Even the best traders had entire years where they took major losses.

"So did you like trading?" Tom asked. I had no way to answer; it felt more like a game of roulette—sure, I liked it when I was winning.

EIGHT

Levels of Support and Resistance

When charting the Market, a trader determines two specific points: one at the top, a level of resistance, and one at the bottom, a level of support. These are usually the points the Market will trade to before it reverses its course. For example, if the level of resistance is determined to be 80, the Market will usually get bought up to around 79, and then drop back down. However, if the Market breaks through the point, if it trades up to 81, then this is taken as a signal that it's going higher—hop on and buy! On the flip side, if the Market breaks through the level of support, it's believed it will then go lower—so you'd better go short, and ride it all the way down.

My little trading experiment made me realize that I needed to learn how to chart the Market so that I could assign some meaning to my trades. The technical trading classes Tara was taking at the Merc seemed perfect, only it was mid-session, so I'd have to wait to enroll. As a consolation, Tara arranged for us to have lunch with one of her instructors, a veteran pit-trader-turned-computer-trader named Max. She enjoyed Max's class, for he was jocular and seasoned with stories of all that he'd seen on the Floor over the years. Max suggested we meet him at the private Merc Club, and we felt posh and privileged to have an invitation there.

One escalator ride up, past the security checkpoint and down the hall, is the Merc Club, a restaurant, bar, and lounge for members only. I had checked my yellow jacket for the day, and Tara and I entered the Club, where we waited at the receptionist's table for Max to escort us back. Max was a slightly round bachelor in his forties, and he led us to a window-side table, overlooking the Chicago River and the glinting skyscrapers along the river's edge. I was anticipating some rollicking stories, but instead Max set the tone with a heavyhearted summation: "You get so self-absorbed when trading," he said. "You're there making the money, but people don't really care about you. There are a lot of brilliant failures on that Floor. A lot of tremendously wealthy zeros. A lot of screwed-up people because you always live with the terror of being wiped out. There are a lot of Captain Nemos."

The Club was crowded with traders. They heartily shook hands as they settled around the white-clothed tables and ordered drinks, which promptly arrived in extra-large glasses. The servers were gracious and attentive, and it seemed everyone knew everyone. Guttural laughs sounded all around, especially from the direction of the large circular bar that divided the restaurant from the lounge. Max's words hung in the air like thick, dark clouds—brilliant failures? Tremendously wealthy zeros? Captain Nemos?

Max and Tara were in the middle of discussing more intricate trading techniques and chart formations, when Max's cell phone rang with a call summoning him back to the firm where he traded. "Just a second," Max said to us. He darted across the room to a table against the wall, where a heavyset woman who looked in her forties sat alone reading the *Atlantic Monthly*. They talked briefly, and then he waved us over.

"This is Alice Kelley," he said to us. "She's a second-generation trader who now trades on Globex." He apologized that he had to run, but said that Alice would be able to answer any questions we had. Alice seemed a bit taken aback, but motioned for us to sit. Our half-finished lunches immediately found us, and the servers slid us into chairs and spread our starched white-cloth napkins over our laps, and suddenly we were lunching with an unsuspecting woman who had simply been minding her own business. However, it was quite a serendipitous move, for Alice, I'd discover, was one of the most technically seasoned, intellectual traders around.

At first Alice was slightly reserved, but it didn't take long for her to warm up to us and start talking. Alice had the rare ability to claim lineage to the Merc, and to trading in general, through her mother, Sonia— or Sunny, as she had been known on the Floor. In 1949, Sunny had been inspired by a circular in the mail touting the money that could be made trading Futures. She became one of the first female clerks, and eventually went on to trade. Throughout her forty-year career, she made a considerable fortune. Even as Sunny was dying, she still traded; she called in her last trade—a Bond Futures trade—from her hospital bed. It was a $50,000 winner. Despite her success, Sunny had discouraged Alice from getting into trading. But after Alice consistently showed interest, Sunny relinquished and bought her daughter a seat at the Merc as a Christmas present.

In recent years, Alice had begun trading on the computer from her apartment in the mammoth rental complex called Presidential Towers, which was a popular residence for traders because of its high-class amenities—restaurants and a supermarket in the building—and its proximity to the Merc. Alice typically traded until around 2 p.m., then she'd put away her charts and graphs and walk the few blocks to the Merc, where her reserved table awaited her at the Club.

I immediately liked Alice; she seemed quirky, entertainingly eccentric, and smart in the way that she could practically quote the encyclopedia. As it neared the close of the Market, several traders who were regulars at Alice's table trickled in. One was a talkative Israeli, Ben, who used to trade Cattle but now traded on the computer. Another was a soft-spoken family man who was also a Fundamentalist Christian, but who, Alice informed us, turned into a fistfighting avenger when he was in the pit. And then there was a thirty-seven-year-old bachelor, John, who could easily have passed for ten years younger. He'd been frequenting Alice's table for several years, and they'd seen each other through fortunes made and lost, and made again.

They all feasted primarily on fried foods—chicken fingers, French fries, cheese sticks—and discussed trading. They asked Tara about her techniques and her goals, which seemed to make Tara uncomfortable, for she wasn't quite sure about either. I, on the other hand, was enjoying every minute. Unlike the other after-work gatherings I'd attended with people from the trading floor, the talk here was witty and current and informative. No one spoke or reminisced about the wild days of drugs and alcohol; in fact, no one even ordered a drink other than iced tea. It was also refreshing to me how no one was rushed or had anywhere else they needed to be. It was 3:30 in the afternoon, and the only thing these people wanted to do was relax and have stimulating conversation. Out of all the places for me to stumble upon such intellectual discussion, I had practically ruled out that it would ever be at an Exchange.

Avoiding rush-hour traffic seemed the only impetus for those at the table to keep an eye on the time, so as it neared 4:30, everyone—except for

Alice, who usually stayed until around 5, then walked home—readied to head out. Alice asked Tara and me when we were going to be at the Merc again. Tara said she came for her evening classes, and other than that, she didn't know. "I'll be back tomorrow, clerking," I said.

Alice smiled. "I'll be here from two on," she said. "So why don't you join me for lunch whenever you'd like."

I took Alice up on her offer, and oddly enough, I would come to view her table as a throwback to the intellectual salons of 1920s Paris or New York. Conversation typically started off about the Market, but then branched into every subject imaginable, from literature to the occult. Before I began coming for visits, Alice was the only woman at her table, and often, the only woman trader in the entire Club. She always sat at the same table, in the same seat, with a pitcher of iced tea, a pitcher of water, and a plate of lemons. She typically opted for the same lunch entrée for days—if not weeks—at a time. Alice knew every staff member at the Club, and on the occasion that she threw a party, she invited many of them. Alice seemed more at home at the Merc Club than at her own apartment.

For me, Alice's table replaced the viewing room as my haven, and I began visiting her a few times a week. It was nice to leave the noisy, sweaty, dirty Floor, take the escalator down one level, and enter into a serene, polite world, where I could watch the boats sailing down the river, where the staff knew me and rushed over with a tall glass of whatever I wanted, and where the only hint of the chaos of the Market was the handful of blue-screened television monitors that silently displayed columns of numbers. I found myself leaving the Floor earlier and earlier to go to the Club. Often, Alice and I would have a good hour to chat before the men started showing up. Alice seemed to know everything there was to know about technical trading, and she said she'd teach me whatever I wanted to learn about charting. "You can give me a chart and not tell me what it is—up to and including the weather—and I am able to give you an opinion, I can tell you what I think this chart will resolve into," she said. "I have literally bought stocks when I didn't even know what the company was—the chart pattern told me it was a buy, and that's all I needed. I remember doing that on a couple of occasions and I made fairly good money. But I became very embarrassed when I recommended the stock to somebody else without knowing what the company did. So now I always make sure to at least look up what they do."

Alice was a child genius who, at nineteen years old, realized: "Just being a genius was not enough anymore, you had to be a genius *at* something." However, what that something was, Alice was not sure. Although Alice loved her mother dearly and spoke of her with tremendous admiration, she often felt she lived in Sunny's shadow. "She spoke five languages," Alice said of her mother. "I can barely speak one." I rolled my eyes when she said this, for Alice had a stunning vocabulary, one that seemed to just roll off her tongue; and yet she didn't intimidate with words. She was able to tailor her dialogue to fit the audience, and, given that the audience was usually traders, it could be quite diverse.

Sunny was also known for her great beauty and her refined spunk. The men on the Floor transformed into gentlemen when she was around. They looked out for her, and wouldn't curse around her. One of Alice's favorite stories about her mother is how Sunny, at nine years old, heard of an experimental procedure at Mayo Clinic that would improve the aesthetics of one's nose. Sunny didn't like her nose, so, in mature prose, she wrote to the doctors involved in the research and stated her case for becoming a test patient. Thinking the letter was from an adult, the doctors wrote back that they'd be interested in speaking with her and that they were visiting Chicago in the near future. Sunny corresponded with a date and time and her home address, where they should meet. When the doctors showed up at her front door, both they, along with Sunny's unsuspecting mother, were quite shocked.

Sunny never received the nose job, but despite that, grew into a beautiful woman. Perhaps there are traces in Alice, although it was difficult to tell. Alice inherited no vanity—she kept her hair in a buzz cut, so as not to have to mess with it; she proclaimed the only time she wore makeup was on Halloween; she loved food too much to be concerned with her weight; and she hid half her face under blue plastic, wide-framed glasses. Alice looked like she'd never pressed her feet into anything that didn't have flat, cushioned soles, and she was happiest wearing sweatshirts to the Merc every day, typically alternating between three favorites.

Alice had lived with her mother in a town house in the city up until her mother's death at age seventy-eight. There was a loneliness about Alice, which she'd never admit—she'd never stand to have anyone feel sorry for her. She'd never been married, nor did she ever want to be, and she had never felt the slightest want for children (in W. C. Fields fashion she described kids as "rather dreadful"). The closest I came to sensing emotion in Alice was when she said, in reference to her childhood, "You can't compete with your mother, so you withdraw and go the opposite way."

Outwardly, it didn't appear Alice had been withdrawn—in high school, she played field hockey and was a pitcher in softball, winning the Regional trophy. Yet, she summed up that period with: "I'm not too serious about games. I could lose and it doesn't bother me." She graduated class valedictorian at the age of fifteen. "I didn't care about all that," she told me. "I threw out all the trophies, threw out the yearbooks. I just didn't care." She began applying to colleges right away, and won a scholarship to Radcliffe, where, despite the fact that her parents were encouraging her to stay in Chicago—her mother had gone to the University of Chicago, and her father to Northwestern—she elected to go. Then Alice's father died, and although Alice had never been close to him, she felt she should stay nearby. She ended up at the private Lake Forest College, where, due to an administrative error, the little fifteen-year-old prodigy got stuck in a dorm with seniors. It didn't bother her for long, for the others quickly adopted her. "I was their mascot, so to speak," Alice recalled. It was there that she ventured into the wildness that accompanied college life during the height of the 1960s. Alice experimented in every way that a young adult (or, in her case, an adolescent masquerading as a young adult) of that time possibly could. She enjoyed LSD and mushrooms, and she decided that, although her dream was to be a writer of historical fiction, she was going to be a trader, much to her mother's dismay.

Alice had always loved mathematics. "I have almost an erotic attraction to numbers," she said. "I can hardly pass by integers without feeling drawn in. I have so many numbers stored in my head. Whole integers are my friends." She talked of numbers the way she talked of food, as if they both were an equally visceral and immensely satisfying experience. She often described things with taste-related adjectives, even though what she was describing had no gastronomic value, such as: "The pattern I had charted was a delicious formation."

One of Alice's oldest memories was of her father explaining Futures trading to her by using a pair of scissors as an example of a commodity the five-year-old likely wanted. However, Alice's most vivid childhood memory was of her mother trying to get out of a bad trade. The year was 1960; Alice was eight years old. Her mother took Alice's hand and said, "We have to go to the Drake Hotel." The Drake was, and still is, one of Chicago's most posh hotels. It was also near the now-extinct Plaza Hotel, where Alice and her mother lived. They walked down the block and into the lobby of the Drake. Lining the wall were private telephone booths, and Sunny and Alice stepped into one and closed the door. "Mom had so much change with her," Alice remembered. "She said, 'I have to send a telegram.' Very elegantly, she sat down and started composing it. I heard her say things like, 'Look out for this. . . .' and 'It's going to be the biggest debacle since the Black Sox scandal in 1919. . . .' She told me she was pretending it was a man writing the telegram. I pointed out one phrase that was not very good, that didn't sound like how a guy would talk, and she crossed it out and rewrote it. Of course, what I didn't know until later was that she was caught short and the Market was going against her. However, a little lie could turn things around. So she was spreading rumors. She wanted to get out with a modest loss rather than a huge one. She ended up with a two-page telegram, and she called Western Union and began pouring quarters down the slot. She was sending the telegram to two people who were very influential and could move the Market. The next day, the Market turned around and went up. Mom made me promise not to tell anybody."

When Alice first came to the Merc, the trading orientation classes alone overwhelmed her. Shy and awkward, she could have written a term paper on economics, but as to the practical aspects of trading—such as how to hold her trading cards—she was lost. One of her mother's friends who was a trader sent his clerk to help her, and only then did Alice end up passing orientation. Of course, she passed the written membership exam with a perfect score.

On Alice's first day on the Floor, she was knocked over during a rush. Her head hit the ground and her glasses flew off. Luckily for her, many traders knew and respected her mother and looked out for Alice. Someone helped her to her feet, and someone else found her glasses and slid them on her face before running off to make a trade.

At the end of the day a man came up to Alice and shook her hand. "I'm sorry I won't be getting to know you," he said. "I'm going home this week-end and am going to kill myself." Alice was stunned, but the other men in the pit laughed him off. "Don't listen to Charlie-boy, he's full of crap, had a bad day, that's all. What? Can't take a bad day anymore, Charlie?"

On Monday, Charlie didn't show. He had done it.

My eyes widened when she told me. I couldn't help but inquire about the other trader suicide I had heard about some months earlier. "Do you remember anything about a young woman who jumped off the roof in Sandburg Village?" I ventured.

Alice shook her head. "When was this?"

"Around the crash in '87."

She seemed perplexed. "I was here, but no, I don't know anything about it."

Once again, the veteran trader's strange admonishment that I would never find out anything more about the woman I referred to as Anne McKenzie rang true. If there was anyone who'd have known about McKenzie, it would have been Alice, for she seemed up on all the details and goings-on around here. "The Merc may look big, but it's a very small world," Alice was fond of saying. Just getting Alice's general overview of the others in the Club at any given moment was like watching a soap opera: She pointed out a woman trader at one table who had been twice married to and divorced from the same man, who was also a trader, and who always sat at a nearby table. Across the room was a trader whose ruthless divorce took an even nastier turn when it was discovered that his wife was having an affair with the ruling judge. At another table, a slick-looking older trader dressed in shined leather loafers and pressed slacks was lunching with his trader son. "He knows where all the bodies are buried," Alice said. She pointed to someone else. "That one's big into nose candy," and then to someone else, "I don't remember ever seeing him sober."

When I once asked Alice to describe herself, she used the word "phleg-matic." Perhaps, for this reason, she didn't care to trade in the pit. "The Floor is a tremendous energy field," she said. "Depending on your mental state, it can either be threatening or incredibly euphoric. You can be intim-idated or you can feel you are part of an elite group. I, however, find the

Floor disgusting. Men are messy! And rude! If they hadn't stolen my charts to look at them, then I'd take the charts into the members-only lounge and even there, I couldn't put them down on the table because it was sticky or dirty or wet. You would think at the very least they would know how to throw their sandwich plates away."

Alice would walk around the Floor, placing orders through brokers. She made money in Gold, but after a while, Gold began losing business. The S&P was the new rush, and she began studying systems and charting the S&P market. She then left the Floor altogether and would call in her trades from a private office high in the Merc tower. Now, with her computer setup, she traded from home, where, she said happily, she could sit all day on her sumptuous posterior. She spent much time researching—trying, like most traders, to attach some sort of logic, some sort of pattern or meaning, to a whimsical system. Alice tended toward more esoteric technical study—she was currently trying to figure out the tonal configurations of a Bull market.

I also learned that Alice was an extremely avid reader—she loved reading so much that she'd rented an additional apartment next door just to store all her books. It seemed she had read every classic piece of literature, along with every book that dealt with trading. She didn't care much for romance novels, although she admitted she did indulge in one series, *The Regency*. "Because," she said, "there's no sex, and they're all about money."

Alice, like almost all the traders I had met, loved money. Although, like most, it was in an odd way. When I visited her apartment once, I was surprised to find it nearly bare. While her view of the city was phenomenal, that was about all there was to look at; I had heard Alice speak of a vast art collection, but apparently she stored it elsewhere. There was hardly any furniture—just a couch and La-Z-Boy chair—and not so much as a photograph or picture or tchotchke of any sort. The only impressive piece was a massive sleigh bed that she said she'd bought for $20,000 on a rash shopping spree. It seemed Alice's habit that, if she'd had a really bad trading day, she'd indulge in a pricey purchase. "On my last big losing day," she told me, "I bought a DVD player from Amazon.com. Not just any DVD, but the tip-top-of-the-line $1,500 DVD, with every possible gadget, most of which I will likely never use. I bought it just because I like to know I still can."

However, Alice was quick to downplay her trading skills—she had more than once mentioned that she didn't want to misrepresent herself as an extremely successful trader. "I came into money, then magnificently lost it," she said. Although from what I gathered, she had more than enough left to last a lifetime.

Alice's friend John, the thirty-seven-year-old bachelor, often found it relieving to shake off the trading day by relaxing at Alice's table over an iced tea, or, if he had big losses, a Scotch or a Martini. John tended to trade large size, so for him a bad day could be very bad. When this happened, he possessed what Alice called "the ten-thousand-mile stare." He'd pull up to the table, lean back in the chair as if it were a recliner, and fix his gaze on nothing in particular. Sometimes it would be several minutes before he spoke, other times it would be an hour.

After about my third visit to Alice's table, I received a phone call at home from Alice. "John would like to know if it's all right for me to give him your number," she said in about as bored a tone as one could manage. "I told him I didn't think you'd mind, but he insisted that I call you first. I'm not sure why he feels the need to be so old-fashioned, but this is how he wanted to handle it." It struck me as funny how deadbeat of a matchmaker Alice was. She had no soft spot for romance whatsoever. I hesitated briefly before giving Alice the go-ahead. Normally, first dates seemed rather harmless to me—I was always open to going, even if I wasn't always that enthused. But in this situation, given the atmosphere of the Floor, I wasn't sure if going on a date with a trader was the wisest thing for me to do. I was serious about learning, and I didn't want anything to portray me otherwise. Oh, but maybe I was overthinking everything; after all, it was just dinner.

A week later, John and I went to a cozy mom-and-pop Italian restaurant. He told me he'd started trading almost straight out of college. He had a degree in electrical engineering, but after one year working at IBM in Cleveland, he tossed that career and came to Chicago to trade. He had known someone who was a trader and touted how much money could be made, and for John, that was reason enough. He started out at the Board of Trade as a clerk for, interestingly enough, Bev Gelman, who at the time was just starting her trading career as well. The two had remained friends ever since. I told John I'd spent some time watching Bev, and had found her mesmerizing, even though I didn't understand all the complexities of the Eurodollar pit.

"Just like every house has a foundation," John said, "the foundation of the Merc is Bev Gelman." Then, just for fun, John and I tried to figure out the monetary value of what Bev traded in a given day. Each contract was theoretically worth $1 million, and she typically traded around a hundred thousand contracts per day. It was too many zeros for me, and I had trouble keeping track. John came up with the astounding grand total: Bev's volume on any run-of-the-mill day: $100 billion.

John, too, had found success on the trading floor. For many years he was one of the largest S&P Options traders. The S&P Options pit was a small pit adjacent to the larger Futures pit. This was where the more studious traders were squeezed together with their noses in thick stacks of rabbit-eared pricing sheets. They looked more as if they'd gathered for a class or a debate than for a trading day. In the Options pit, John had days where he made a million dollars—in a *single* day. Granted, he'd had a couple of days where he lost a million dollars in a single day—but the winners outweighed the losers, and really, how many winning million-dollar days does a person need? I could be happy with just one.

Options trading, however, requires constant—often all-night—monitoring, since positions are held for longer terms. After several years of sleepless nights, John was drained. Besides, in Options it was customary to work for a firm, and John yearned to be his own boss. He left Options and moved next door to the S&P Futures pit. Despite the fact that he was a big trader on the Floor, he still had to start out in the soup of the pit—real estate there was worth more than a penthouse on Lake Shore Drive, and each pit required a trader to *earn* his way up, no matter who he was.

John quickly learned that going from Options to Futures was like a mathematician switching his career to that of construction worker. Options is precise and detailed; Futures is instinctual and chancy. Alice maintained that the brains of Options and Futures traders were completely different. "Options traders are more in tune to subtleties, gradations, shades," she said. "They need to be able to make calculations way out of the current Market, so they need to be cerebral. Futures, on the other hand, is direct."

A year and a million-dollar loss later, John quit the S&P pit. He took months off—he traveled, he fished, he golfed, he camped. As a testament to his success in the Options pit, he could still afford the time off even after taking a million-dollar hit. Eventually, he decided to trade again; this time, on the computer. He had a Globex machine installed in his home—only, the twenty-four-hour Market reminded him too much of his Options days. He found himself in front of the screen at 2 a.m., unable to break away. So he had the machine and all the cords and phone lines ripped out, and he began trading on a Globex machine on the Floor. This way, he could still set his own hours—going into work at noon, if he felt like it—but at the closing 3:15 gong, he was out of there. From what I could gather, he was doing quite well, although I would learn that John generally made a conscious effort not to flaunt money. He drove an SUV; he eschewed trendy, overpriced restaurants and clubs; he wore jeans and beat-up hiking shoes everywhere he could get away with it; and he took pride in describing himself as "just your average guy." Because of this, I doubted that he was bothered by the fact that our date was, well, just average—no sparks and nothing much in common. He liked Arnold Schwarzenegger movies and deer hunting. I didn't.

The next day, John called to tell me he had talked to Bev and had asked her if she'd talk to me about trading. At first she had responded with a flat-out no, but John pushed. "Can you do it as a personal favor to me?" he asked. "It's a girl I'm dating."

I didn't know if I was more taken aback by the thought of actually having a conversation with the legendary Bev Gelman or by the thought that John had announced that he and I were officially dating. In the past, I would have been flattered by someone's proclamation and willingness to help me after only one date. But now, it made me nervous. I knew how gossip at the Merc spread, and what was I supposed to do come Monday when I was on the Floor in my yellow jacket and there was John, trading away? I was still learning everything and trying to meet people, and I wasn't sure that I wanted our dating to be a declared thing—or even anything at all. I knew that on the Floor, whoever a woman was with determined who *she* was, and I didn't yet know John well enough to decide if I wanted him as my new label. But it was too late. So I pulled what it seemed a typical male would do with a zealous girl—I backed away. I thanked John and told him I'd like to wait until I learned more about trading before I talked to Bev so that I didn't sound like a complete idiot. "Maybe we could all go out in a group," I suggested. It wouldn't be long before I was taken up on that.

Party at Bev's the dainty green-checkered card with little cloth roses announced. A tuxedoed butler welcomed us into Bev Gelman's regal brownstone, which sat in the middle of a row of multimillion-dollar homes in the Gold Coast section of the city. Bev was in a fitted lime dress, which happened to match the invitation, and also happened to be a similar shade to her trading jacket. Over a hundred people caroused around Bev's dark-wood house. A full bar filled the foyer and a catered banquet was laid out in the dining room. I couldn't quite believe that I was in the home of Bev herself. I was dining among the top tier of traders in the world. The worth of the people in this room, the financial significance under this roof, the influence, the clout—just thinking about it made me dizzy, but John came to my rescue with a Cosmopolitan.

Bev had grown up one of three girls in a small town outside of Philadelphia. She'd attended Brown University, and then moved to Chicago, where she began as a clerk at the Board of Trade. I knew she was a spitfire, and I grew nervous when John went to pull her over to introduce me. I felt as if she might laugh in my face if she found out I was a clerk—a lowly clerk at *the* Bev Gelman's party! But off the Floor, Bev was a different person. She was extremely smiley and quick with self-deprecating humor. Still, I felt as if I was in the presence of a celebrity, and I had the need to brandish some lame compliment—I told her I liked her dress. She said, "From the back, I look like a twelve-year-old boy." She cinched the lime fabric tight across her waist. "See," she said. "No shape." I'd heard, however, that she hadn't always been this way—traders who'd started out with Bev years ago said she was chubby, and that it was the stress of trading that caused her to shed just about every ounce of body fat.

Bev spoke very quickly, with short, terse snippets of sentences. She talked about her six-year-old daughter, Sarah, who was prancing in and out of the rooms. Bev's ex-husband was at the party, and he joined our conversation, adding that their daughter was the most competitive first-grader he knew. "At school, she *must* be first in line," he said.

"Are you insinuating she gets this from me?" Bev joked. A waiter bearing a tray of Martinis arrived, and we traded our empty glasses. Bev let out a sigh of resignation about her precocious daughter, although she seemed more amused than worried. "She's such a pretty girl," Bev said, "beautiful, really. But I'm actually hoping she'll eventually go through some awkward, gawky stage. I just think it will ground her."

"Bev, do you want to go fly-fishing with us next month?" John asked.

Bev faked a yawn. "I have all the equipment, you're more than welcome to borrow it if you like, but I don't fly-fish."

"Well, at least come camping with us later," John said. "Bring Sarah, she'd love it." Bev gave him a you've-got-to-be-kidding smirk. "I have great camping equipment; again, you are more than welcome to borrow it, but I don't camp," she said. "Come on, can you see me camping? Puh-lease. And Sarah doesn't camp either." She chuckled at her declaration of what young Sarah's principles ought to be.

I soon forgot that I was talking to the Merc legend, and no one else at the party appeared overly conscious of it either. Her guests seemed to be a loyal network of long-term friends. The only person who was missing was her boyfriend and fellow trader, Sean, who was out of town. I mentioned that I'd watched the two of them in the pit. "Everyone in that pit is sort of scared of me," Bev said. "Which is kind of nice. I like being in that position. When they start really getting on my nerves all I have to say is, 'Fine, guys, I'm just taking the next week off.' Then they shape up. It took a long time to get to where I'm at, though. It certainly wasn't always that way. But I'm tough in the pit. I step in there and all of sudden I don't care about anyone else. Except for Sean."

"How long does it take after the bell for you to shed that?" I asked.

"About thirty seconds," she said. "I owe most of that to Sean too. He keeps me grounded, reminds me about what's important. It's great."

Bev was pulled to another conversation, and John suggested we mingle. "Here, if a guy's wearing a wedding ring," he jokingly instructed me, "it doesn't really matter!" He introduced me to a man in his late thirties who was dubbed the "$300-Million Man," after the recent sale of his trading firm. One of John's closest friends, Scottie, who'd retired from trading in his early thirties, was teasing 300 Mil. "I would have been a sucker and when they said, 'Two hundred million!' I would have shouted, 'Sold!' " Scottie said.

"Yeah, that would have really been selling out," Scottie's wife facetiously offered up.

"So how did you know to hold out?" Scottie asked. "How did you know to up the hundred-mill offer, and up the two hundred-mil?" Three hundred-Mil smiled knowingly. "You just keep your mouth shut," he said.

John introduced me to a Nasdaq pit trader who had a woman half his age clinging to his arm. He spoke like a newscaster, stilted and cocky. She said she was a model, although she lived on a farm in southern Illinois with her parents and commuted to the city to stay with her boyfriend in his condo above Saks Fifth Avenue. She told me that she'd been to the Merc once to have lunch with him and that another trader started calling after them, "Hey, I make more money than *he* does!"

John then pointed out a trader with graying temples. "That guy gets degrees in his spare time," he said. "He has a law degree, a Ph.D. in literature, and an M.D., and now he's having his best trading year ever. He's up $40 million. He's making Bev look like, well, like me."

"Why don't these guys retire?" I asked.

"It's hard to stop when you're doing so well," John said. "I think he's going to finish out this year and then buy a house in the Berkshires. When I heard how much he was up for the year I went home and I was so depressed. Really, it's depressing."

I wasn't so sure what John could be that depressed about. For all his ups and downs on the Floor, it seemed he always managed to finish very much on the upswing. But it was all relative, I supposed. John said everyone on the Floor tried to increase their annual income by 10 percent a year. So if someone made a few million last year, but was only at $800,000 this year, they were going to be complaining that they were down. Because of ridiculous self-set standards such as these, traders tended to indulge in a significant amount of whining.

John and I took our drinks outside to the courtyard and walked down a stone path to a little bench. I wondered how it was going to be on the Floor if I ran into any of these traders—I felt a bit as if I were living a Cinderella story, and while I had my glass slippers on now, come midnight I'd turn back into a yellow-jacketed peon. It seemed ridiculous that just the thought of my yellow jacket made me feel inferior to everyone else here—and yet, the hierarchy of the Floor was so pervasive that that was exactly how I felt. But John didn't make me feel that way. At some point during the night we had the "let's just be friends" talk, which was exactly what I needed—I finally had my friend on the Floor. Then, John spilled my Cosmopolitan, and I spilled his Martini reaching for my toppled glass. Before we could stop laughing, a tuxedoed waiter was rushing over with napkins and new drinks for us both.

$ $ $

Conversation at Alice's table typically focused on current events, the stupidity of specific items of popular culture, trivia, television documentaries, movies, stocks, and occasionally, gossip. However, the common thread linking all the topics together was numbers. Traders *loved* to infiltrate numbers into everything. You get a bunch of doctors together and they're bound to fill their talk with medical terms. You get a bunch of traders together, and the talk turns to numbers: market numbers, statistics on this, percentages on that, ratios, values, probabilities, possibilities, record breakers. How many countries are there in the world? If you were stranded on a desert island and ate nothing but bananas, how long would you survive? What is the minimum amount of money you think you could live off per day? (John said, if he moved to a farm, 49 cents. Alice disagreed, insisting it would be at least 75 cents.) How much do you think you'd need to retire right now? (John felt $8 million in the bank, to do it happily.) How much did you pay for your car? (Alice and John were both buying new cars; Alice had quickly settled on a sedan, bought it, and within two weeks decided she didn't like it and took it back. "I told you you should have test-driven it first," John had reprimanded her.) How much you had overpaid for something. How much the vacation was costing. How much your clerk blew at the Merc Club on your account. How much you dropped this weekend. How many shares you bought of this stock, how many you should have bought, where it's at, where it was at, where it should be at. It was as though they needed to assign a numerical value to everything in order to make some sense of it. For traders, numbers are black and white, and they feel comfortable with them. They are also not afraid of appearing gauche by talking prices. A group of doctors won't likely discuss what each one is earning, or their raises or pay cuts. But traders will. It was odd, at first, to hear them spouting their wins and losses in monetary terms. Just as it was odd to hear them ask what things cost and how much you paid for something. But that was the norm. And it was precisely the conversation one day at Alice's table. We were discussing monthly fees—that is, four traders were discussing monthly fees, while I was trying to mask my astonishment by casually, and silently, sipping an iced tea. With clerk fees, clearinghouse fees, seat fees, and commissions on each trade, the monthly total that a Local must pay can soar astronomically.

The topic came up when one trader was complaining that his clearing-firm commissions were being raised. He had been paying twenty cents per contract he traded, and now they were upping it to twenty-five cents. This didn't seem significant until you considered that he typically traded over $100,000 contracts a month. Calculate it out, and it was somewhere around an additional $5,000 a month. Now add all additional costs—clerks, seat lease, trade-checker, etc.—and the grand total was $45,000 a month that this trader must pay as the base cost of doing business. He was apparently clearing it, although not happily. Everyone else at the table weighed in with their monthly fees, along with a rundown of which clearing firms charged less or more, plus the calculations of an eighth-of-a-penny difference over a month, and the calculations of half-a-penny difference. The numbers were flying: "I pay $1,000 a day in commissions." "That's nothing, I'm up to $1,500!" My stomach was twisting—their five-figure monthly fees were my not-too-long-ago yearly salary.

Alice turned to me. "So Cari," she asked, "does this make you feel richer or poorer?"

It was after the Close, and Alice, Ben, and I were lounging at Alice's table. Ben noticed a trader across the room and proceeded to tell us a story about him. "There's this guy I've stood next to in the pit for some time," Ben said. "Every day, he's there, I'm there, and we trade. Well, I saw this guy while I was on vacation in Florida. I walk up to him, I say, 'Hello, isn't this funny!' and he looks at me with this blank face. 'Do I know you?' he asks. Know me? We've stood next to each other for years! Do I know you! Some of these people, they don't care about anyone but themselves. So the next time we are both back in the pit I turn to him and say, 'Hey, *now* do you remember me?' "

I spotted another example of the stereotypical self-centered trader when I glanced over at the Club bar. His name was Billy, and when I saw that his badge was BDOG, I chuckled at the appropriateness. Billy was in his mid-twenties, and I'd happened to meet him one weekend at a trendy steakhouse/bar called Gibson's. Gibson's is in the heart of the Rush and State Street intersection—a strip otherwise known as "Viagra Triangle," since everywhere you look an older man, dripping with money, has a beau-

tiful woman, half his age, hooked on his arm. It seemed that a disproportionate number of those men were traders, and that Gibson's was a favorite
spot. One trader from the Board of Trade had his own personal table
there—it was his every night, and if he didn't show, the prime table
remained empty.

The night I met Billy he was trying to be as smooth as possible, for my
blond friend was his sudden object of desire. He gave her all the lines and
invited us to a barbeque at his apartment that Sunday. Out of curiosity, we
went, only to discover there was no food to grill, nor was there even a single piece of silverware in any drawer, just a bottle opener and a lot of
crumbs. While Billy and his friends were dancing to blasting music, we
made a quick getaway.

$ $ $

At the Club, Alice ordered the calamari salad, which arrived as a double-
sized, heaping plateful that the chef had made especially for her. Alice
tucked the starched, white napkin into the collar of her shirt, fanned it over
her chest, then dug in. It was around the fifth time in a row that I'd seen
Alice have the calamari salad. When John walked in, he looked worn out
and cranky. He glanced at the pyramid of salad. "Trying something new
today, Alice?" he said.

It was no secret that Alice was big on routine. Soon after the calamari
salad trend, a new one started: cheeseburger and fries. Once, when I turned
the corner to Alice's table, I was shocked to find her not there. Instead, the
staff was clearing her table and she was seated at the table next door. "This
is new," I said as I sat down.

"Oh, there was a large party and they ran over," Alice explained. Her
meal arrived—sure enough, cheeseburger and fries—and she dug in. As
soon as the staff finished setting Alice's usual table, they came to her and
apologized for the delay. To my surprise, Alice got up and moved—along
with her half-eaten plate of cheeseburger, her pitcher of water, pitcher of
iced tea, plate of lemons, and her numerous napkins—to her usual spot, as
if it would not be possible to spend a single afternoon at a different table.

When Alice threw a party, like she did for the 2000 presidential election, she
threw a top-notch affair at the Merc Club. Tara and I were invited, and we

dined on jumbo shrimp, enormous lobster tails, duck confit, and legs of lamb. Alice had shed her sweatshirt for a solid-forest-green pantsuit that made her look like a little spruce tree.

The waiters hovered over everyone's wineglass, champagne flute, Scotch tumbler, rendering everyone absolutely unaware of how much they were imbibing since all drinks were perpetually full. The bartender would report to Alice the next day that all her guests were extremely nice, but boy, could they drink! And this, coming from a full-time Merc Club bartender who served a population of men known to guzzle alcohol both to drown a losing day and to toast a winning day.

Tara and I were the youngest at the party, and most likely the poorest, although a handful of Alice's relatives balanced out the crowd, so it didn't seem as Merc-elite as Bev's guest list had been. We listened to people's war stories of the pits, the money made, the money lost, the staggering figures, dropped like something that was read in today's newspaper and not personal fortunes. We pretended that we, too, were a part of this segment of society in the high-income bracket, and we reveled in the decadent private-club mentality where nothing was scrimped on. In every corner of the Club, the television monitors that usually displayed Market numbers were tuned to the election. With each swing state's poll results, John ran and checked the Market for fluctuation. "We're up a buck and a half!" he'd report. Alice had also devised a guess-the-number-of-electoral-votes contest, the winner of which would receive a bottle of Dom Perignon.

After the party, John, Tara, Alice, and I stumbled down the street to Alice's apartment to watch the end of the election. "Now I don't want to hear any comments about how sparse it is," Alice reminded us as we approached her door.

As the election dragged on, the talk turned to trading, and Alice and John began questioning Tara. "I only want to make $30,000 a year with trading," Tara revealed, "just enough to cover my costs so that I can do my music."

John made a face. "Then get some other job. Trading is only for people who want to make millions. That's the only way to make the stress worth it."

"It's true," Alice agreed.

"And even then," John added, sipping his—fourth? tenth?—Scotch, "it's never enough."

"But I don't need a lot of money," Tara said. "And what if I can make what I want in just a few hours a day?" I should have spoken up, too, for this was along the lines of my game plan—to trade for supplemental income. But Alice and John were in a different league, they traded large size, and John, at least, tended to discredit the measly one-lot trader, so I just sat there silently.

"Listen," John said. "Anyone who is not after the money when they trade, shouldn't be trading. Trading is for ex-athletes who have a fierce sense of competition." John had run track all throughout college and never lost that sense of winning on your own, of beating your own best time, of gaining achievement in a solitary sport that revolved around others, but didn't *depend* on others—much like trading. Tara didn't mention that she was a former gymnast. "You take on all this risk for hope of the reward, but the reward has to be worth it," John went on. "Besides, with trading, you always have to pay your tuition at some point." He let out a bitter chuckle. "I went to Harvard."

He began detailing his early years and the top price he had paid as a right of passage, a toll of sorts to the trading gods. I knew he had lost a million dollars in the S&P Futures pit, but I didn't know that years earlier he had suffered another monumental loss. He was at the Board of Trade, in the Bond Options pit, where he had been doing very well—until the day the Gulf War began. He got caught on the wrong side of a market that suddenly exploded into a vicious tidal wave. He called that day his Gray Day—for in a split second, all color was gone and the faces and bodies around him were nothing more than gray blobs. And then everything—all the gray blobs—started spinning, not the kind of merry-go-round spinning the room does when you've had too much to drink or when you turn in circles and get dizzy, but a vertical spinning, where the bottom flips to the top, where the floor moves toward the ceiling, where you're falling upside down. He shoved his trading cards to the broker next to him, muttered three words, "Get me out," then ran out of the pit, out of the building, outside to the sidewalk, and right there, in the middle of the bustling downtown Loop, he threw himself into a snowdrift and lay there until the sky returned to where it was supposed to be. He lost a million dollars that day. He never went back to the Board of Trade.

After taking several months off, John returned to trading, this time in the S&P Options pit. Eventually, he worked his way up to become one of the largest and most successful traders. He was known as "Take 'Em All!" for that was often his response when a large order was dropped. He'd swipe the air with a muscular arm. "Take 'em all!" he'd shout, and the others, the little guys, screaming and vying for a two-lot, a five-lot, a ten-lot out of that order, would be stopped cold, out of luck, cowering in John's shadow.

But even though John had made a stunning comeback, he admitted to us, while pouring another glass of Scotch, that it still wasn't enough. "I used to feel frustrated in the pit because I was standing next to guys who were making $10 million a year and I was only making a million," he said. "I would feel bad about myself. I'd be like, what's *wrong* with me? But then I turned it around and I thought, hey, I'm making more money than 99 percent of the people in the entire world. It's amazing how warped everything is on the trading floor, that you can feel bad about yourself because you're only making a million."

Tara didn't want to listen anymore. Must everyone try to discourage her? To her relief, the election finally ended (for the night, at least), and, exhausted, we left for home.

Even though I had much the same goal as Tara, the time I'd already spent on the Floor made me feel that Alice's and John's philosophies were cogent. The more I learned, the more it was becoming clear that to be a trader, you pretty much either had "it" or you didn't. Of course, there were things to learn and guidelines to follow, and plenty of errors to be made along the way, but it really did seem like there was some innate quality that you had to possess—something that couldn't be taught. I had yet to determine if *I* had it, and I hoped that a full tutorial from Alice on technical trading would shed some much-needed light on my own direction in this world. For Tara, however, trading was riddled with stress and panic attacks, and provided very little that was positive. She was so talented in other areas, such as her music, and I couldn't help but wonder what she was trying to prove by sticking with trading—and to whom she was trying to prove it? Ironically, this tenaciousness was the quality in her that most resembled a trader.

The need to prove oneself appeared to be an integral facet of many traders' personalities. This could manifest itself in various ways, but the most obvious and most common seemed to be the amount of contracts you traded—

as if large contract size was somehow a testament to a trader's virility and adeptness. A Dow Futures trader once explained to me, "There's a point in your early career where you just have to take the plunge and make a colossal trade and think, 'This is either going to make me, or this is going to blow me out of the water, and then I'd know I shouldn't be trading anyway.' " Luckily for him, his philosophy panned out, for after his do-or-die trade, he remained standing.

John had told me that his secret to making multimillions on the trading floor boiled down to two things: (1) knowing how to take advantage of others' fears; and (2) assuming a larger-than-life persona. "This is why I was known as 'Take 'Em All!' " he said. "Intimidation is key." I'd heard other stories of intimidation on the Floor. Tom told me about a trader, whom I'll call Carl, who lived a high-profile, party-with-celebrities life. "Carl hardly comes down to the Floor anymore," Tom said, "but when he does, he pushes everyone out of the way to claim his spot, even though he may not have been in for nine months. He looks like a heavyset Rod Stewart—his hair is half lion, he has a fake tan, his shirt is unbuttoned. He puts on three-hundred-lot positions—that means for every tick, he's up or down $7,500. This guy has balls the size of Jupiter. He just walks in screaming, 'Fuck you, sell! Fuck you too, buy!' And everyone just stares."

Not only are most traders obsessed with throwing around large numbers, especially if it will gain attention, but several of the men at the Merc expressed annoyance with those who traded just a small number of contracts at a time. John and another trader both bemoaned having to hear a woman call in her measly one-lots. "All day long," they complained, "I have to watch her jumping up and down, 'One! Sell one!' She acts like she's trading one-hundred-lots."

"Would she bother you if she was jumping up and down all day going, 'Sell ten!'?" I asked.

"No," they agreed in unison, that was a respectable enough amount for her not to bother them.

$ $ $

John sometimes wore a headset while he was trading so that he could arb with a broker in the pit. Recently, he'd begun sharing his broker with another trader, so that they could split expenses, but yesterday the other trader stole John's trade—which was a $4,000 trade—and they both knew it. "You fucker!" John yelled, and the guy, realizing that what he'd done was slimy, said, "I'll make it up to you—I'll buy you a hooker."

"A good hooker's gonna run you around four-hundred to five-hundred bucks," John said.

"I know," the guy answered, as if it were no problem.

John thought it over. "I'm gonna have you get me a fishing rod instead." A few days later, John picked out his new fishing pole. With that, and a handshake, the stolen-trade incident was forgotten.

Male traders all tended to agree that they were better suited to a detached attitude than the women. The men believed that the castigating environment of the Floor was no big deal—that is, once the closing bell rang. But what bugged them was that most of the women here thought it *was* a big deal—even *after* the bell rang. They offered up that women would hold a grudge, stew, demand an apology, fume, become bitter, complain to everyone about each and every incident, hound the man until he gave in, and, basically, never let it go.

Alice told me about a woman trader who'd managed to come up with a reason for hating just about every man at the Merc. She eventually became so emblazoned that she began referring to all men on the Floor as "rapists." It didn't take long for this woman to leave the Merc, and trading, altogether.

In order to prevent things from going this far, one woman trader, Jen—JNN—made the decision not to trade in the pit, but rather to stand directly outside of it and place trades through a broker. "I didn't like getting picked on by people in the pit and then having them slap me on the back and say, 'Can I buy you a beer downstairs?' " she said. "I'd get very frustrated by that. So if I go through a broker there's no one to blame but myself. Someone didn't tick me off, someone didn't stuff me, someone didn't screw me over. I don't have to feel like I got pickpocketed. There are people here who want you to do badly, but then at 3:15 they're your best friend."

Alice, however, was a woman who had perfected the art of detachment. I knew she was about as far as one could get from a romantic, but just the thought of intimacy seemed to disgust her. She readily professed to "arrested development" and "lack of emotion." John, too, confessed to an emotional void. "I was remarkably born without any feelings," he once told me. Which is just another curious quality that likely made the both of them successful traders.

And yet, despite their professed callousness, I noticed that actual feelings started to surface when a stock that both Alice and John held suddenly plunged. John had fortuitously sold off a large portion not long before, but Alice hadn't. And then, Alice was hit again, this time on her largest stock holding—she suffered a million-dollar-plus loss. Although she denied the correlation, she began experiencing fluke physical symptoms, such as wheezing and fatigue, which landed her in the hospital, where all they found was high blood pressure. They released her with the recommendation that she speak to a psychiatrist.

Reluctantly, Alice met with the psychiatrist, who, among other questions, asked if Alice was prone to binge spending. "I don't think so," Alice said.

"What was your last big purchase?" the psychiatrist asked. Alice replied meekly, "A bed frame."

"How much did you spend on it?"

Alice shifted uncomfortably. "Twenty thousand dollars." The psychiatrist looked at her knowingly. "But I did have a few hundred thousand in my bank account at that time," Alice added, but to no avail. The doctor arrived at the diagnosis of manic-depression. She wrote out a prescription, which Alice never filled.

Alice then took a break from the Merc Club and from trading in general. She still, however, spent much time analyzing various charts of the Market, for she found that to be a very relaxing activity. Alice never told the psychiatrist that she hadn't taken the medication, but, as the weeks passed, the psychiatrist was quite pleased with Alice's progress. And after a couple of months, Alice returned to the Merc Club.

Her first question of the day for all of us was: "What was your last big purchase?" John thought for a second. "Over $1,000 of fishing gear," he said. She asked another trader, "An $8,000 watch." She asked me. "Uhhh, a $200 plane ticket?" I offered.

"Oh please," Alice groaned. "And it was probably a work-related trip." I smiled feebly. "Well," Alice said to me, "I suppose you're the only one at this table who's not manic-depressive."

Even though Alice was feeling better, there was something different about the aura at her table—it seemed to take on a bitter tone. I got the feeling that everyone was telling one another lies. If they'd lost money (and many of them had), they said they hadn't, or if they'd made money, they exaggerated it one way or the other. Alice started becoming officious with John, and the more he felt she was prying into his personal life, the more he began lying about it. Alice lied too, and freely admitted to me that she would often transpose her winning and losing days, and that she would exaggerate those wins and losses—only, not in the way one might think. If she had a winning day, she'd say, "It was tough, a rough day"; if she had a losing day, she'd say, "It was pretty good, I did okay." I asked her what the point was. "Because," she said, "I learned early on that everyone loves a loser."

But the oddest thing was that they all pretty much knew that they were all lying to one another. "Doesn't it bother you?" I asked Alice.

"I have no problem if someone needs to sit there and tell me lies to make themselves feel better," she said. "Why should it bother me? In fact, I don't understand why you feel it would bother you, Cari. I think that's quite oversensitive of you, although you do have a tendency to get all worked up over things like that."

That was the uniqueness of Alice's table, and the trading world in general. What, from one view, seemed like support, was, from another view, a form of resistance. What constituted a true friend, someone whom you could trust? Wouldn't a major factor be that they didn't lie to you? Or was a good friend someone who allowed you to lie? Who didn't care that, for whatever reason, you needed to lie?

I remember, at first, being greatly taken aback by the typical trader's brash, blunt, whatever-goes attitude. But as time went on, I began to find something oddly refreshing about it. Here, you could say whatever was on your mind, and you could expect that no one would take it personally. You could be as craggy and crass as you wanted, and there was no need for political correctness. You could scream and call someone names, and then meet them for a drink after the bell with no mention of the scene that had occurred earlier. Where else could you find a group of co-workers so unwilling to hold a grudge? You were accepted here, faults and all. Because of this, deep bonds of friendship developed. These were the people you invited to your home for holidays, or went on vacations with, or with whom you bought adjacent summer homes. These were the people you designated as your children's godparents. And you could count on them. All of the people at Alice's table were loyal friends to one another—and they'd even begun to extend themselves to me.

But it was now that I learned how friendships here had their own set of rules—for everything instantly changed when it came to trading. The pit resembled a huge poker table—you had to be wary of everyone, you had to be adept at bluffing, and no matter how good a friend you were with someone, the bottom line was that from the moment you stepped into the pit, the only thing you could be concerned with was yourself, and how *you* were going to get the chips. If you were up, your best friend could be down. Or, it could be the other way around. And that was where all the lying came in.

What it all boiled down to, I believed, was that traders needed to adopt certain defense mechanisms to deal with an environment that promoted such an intense, self-centered instinct for survival. And what I had witnessed was the bizarre, push-and-pull behavior that ended up surfacing when money became just as—if not more—important than people.

NINE

The O'Hare Spread

The O'Hare spread was created by some devious traders who hated playing by the rules. These were the overbold boys who traded large—sometimes larger than the limits imposed by their clearing firms. When this happened, they would do a trader form of doubling down by putting on a new position in a different market. The point of this spread was not to hedge or protect themselves—but to go for broke. This is where O'Hare—as in O'Hare Airport—comes in. The stress of going for broke is great, and the traders devised a superstitious way of killing time while waiting for the verdict on their two positions: they would head out to O'Hare. From there, they would call in to the Floor. If the trades were good, they would dash out of the airport and back to the Floor to take their profits; if the trades were bad, they would hop on the next flight—to anywhere.

t was a busy Friday and I was on the Floor trying to figure out why the Market had suddenly rallied. Earlier today, many reports with numbers that could affect the Market had come in: Housing, Loans, Producer Price Index (an inflation indicator), Consumer Sentiment, and Industrial Production. Also, today was what's known as "triple witching," where the simultaneous expiration of Stock Index Futures, Stock Index Options, and Stock Options could make markets more volatile than usual. A helpful clerk informed me that the rally was likely due to the Unemployment number, which had just been released. It was higher than expected.

"But if the rate of unemployment was higher," I asked, "why would the Market go up?"

"Yeah, a high unemployment rate reflects poorly on the economy," the clerk said, "*but* it signifies the Fed will likely cut interest rates again in a couple of weeks, so the Market likes that." He tapped his finger to his head to flaunt his braininess. "Sometimes bad news is good news to the Market—and good news can be bad."

I verified this all with Tom later. "Yep," he said, "the Dow had a knee-jerk reaction and actually went up." How can you be two steps ahead of everything and factor in the future, *now*, in the present, I wondered? Tom explained that it hadn't always been like this. It used to be that just a select group of insiders knew information about the Market. But now information was immediately available to the masses; plus, history had a tendency to repeat itself, so more and more people knew what to expect. Trading had become a big chess tournament, where you had to see all the steps ahead of time and anticipate your opponent's move—in this case, anticipate the public move. "But you get used to it," Tom said. "See, there's this traders' adage: 'Buy the rumor, sell the fact.' The public usually sits there and waits until whatever talk—a merger? a new product launch? a possible announcement? bankruptcy?—is confirmed, but we pros know that by the time it's reality, it has already been, as they say, *factored* into the price. For amateurs, that means: you missed it. See, I have my own motto: 'When everyone's cryin', I'm buyin'. When everyone's yellin', I'm sellin'.' "

Most traders, I'd found, had their own adages or mantras or little sayings, and I'd even seen some who had them printed on a trading card, which they kept with them in their jacket pocket:

- Buy into strength, sell into weakness.
- The trend is your friend.
- Being a bottom picker or a top picker is like fighting the tape.
- You're only as good as your last trade.
- Don't let losses run.
- Never add to a loser.
- Lose the ego, detach your emotions. No what-ifs, no fear, no guilt.
- Scared money never wins.
- Stubbornness is the bane of all traders—you must quickly admit you were wrong.

Alice told me the best phrase she'd heard about trading was from a trader and author named Jake Bernstein, who said: "The worst thing about a bad trade is that it keeps you out of a good trade."

"It rang true to me," Alice said, "but then again, I practiced a much different tactic from many male traders when I was on the Floor—I was smart enough to almost always assume I was wrong. If I have a trading motto of my own it's 'Question all accepted wisdom—hold it in deep suspicion.' "

But did all these proclamations and recommendations really help when you were in the middle of the pit and the veins in your forehead were about to explode? Did you pull out your printed trading card and repeat your mantras? Did you call upon words of wisdom from experts in the field? Did you furiously flip through your charts and graphs and figures?

No. Pretty much, you resorted back to your most primal of instincts. As I was learning, plain old superstition was a force greater—and perhaps far more adhered to on the Floor—than most any other trading principle. It could be traced back to the origins of time, to beliefs in signs and clouds and omens, to talismans and sacrificial offerings. It was the unshakable sense that your presence in the world—your every move, every decision, every temptation—could trip up or appease the powers that be.

It had happened more than once: a shipment of pens with the trading-firm logo arrived on schedule, but upon opening the box, it was discovered that the pens were—gasp!—not black ink, but blue, and the whole shipment was immediately removed from the office and sent to the incinerator where all blue—and God forbid, red!—ink belonged. To have anything but black ink was inviting trouble—after all, you wanted to be in the black, *always*. When you were at a restaurant for dinner, no matter how posh the place, you did not sign the bill if they provided you with a blue pen. A real trader always carried a black-ink pen, rather than risk an occasion such as this. But if you happened to forget, well then, someone else at the table must sign for you—and if you were with only traders, then you had a problem—*excuse me, waiter, I need a black pen . . . yes, another pen, but . . . no I'm sure this one works, it's just that I need a* black *pen*—because blue ink on your fingertips, blue ink forming your signature, was a bad omen. If this sounds like poppycock, hogwash behavior, then you don't know traders. Many of them possess the black-ink-only hang-up, and even those who don't are quite sensitive to those who do—it's been melded into the collective consciousness of trader mentality. It's so prevalent that it no longer seems odd. Just as it is not odd to see a trader waiting for a specific turnstile, or, so I've heard, a certain urinal or bathroom stall.

It was also not unusual, back when traders were required to wear ties, to see someone wearing the same tie every single day. He likely checked it with his trader's jacket, and every morning slung the ratty thing around his neck—not *tied*, but slung, just slipped the already tied, tattered, stained thing over his head—and caught the escalator up to start the day. It was quite common behavior to associate a winning trading day with a specific tie. These winning ties would end up ripped and frayed, with the stitching and seams coming undone—but it didn't matter so long as the trader observed the tie-wearing regulation at the time, which proclaimed the tie had to maintain some sort of knot above the second shirt button. Alice recalled a Pork Belly trader who wore the same threadbare, raggedy tie every single day, and would declare: "When this tie goes, I go!" "I had thought that dreadful tie had gone ten years ago," Alice quipped. Another trader and former executive of the Merc, a brilliant man who had made millions of dollars by meticulously charting algorithms, never failed to wear his blue tie with red diamonds on the day of a big trade. He had an Ivy League law degree and held a top position in his field, gained from years of tedious studies and consistently accurate reports of the Market—yet he believed in a lucky tie, relied on it, *needed* it.

John told me that he used to have a thing with ties, too. For him, it wasn't a single lucky tie, but rather it became *unlucky* to wear a tie that cost more than a dollar. He set about buying not just cheap, but ludicrously cheap, and not just ugly, but ludicrously ugly ties. John's friends and family joined in, splurging 99 cents on him if ever they were lucky enough to spot a beauty.

I was at Alice's table one afternoon with several other traders when Alice, for no apparent reason, pulled a wad of cash from the pocket of her red polyester, wide-collared jacket and dumped it on the table. It was a crumpled mess, and by the looks of it, I'd expected it all to be singles. But as she rifled through, unfolding the bills, there were tens, twenties, a fifty. Alice suddenly stopped. "John, do you have change for a fifty?" she asked, sliding it toward him as if she didn't want to touch it for very long.

"Do you have something against the fifty, Alice?" John asked.

"I just don't like it."

John pulled cash from his pants pocket, from his wallet, then from his trader's jacket pocket. It seemed that both of them haphazardly scattered large bills the way I did Kleenex or spare change. The table was covered with rumpled money. He handed her two twenties and a ten, and, now contented, she resumed counting her bills.

When she was done, she pocketed the money, then launched into a story about a man named Harold, who had been a friend of her mother's.

"Harold traded a little and one day said to my mother, 'You know, Sunny, I think I'm going to put on a huge Silver position. I'm going to sell.' He called in his trade and then got the call back to confirm. 'Bought?' he yelled into the phone. 'I gave you a sell order!' Then, he got weirdly quiet, as if the mistake was an omen of some sort. 'No,' he said, 'just leave it.' And not more than a few days later was the start of a huge run-up of Silver. Harold ran it all the way. His mistaken trade was a multimillion-dollar winner."

The others at the table only half listened, hardly as amused as I. For every story like this, there were a hundred more, and they'd heard these stories a hundred times. Besides, no one was in the mood to hear about the lucky ride of some trader long ago. But I understood that Alice was telling this story to demonstrate to me how commonplace superstition was among traders—and that, no, her thing against the $50 bill did not mean she was nutty.

Later, when it was just the two of us, Alice informed me she also had a "yellow straw issue." "I had this very big losing day," she confided. "And when I went to the Club later, I became appalled that there was a yellow straw in my drink. I didn't tell anybody, but I had to switch it. The reality is, a lot of things happened that day, but I chose to focus on the yellow straw. Of course, I know I am being obsessive-compulsive, but you better believe that if I get a yellow straw I am going to switch it. Now this is not to say that removing a yellow straw precludes a bad day, because then I start thinking that it will be the day *after* that will be bad. I finally announced to the Club staff that I won't have any yellow straws. They're very careful now about what color straw they give me—hey, I'm not the only person in the Club with weird things."

Some time ago, while surfing the Internet, I'd discovered a website called TeachTrade, which was run by a top trader at the Merc. When I signed on today, I was surprised at the aptness of the commentary, for it tied in perfectly to Alice's and my discussion of traders' unique philosophies:

Given these uncertain and frustrating market conditions, it was time to share with you the highly secret methodology. It's all in the cards, the unofficial "Ouija" market cards.

1. Take a trading card—the kind we use in the pit to record our trades, with buys on one side and sells on the other. Toss it in the air. If it

lands on the "buy" side, then buy. If it lands on the "sell," then sell. More sophisticated traders may want to use this as a contrarian indicator, buying when it lands on sell, and selling when it lands on buy. Works equally well both ways.

2. Use the elevator rule. If you get on the "up" elevator when you mean to go down, buy the market. If you get on the "down" when you want to go up, then sell the market. For at-home traders, adjust to your own, specific parameters. If you leave the garage door open, then sell the market. If you go to the refrigerator during a market lull to find you're out of milk, then buy the market. This can be adjusted for any scenario or idiosyncrasy without changing the accuracy of the indicator.

3. My mentor, Maury Kravitz, used a dreidel. By spinning it, he could know to buy, sell or stay out of the market, depending upon where the dreidel landed. With proper training, this method can also be used with a handful of coins (two heads and a tail then buy, two tails and a head then sell) or even dice. (If the dice add up to seven or more, then buy. Seven or less than, sell. Seven? Sorry! You've crapped out.)

So, what was it, after all, with the need to attribute some event in the pit to something else completely unrelated and completely happenstance? Perhaps it went straight to the core of one's need for security, for something to believe in, whatever that something may be—a threadbare, smelly tie; a certain door; a yellow straw as a harbinger. Maybe the bottom line was: if you credited your winnings to something outside of yourself then you could credit your failings to something outside of yourself too. If the good wasn't all that personal, well, nice for you, then neither was the bad. But I believed there was more to it than that. If, on your good days, you said: *I'm a success story! I am a great trader!* then, on your bad days you had to say, *I failed, I am a terrible trader.* If you're alternately beating yourself up, then patting yourself on the back in accordance with your good days and bad—which, in this field, are in accordance with the highly volatile Market—you are going to be one very unstable person, a walking bipolar mess. So instead, you refrained from thinking of yourself as a failure when you lost money; and when you had a great day, when you walked out of there up an average Joe's yearly salary, well then, it must have been that new cereal you ate for breakfast.

Of course, much of trading was a game of chance, and the truth may be, plain and simple, that you had your winning streaks and you wanted to do whatever you could to keep them rolling, you didn't want to tempt fate, you didn't want to change much, because YOU WERE WINNING, so you should just keep doing exactly what you were doing—even if it meant washing the same pair of underwear every night and wearing them day after day after day. Even if it was bestowing twenty bucks on the vagrant outside the Merc every morning, as some traders did.

Sometimes, the amulet would find the trader—when Jen, JNN, was still a clerk, she would on occasion help out an S&P trader named Howard. Every time she clerked for Howard, it seemed that the Market would break—only Howard felt this was no coincidence. "Howard started calling me his good luck charm," Jen recalled. "He would rub his cards on my head every day. And then he offered me a job. I've been with him for six years, and he's the one who put me in the pit."

On the Floor, no one so much as paused at any type of odd, fanciful explanation of behavior—for example, it was a given that many traders did not work on Friday the thirteenth. No one cared what your superstition of choice was, and all seemed to be granted due respect and consideration, no matter how loony.

At the Board of Trade, the old boys of the 1950s and '60s remember the Voice of the Tomb. According to Floor legend, there was a millionaire Wheat trader who had made most of his money by placing Wheat trades on the same exact days, year after year. Of course, his strategy was shrouded in secrecy, and he would never announce the precise dates of his fortuitous trades. As it happened, the trader's wife died and he was left to raise their three children. The children had become accustomed to a wealthy lifestyle, and as the years went on, the trader felt that his children were spoiled and wasteful and took everything for granted. As good as any best-selling paperback saga, the story goes that when the trader was on his deathbed, he amended his will so that his vast wealth went to charities, and not to his children. What he did leave them, however, was a cryptic message, along the lines of: Sell March Wheat on January 10, Buy May Wheat on February 22, Sell July Wheat on May 10, Buy December Wheat on July 1, Sell December Wheat on September 10, Buy March Wheat on November 28. The dates were included with a moral for his children: work hard and strictly discipline yourself with these dates, and the fortune that you automatically assumed would be yours will eventually come.

No one knew if his children ever followed these dates, or even placed trades at all, but what did happen was that other traders took his dates and began trading by them—and still do, calling them Voice of the Tomb trades. As the years went on, Voice of the Tomb went the way of most other gossip, and the details grew careless and twisted. Today, traders argue about the exact dates, and the ones listed here may not really be the correct ones—only the Voice knows for sure. But followers swear by them, citing excellent track records for whatever dates they're trading.

John had been having a lousy trading streak, and one day, with nothing I could think of that prompted him, he announced that it was me who was bringing him this bad luck. He claimed that ever since I'd come on the Floor, he'd been losing money on a much more frequent basis. He wasn't kidding around either; he had actually pondered this correlation. He put forth a remedy: I was forbidden from standing on the landing that I'd come to designate as "my spot." Why? Because my spot overlooked his trading booth.

Although that spot provided me with a perfect view of the S&P pit and the agricultural pits, I could somewhat understand John's beef about me standing there—he was having a rough time trading and I'd been watching him throw his cards, punch the air, and occasionally kick a chair. No one wanted to be watched when they were losing. So I agreed I wouldn't stand there. And for the next couple of days, I didn't. But he wasn't appeased for long. Next, he insisted that I couldn't walk up the main staircase near his booth either. In other words, he didn't want to—couldn't!—see me *at all* when he was trading. "You have to take the back stairs," he informed me.

"I don't know of any back staircase," I said, growing perturbed. "So unless you want to personally show me—"

"Oh, I will!" he snapped.

I didn't even try appealing to anyone else to talk some sense into John because chances were that any other trader would side with him. So, in order to avoid John, I walked a roundabout way onto the Floor, past the S&P pit, past the winding staircase that runs alongside John's booth, past the rows of brokers at the phones, past the dozens of clerks at computers, and down a back corridor that was surprisingly quiet and less trafficked. There, a row of clerks sat silently staring at computer screens. They appeared deep in concentration, although as I passed, I noticed a woman clerk sending an e-mail entitled: The Friendship Bracelet. Several other clerks were huddled around a big-screen laptop, their mouths slightly dropped open—only, it wasn't Market commentary or graphs or charts they were watching, but a Jim Carrey movie. Farther on down the aisle, a woman clerk was on the phone. "You said you'd pick me up at seven. Not seven-fifteen, not seven-thirty. I don't go for that. You say seven, I better see your sweet face at seven."

I headed up toward the Russell 2000 pit, where the gridlock began to kick in on a narrow staircase. Two traders and I did a little sidestepping. "Just push the lady out of the way, why don't ya?" one trader said to the other, who had barreled right past me.

I eventually found a new spot, leaning over a railing that overlooked the entire Nasdaq pit. I was directly behind the chair of a short, balding, red-jacketed guy trading on a computer, and I had the feeling my presence—someone lurking behind him—was disconcerting to him, but hey, this was a place with zero respect for personal space, so what was he going to do? Here, I'd learned, you staked your spot, and you didn't budge. Even your Globex booth wasn't solely yours, even though it was clearly labeled with your badge acronym. If John, for example, didn't come in to work for the day, or if he came in late, someone else—a floater—would usually be borrowing his computer. It was common practice, and no one seemed to find it as unnerving as I would to come into work and have to kick someone out of your own space—someone who'd been pounding on your keyboard and spitting into your phone as they screamed orders. In any other business environment you'd likely be appalled if you walked into your office and someone else had his feet propped up on your desk. But you couldn't mind that here.

The trader in front of me kept tossing me looks, trying to gauge what some clerk would be doing hanging around the rails behind him. But I ignored it—I liked this new spot, and most important, John couldn't see me—although I realized that if I stood on tiptoes, I could see him. He said something into his headset, waited for a response, then jammed his Timberland shoe into his chair. *Maybe I shouldn't have looked*, I thought, then rolled my eyes at the notion that I could get caught up in all this. The trader behind John—whom I didn't know—was faring no better and was bouncing in his seat with such nervous energy that it looked as if he were doing an angry kind of rhythmic rain dance. He then made a megaphone with his hands, and screamed toward the pit, "Fuck you, Skippy!"

Not everyone was having a rough time—I watched as one trader at a computer clasped his hands and flipped them over each shoulder like he had just won the championship trophy.

After the closing bell I waited for John to gather his things and leave his booth. When the coast was clear, I milled with the crowd, down the forbidden staircase, around the pit, and off the Floor. I rode up the escalator, checked my jacket, then headed to the bathroom to scrub the grime from my hands. Back down a couple of escalator flights—I felt as if I already needed another disinfecting scrub—and I arrived at the Club.

John was already at the table, and he had the ten-thousand-mile stare. I was afraid to speak at first, but come on, this was stupid. I had traipsed all over the Floor making sure he didn't *see* me, and while I felt bad for him that he'd still lost money, that was the nature of the game. So he'd had another bad day. It happened. "So it's not me," I said, hopefully. John shot me a look from the corner of his eye. "Oh, it's still *you*," he said.

TEN

Head and Shoulders

The head-and-shoulders charting pattern is probably the most well-known and frequently used way of trying to predict the Market's next move. It's called a reversal pattern, and it forms three curves, looking like a shoulder, a head, and another shoulder. Through a bunch of connect-the-dots, this pattern, if it's facing right side up, indicates that you should sell the Market at a certain point. If it's a bottom head-and-shoulders pattern, that is, if it's upside down, it indicates a buy.

In the mid-1980s, an influential Futures analyst named Robert Prechter, who formerly worked for Merrill Lynch, was conducting in-depth analysis using a trading theory called the "Elliott Wave." It was derived from a series of ratios, a recurrent formation of waves that could actually be applied not just to the Market, but throughout nature—to the human face, to the Mona Lisa, or the statue of David, to the ocean, or even to a head of cauliflower. One of the main numbers in the Elliott Wave was .618, and, the theory stated, when something is .618 of the whole, the overall effect was harmony. The number .618, through a bunch of difficult and abstruse computations, was also determined to be a very important and telling figure regarding the Market. As the story goes, Prechter applied these difficult and abstruse computations to the Gold market and discerned that Gold was going to have a good pop. He made an official announcement that he was recommending to buy Gold, and he bought some himself.

A few days after his announcement, a huge robbery in France occurred and the thieves made off with a large amount of gold. On news of this, traders panicked and began buying Gold—the Gold market leaped to Limit Up, the maximum amount the Market is allowed to move in a day before trading is halted.

Back at Prechter's office, his phone was ringing off the hook. In all of his analysis, his poring over graphs and ratios and equations, he had been, eerily, correct. Only, the callers weren't interested in his studious findings—all they wanted to know was "Did you stage the robbery?"

This was the first story Alice told me during my initial lesson on technical trading. We were at Alice's table, and in front of her was a heaping plate from the buffet. For some reason, she was picking the fried breading off the chicken fingers, one by one. She began describing how the founder of the Elliott Wave, Ralph Nelson Elliott, had gotten his start in technical studies. Elliott had been leading an adventuresome life, serving, in the mid-1920s, as the chief accountant of Nicaragua. But while in Central America, he contracted a dangerous parasite. He returned to the United States, where he became bedridden for years. During that time, one of the few ways he found to pass the hours and engage his mind was to study and chart the Market. He sent letters that detailed his findings—such as the use of .618—to several influential people in finance. They were all impressed, but nothing ever hit the mainstream. Elliott never did any trading himself, and he ended up dying in abject poverty. Years later, it was Prechter who, while studying psychology at Yale, happened to hear about Elliott's theories. Prechter buried himself in the study of Elliott's all-but-forgotten writings and now bears the credit for resurrecting the Elliott Wave. Today, many traders swear by it, and most utilize some facet of the Elliott Wave in their trading.

I had long been anticipating delving into concepts of technical trading, but after hearing about the Elliott Wave, I felt disappointed. Sure, I was learning merely a general overview—people spent years and years studying these concepts—but I couldn't help but admit that what I'd heard so far struck me as somewhat far-fetched. I understood about the symmetry of .618—and it was certainly an interesting, perceptive concept—but really, I wondered, how could it consistently have something to do with the Market, which was heavily influenced by random world events? Of course, many technical traders believed there was a pattern to everything, that the world followed cycles—cycles of droughts, floods, coups—and they quoted Market run-ups and run-downs to prove their point. However, I had trouble completely buying into that philosophy, at least enough to wager my money on it. All this time, I had thought charting would help me assign meaning to the chaos of the Market, but what happened when the charting itself seemed contrived and delusive? How could I risk my cash and my time on a technique that applied just as much to the Market as it did to a cauliflower?

Next up was Alice's favorite, a bizarre and abstruse theorist named W. D. Gann. "When I first became interested in trading, I asked Mom what I should study," Alice said. "She thought about it for a bit, then said, 'Gann.' She herself only did one little Gann technique, even though he has a whole basket. I kind of wish she hadn't said that because I spent the next ten years absorbed in Gann. The funny thing is that you can make an awful lot of money analyzing and following Gann, but there are a lot of other ways you can make the same amount of money more easily. However, the thing Gann will give you that many other techniques won't is ego satisfaction."

When Alice spoke of Gann, she talked as if she knew him personally— sort of like a student/teacher, love/hate relationship, where she was at the same time mystified and frustrated, and yet the combination was exhilarating. Gann had been born into poverty in 1878 in Texas. With nothing more than an eighth-grade education, he went on to become a hugely successful Market speculator and the author of numerous books on predicting the markets. "He was an incredibly secretive and idiosyncratic man," Alice said. "Purple is popularly considered to be the color of mysticism, so he drew all his charts in purple ink, and he also drove a purple Lincoln. Gann was a devout Mason and he liked the rituals, where everything was done geometrically; it was like a religion to him, and he believed God was a geometrist. Gann was big on angles and when they would have their Mason meetings everyone would stand at certain points. He literally transferred some of these important angles into trading charts. See, angles are nothing more than fixed moving averages, from lows and highs and midpoints. He found that when bunches of angles would coincide, the Market would hold or resist."

Alice poured us both some more iced tea. "Gann was also interested in financial astrology," she continued. "This is an arcane method that won't make you a dime if you do it by yourself because you don't have enough examples—the stars don't technically come into sync for years at a time, so it's very difficult to say, 'Oh, the last time Venus and Mars were doing this, such-and-such happened in Soybeans.' They now have computer software programs that will go and search that very thing. They combine data from the Market and all the data from the planets, so you can determine, 'The last time Pork Bellies did this, the planets were in this alignment.' It's interesting, but, believe me, there are easier ways to make money. Astrology is its own discipline. It's like adding another study onto everything. And whether you believe in it or not, it's very complicated. It's not just looking up your sun sign and your horoscope every day. Gann worked with an astrologer and it was believed that he received much information from him. The story goes that the astrologer wrote a book and after reading it, Gann said, 'You must burn this for it reveals all your secrets.' The astrologer did not burn it, but hid it. No one has found it since, and it would be very useful because Gann writes so peculiarly and so eccentrically—really, his stuff is weird. I had a Gann club at one point, and this one Gann fanatic and friend of mine, Fred, told me, 'Even though I'm an atheist, if there is an afterlife, I'm going to find that Gann and I'm going to grab him by the collar and say, "Listen you sonovabitch! What did you mean by this, and what did you mean by that, and why did you say this?" ' " Alice chuckled. "Knowing Fred," she said, "he's probably done it. He was the type who could get intellectual satisfaction just from knowing."

In 1927, Gann wrote his first nontrading book—a novel entitled, *Tunnel Thru the Air*. Gann touted the book as a "futuristic romance novel," although he claimed that if you read it three times, you would uncover priceless Market discoveries that he had hidden throughout the story. When I asked Alice if she had read his novel, she answered with an enthusiastic "Of course!"

"Did you read it three times and uncover trading secrets?" I asked.

"I don't know anybody who could get through that horrible novel three times," she said.

Gann traded heavily in Cotton and Wheat and eventually became a member of the Chicago Board of Trade. In 1936, he was the first American to purchase a private, metal airplane. He called it "The Silver Star," and he would fly—with an attractive female copilot, who was not his wife (he had been married three times)—to check out farms and the status of crops.

"In the 1920s, Gann had a phenomenal number of consecutive good trades," Alice told me. "Then he declared: 'Wheat will reach a certain level on this date when the contract expires, or all my work will have been for nothing!' The level was a good deal higher than where Wheat was trading. Then Wheat dropped even more and it looked like all his work was going to be for nothing. But as it neared the date, Wheat started going back up and then went Limit Up, and sure enough, it hit Gann's point.

"There have been times when I've been able to tell the guys, 'The S&P will be trading five points underneath this, so at this level it's a sale.' " Alice went on. "And it won't have been an obvious point on the chart, or a point of support or resistance, but I can tell this from certain Gann harmonics that I do. So the guys think I'm a genius because the Market would hit that point and then go right down. Every once in a while Gann will let you do that, but you have to really work at Gann to get that good. Again, you can do things another way with much less work and make just as much, or more, money. But Gann gives you a certain intellectual satisfaction because you really start to glimpse how the Market works. It's sort of a dance, it's musical. And once you see that harmony and symmetry, it can be very satisfying on an intellectual level. I don't think many of the guys look at it that way, and this is not how anyone in the pit trades. They know how much a tick is worth and they're going after it."

As far as technical skills went, I was learning, a trader could choose from dozens upon dozens of charting patterns and signals: head and shoulders, descending triangles, ascending triangles, symmetrical triangles, retracements, pennants, flags, continuous patterns, reversal patterns, double tops if there's too much supply, double bottoms if there's too much demand, and more. Along with dozens upon dozens of methods by which to read a chart: stochastics, the Elliott Wave, Gann, Fibonacci numbers, Japanese candlesticks, directional move indicators, moving averages, the square of nine, the list went on and on.

Tom utilized technical analysis, and when he showed me his chart of the Market, it looked like an erratic heartbeat—up-down, up-down. His idea of a winning combination was: "You need to combine technical skills with balls the size of grapefruits."

Traders would also go by historical case studies. In the *New York Times*, on November 1, 2000, a blurb stated: "GORE HAS DOW HISTORY ON HIS SIDE: If the Dow Jones Industrial average has anything to say about it, Al Gore is headed for the White House. When the Dow rises from the end of July through the end of October, the incumbent party historically keeps the White House. But when the Dow goes down, the insiders get thrown out. The Dow . . . has correctly forecast 22 of the 25 presidential elections since it made its debut in 1897."

Oops . . . make that 22 of 26. Maybe I was just being skeptical, but a lot

of the technical theories seemed to be a matter of coincidence, or perhaps
nothing more than a "well-chosen example." Couldn't you pretty much
assign a correlation—right or wrong—to just about anything? I'd heard a
story about a well-known trader who one day made a sweeping announcement on the Floor: "Tomorrow," he said, "at 10:54 a.m., the Market will go
up." He had declared it with such staunch vivacity that at 10:54 the next
day, the Floor was watching and waiting. Amazingly, at that precise time,
the Market went up. That was the first time he called the Market like that—
the next time, he generated even more fanfare, and who knows how many
traders jumped on for the ride. Unfortunately, he was wrong. Today, he
earns a living by driving a bus.

Alice spent hours with me, explaining and diagramming. I knew she
studied the Market the way one studied for a Ph.D., and yet I found that
much of it—too much of it—still seemed hokey. Either that, or it seemed
like a bunch of complicated ways to arrive at a rather commonsense pos-
tulate; or, it appeared completely luck-related—after all, you had a 50 percent chance of calling at least the direction of the Market correctly. I
mentioned to Alice how Tom had said that he believed a monkey could
trade for a living.

"A pigeon, Cari," Alice corrected. "A pigeon could trade."

"So you spend the majority of your time investigating all these systems
and plotting them out and putting money on them, even though you
believe a creature with a brain the size of a pea could arrive at the same
outcome?"

"What it essentially boils down to," Alice replied, "is that you need
things like charting to hold on to psychologically when you trade. All I can
say is, I think there is something more to it than just chance. There is
a propensity for the Market to support on these levels. But, it *is* just a
propensity."

"But wouldn't that happen anyway if enough people were following by
these rules?" I asked.

"It is a self-fulfilling prophecy to that extent," Alice agreed. "Just look at
the high, low, and close of the Market every day. This can give you a mental pattern. Most people in the pit can give you the last two days—this was
the low yesterday, and the low the day before was two ticks above that, so
you know that where the level gets thick is where the buying comes in. Are

we trading above the open or below? Above yesterday's close or below? They do these things in their minds—we're strong above this level, we're weak below, so I'll be a seller below. They try to read brokers' faces. There will be a rumor that a broker's going to come in and sell a lot at this level. Some guys will believe it and trade by it. Sometimes it's a false rumor spread by somebody who wants to sell a lot.

"With a little application, you can learn to be a pretty good chartist in one year," she said, then rolled her eyes. "Pit traders think they're real good chartists if they spend ten minutes every night looking at a chart. I find that it settles my mind to look at charts. It's a little addictive, actually. It's like doing chess problems. But then people like me can fall into the trap where you've done so much analysis, that you're too wiped out to trade. It's paralysis from analysis. That's why some traders form partnerships, where one does the analysis and the other executes the trades.

"But you can't be like Tara, who negates all her chart work by being unable to pull the trigger," she warned. "That's a woman's most common failing. If a woman doesn't have a problem pulling the trigger, she will make a significant amount of money because she will study the charts a lot more than a man. To a guy, charts are too much like homework. A woman's not going to make her presence on the Floor by yelling at a man—she's got to outthink him."

I soon realized I was in the minority for considering technical trading systems to be packed with a lot of fluff. Developing systems was big business, and technical traders recruited computer and mathematical geniuses from all over the world to fiddle with theories and programs, to compute masses of numbers, and to seek out the most intricate of patterns, all for the elusive—perhaps impossible—goal of coming up with something that could beat the Market. Because of this, a new breed of trader developed. It used to be that there was no spectrum of trading personalities—the typical trader was the pit trader, the Jock: gruff, callous, intimidating, and impatient, although with the ability to handle numbers quickly and make split decisions. Most of the pit trader's computations involve on-your-feet addition, subtraction, and multiplication—not amazingly complex, but speed is the key.

But now, with the computer it was possible to be quiet and introverted and still be a great trader. Enter the Geeks, who have in recent years been giving the Jocks a run for their money. While the Jocks duked it out in the pits, the Geeks sat in private offices high above the Floor, earning themselves the title of "Upstairs Traders." Ironically, if you introduced a pit trader to an upstairs trader, the pit trader would often feel insecure, wondering, "What does this Geek know about the Market that I don't?" The upstairs trader would likely be intimidated too—"Is this Jock going to beat the crap out of me?"

Somewhere in the middle of the spectrum were traders like John, who withstood the chaos of the Floor while still spending the majority of the trading day in their heads. One evening, at a social gathering at my apartment, a friend introduced John to her date, an upstairs trader named Charles, who fit the mold to a tee—shy, awkward, thick glasses, a mind whirring so fast that he occasionally stumbled over words because he couldn't get them out quickly enough. John boisterously kept calling Charles "Charlie," and Charles kept pointedly, yet quietly, correcting him, only John never seemed to notice. It struck me how both men had spent their entire adult lives immersed in the same field, trading the same markets, and yet you couldn't find two more disparate people. Charles later admitted to me that he felt the Jocks were still the ones who usually won at trading. "They can trade off of something the guys upstairs can't," Charles said. "Gut. The pit has a feel and a motion and a momentum all its own." Even Alice, who was forever charting and would certainly be categorized as "upstairs," agreed. "Although a pit trader will bring in his own foibles," she said, "a trader with touch will outdo any mechanical system."

Alice's latest reading genre was books on gambling. "I just want to call up these professional gamblers and tell them to try trading," she said. "One guy developed this whole complex system of counting cards, and was consequently banned from casinos in Vegas. I want him to come and trade because there is no one who is going to say to you, 'No, you can't derive a system.' So instead, he has to use all this camouflage and tip the dealer, because he is under surveillance at many casinos. He belongs on a trading floor." She sighed. "However, the casino's conditions are nicer, not as smelly."

Not long ago, some Merc traders stumbled across this same idea. They were in Las Vegas and happened to meet a professional poker player who was brilliantly calculating and had a knack for remaining calm under pressure. The traders reasoned that he'd make an exceptional Options trader and offered him a deal in which they'd back him if he came to work at the Merc. The poker player agreed, and ended up making them, and himself, a lot of money.

However, you should never say to a trader that trading is simply a form of legalized gambling. The trader will scoff at you. As one top trader, Victor Sperandeo, who was profiled in the 1992 book *The New Market Wizards*, said, "Gambling involves taking a risk when the odds are against you. I think successful trading . . . implies taking risks when the odds are in your favor." So traders pull out charts and textbooks and theories and computer programs and trading modules, and rattle off historical examples to support their data—and it's all intended to prove that it takes a lot of study and know-how, and a lot of talent, to determine when the odds are in your favor.

And yet, there is no denying that a certain degree of guesswork will always exist. A trader can never place a trade with 100 percent conviction that it will be a winner. Perhaps the gambler is correct; perhaps the trader is. More likely, they both are. And therein lies the rush, the energy, the addictiveness of trading. "Trading's about temptation," one woman trader told me. "People are trying to give you money. It's up to you to know when to take it."

$ $ $

One thing was definite—whether you were in the pit or upstairs—all traders were looking for their own winning system, their own edge, their own secret formula. Trading methods were almost as diverse as traders themselves. There were scalpers, like Tom, who made hundreds of quick trades in a day; then those like John who held larger trades for twenty minutes or so; and then there were position traders who held a trade for days, weeks, even months at a time. Alice's mother was a position trader, and if she had a winning trade, she would keep rolling it over and adding on contracts. When she'd finally liquidate—sometimes more than six months later—she'd have made several hundred thousand dollars.

Of course, each pattern of trading had its downsides. John's style could be categorized as heart-attack trading—he took on huge positions and would add to them along the way, even if the position was going against him. "That much risk kills your body," Tom once said of John. "But he'll be able to buy himself a real pretty box." I wasn't convinced that Tom's style was much better—it was blood-pressure trading, the quick, edge-of-your-seat decisions, the furious surges, the constant reactions. Alice, on the other hand, engaged in ulcer trading, where the slow burn of holding a trade long-term could often keep you up at night, worrying and checking the Market.

It's been said that one's trading style is directly linked to one's personality. Some traders—the pessimists, perhaps?—prefer short positions, perpetually thinking the Market's bound to drop. Other traders maintain a more optimistic view—the Market has to come back up sometime!—so they favor going long. Many traders also believe that all trading problems are personal problems manifested—and that if you haven't mastered your own mind, you'll be lost. A common saying among traders is: "If you don't know who you are, this is an expensive place to find out."

Tara had begun to admit this might be true. "I realize I need to take a big step back," she said to me one day. "I've been trying to trade the way Tom does, but that's a very specific style and not everyone can trade that way. I guess I connect trading with him and that's making me too dependent on him."

To try to remedy this, Tara attended—by herself—a daylong technical-analysis conference at a hotel near O'Hare Airport. Ostensibly, the conference was to sell a trading system, but Tara was also viewing it as a networking possibility. Within the first few minutes, she'd met someone—a husky, garrulous man who settled into the seat next to hers and introduced himself as Ray from Alabama. "Do you invest?" he asked, which struck Tara as an odd question, seeing they were at a conference on technical analysis. "Yes," Tara said. "Do you?"

"I *trade*," he boasted. Tara was one of only a handful of women at the conference, although, when they went around the room for introductions, all the other women begged off as wives or girlfriends of attendees who were essentially dragged along. The lecture was intense, a lot of talk about algorithms and Elliott Waves and algorithms of Elliott Waves. Alabama seemed thoroughly confused and turned to Tara for a little company. "You're not getting any of this either, are you?" he asked.

"Well, I'm actually a little familiar with some of the theories and have been studying them for almost a year," Tara said modestly. Alabama was taken aback. He shifted uncomfortably in his seat, then said, "I think it would be in my best interest to keep in touch with you." So much for trying to build a network of her own so that she could declare independence from Tom—she'd wanted to come away from the conference with contacts who could help *her*, not the other way around.

So she tried another angle: She began consulting with a trading therapist. I had no idea there was such a thing, but she'd found a therapist's name online. The first thing the therapist did was have Tara take a personality test to determine what type of trading style would best fit her. He analyzed her decision-making processes, her coping mechanisms, and her general psychological makeup. From this, he concluded that she often second-guessed her decisions (true) and had difficulty arriving at those decisions in the first place (also true)—both of which were severe impediments for a trader. So what Tara now needed to do was to start over from scratch—the goal was not for her to try to perfect existing skills, but for her to try to gain and develop new, necessary skills.

When she told me this, it further enhanced my growing conviction that trading required innate characteristics—none of which, I was beginning to believe, I seemed to possess either. Math professors have tried trading and fallen flat on their faces. So have Harvard and Wharton MBAs, proving that trading is far more about instinct than intellect. One woman pit trader, Denise Hubbard, HUB, had been successful in the Currencies before becoming the head of hiring and training of new recruits for an Options trading firm. "We don't really want people with Options experience because we want to build them from the ground up," she said. "We want people with no bad habits to break. We also use the athlete profile. We figure that if you were an athlete, you're going to be aggressive and competitive, you're going to want to trade more than the guy next to you, plus, physically, if you're fit or bigger it tends to give you an advantage. While some of these big guys are not the most agile, you can certainly see them from across the pit."

Possibly the best-known experiment concerning this kind of nature-versus-nurture was instigated in the mid-1980s by two former high-school buddies who both became traders, Richard Dennis and William Eckhardt. They had a long-standing debate: Eckhardt believed that successful traders were born, that there were intrinsic personality traits and a certain intuition that good traders naturally possessed and bad traders didn't. Dennis, on the other hand, believed good traders could be made, conditioned, nurtured like the fighting turtles he had seen while vacationing in the Far East. Thus, the Turtles experiment was born. Dennis—described by the *Wall Street Journal* as "the legendary Chicago commodity trader, who turned a grubstake of $400 into $200 million in 18 years"—ran classified ads in the *New York Times*, the *Wall Street Journal*, and *Barron's*, searching for people with no real trading background to participate in the study. Each person would be required to move to Chicago and would be given a small salary, along with a $100,000 trading account, out of which they would receive a percentage of any trading profits—so long as they adhered to a set of trading rules, or systems, that Dennis and Eckhardt had devised. The responses were overwhelming, thousands of applications were received, and out of those, Dennis and Eckhardt chose forty people to undergo an elaborate interviewing process. The final ten chosen ones were dubbed "The Turtles."

An air of mystique and secrecy surrounded the experiment. What was leaked, however, was that the resulting Turtles were a diverse bunch: two professional gamblers, a Dungeons and Dragons designer, an actor, a security guard, a bookkeeper, an accountant, and, out of the whole group, only one woman, who had been a trading clerk. And yet, there was one characteristic the Turtles all had in common: they all played chess.

The initial training process, steeped in confidentiality, took two weeks. The trainees learned the rules and discipline for the trend-style trading that Dennis followed. They were taught that they couldn't feed into their emotional satisfaction because, in trading, what felt good was usually not the right thing to do. After training, the Turtles were on their own, each with $100,000 of Dennis's money.

Dennis and Eckhardt then conducted the identical experiment the following year—ads were run, people were interviewed, and ten were chosen and trained.

In the end, Dennis won the debate—and it was even surprising to him how overwhelmingly he'd been proven correct. Over the two-year run, there were twenty-three trainees altogether (three people were dropped early on because, Dennis said, they "didn't do well"). However, he reported, the remaining twenty averaged about a 100 percent profit per year.

John had been one of the thousands who had tried out for the second round of Turtles. He had filled out the application, which asked detailed questions regarding your hobbies and if you played any board games. John noted that he was an avid chess player and had been champion of his high-school chess team. He received a callback and proceeded to the next step, an in-person interview. There, they asked him what seemed like bad first-date questions that he was required to answer with one sentence only: name a book or movie you like and why. Name a historical figure you like and why. Name a risky thing you have done and why. Explain a decision you have made under pressure and why that was your decision.

Next up was a series of reasoning and logic questions, one of which he tested out on me: "If you are on a boat in the middle of the ocean and you drop a cannonball in the water, how long will it take until it hits the bottom?"

I thought for a few seconds, then shook my head. "There's not enough information," I said. "How'd you answer it?"

John's answer: "Imagine you're not on a boat, but you're at the edge of a swimming pool, and you drop a bowling ball into the water. How long will it take until it hits the bottom? Picture the bowling ball falling, and count, 1-1000, 2-1000. I imagine it would be around two seconds until it hits. So that means it traveled, what, ten, twelve feet in two seconds. So let's say the ocean is a mile deep, that's around five thousand feet. So if it took two seconds for ten feet, then it's one thousand seconds for five thousand feet, which is around twenty minutes."

"So that's the answer?" I asked.

"Well, I studied engineering in college," John said, "so I know that to really figure it out, you'd use some equation for travel, and some equation for surface area, but I've forgotten all those formulas, and besides, that wasn't what they're looking for. I'm sure my answer of twenty minutes is not correct. The ocean may be five miles deep, I have no idea. But they wanted to see how I reasoned the problem, because that's how trading is— you are never given all the information. You've got to take the limited information you do have and apply logic to it. It's up to you to figure out how to approach the problem."

"So the fact that I answered, 'There's not enough info,' proves that I am not cut out to be a trader?" I asked. John avoided a direct response. "Go ask

Tom, and then ask Tara this question," he said, "and I'll bet you they go about answering it in completely different ways."

I did. Tom pondered it, then declared, "Ten minutes."

"How'd you get that?" I asked. "Is it right?" he asked eagerly.

"I don't know."

"Then why'd you ask me?"

"Tom, tell me how you came up with ten minutes?" He shrugged, then took me through his reasoning process, which was similar to John's—he had estimated the measurements and made his calculation.

Tara, like me, didn't know.

"I told ya!" John said triumphantly when I reported back.

"What's that supposed to mean, that women aren't going to get this?" I said. "Maybe we should ask Bev."

John, who'd known the legendary Eurodollar trader for over a decade and a half, laughed at my suggestion. "Now Bev," he said, "would answer like this: 'What in the hell would I be doing in a boat in the middle of the ocean with a cannonball?' "

For reasons unknown, John didn't make the final cut of the Turtles. Alice's mom had also brought home the Turtles application for Alice, although she never filled it out.

"I remember the question 'Do you have any hobbies?' " Alice said. "And I knew what they were looking for. Chess players make good Options traders, but I think they are the last person you'd want in a Futures pit. They'd be working out this abstruse strategy for a trade that lasts thirty seconds. In chess, one move leads to another, whereas one trade does not lead to another. I think blackjack is probably the best determinant because you are forced to go with the flow."

So had Dennis and the Turtles experiment proven my inkling wrong? Had they proved that traders could be *made* after all? Well, five years after the first round of the experiment, many of the Turtles had gone on to be fund managers and traders on their own. According to Dennis, they each traded, on average, with around $2 million. The lone woman Turtle, Liz Cheval, was just one of the group who went on to start her own money-management firm. She called herself "a high-volatility trader," and by that she meant that she would watch her fund dart and dip—down 42 percent for several months, then up 300 percent, then down, then up. And yet, she stated in a trading journal: "A theoretical investment of $1,000 made in January 1985 was worth more than $61,000 at the end of 1990. Maybe not such a bad ride after all." She was also very careful to mention that her "approach is not for the weak of heart." Anyone who invested with her had to be able to withstand the pressure, she said, and could not bail out early. "If investors come to me with $1 million and say they understand that all of their money is at risk, that they could withstand a drawdown of fifty percent or more and that they can comfortably sit through a drawdown of thirty percent, then I would welcome their account," she stated. In her bio on the Turtles website, she wrote: "I think the key to becoming successful is to love the game more than the result."

Liz Cheval's firm was one of the handful that had remained alive and well. As the years went on, the crash-and-burn rate of the Turtles on a whole seemed to increase, and the figures given were no longer based on the initial group of twenty Turtles, but rather on a dwindling set. One well-regarded independent trader and lecturer devised a trading technique she called the "Anti-Turtle Strategy," which worked on an opposite premise of the theories Dennis preached. Even Dennis himself retired—after reportedly running his fund into the ground. As Tom eloquently summed up, "The Turtles were taken out back and shot."

Dennis's demise was the topic of discussion at Alice's table one day. "The Turtles are overrated," Alice said.

"Their technicals stink," Ben added.

"Dennis's trading career was based on luck," Alice said. "It's luck for a lot of people. They just have good timing—they hit a bubble or a drought and they ride it, and then they think they're a good trader." She shook her head. "The gist of Dennis's trading philosophy is waiting for the Market to make a large move in one direction, and then hopping on it full force. They set their stops so far out there that their only hope is catching a mammoth trend. This happens about 5 percent of the time, so 95 percent of the time they're wrong. But when it's their 5 percent, the payout will be so great, it will make up for their losses. Dennis believed that if you had discipline, you could be taught to trade. However, with a 5 percent accuracy rate, it almost makes you think you could blindly guess and do better." Alice rolled her eyes.

$ $ $

So, is trading well based on intellect, gut, or discipline? Does it take a certain talent, an artistry, to grasp the feel for the Market, to ride its ebb and flow? A common Floor saying is: "I was like a surgeon today," which means a trader had swiftly and precisely extracted a chunk of money from the Market, and then left. And yet, there are days when a trader can do everything right and still end up losing. "Although the beauty of trading," a veteran trader friend of Tom's described to me, "is that you can be wrong the majority of the time and still make a ton of money."

And so, traders like Alice pored over their charts and tested new systems and prophesied about ways to assign meaning to what others believed may not be much more than a random walk. Alice noted offhandedly that her analytical apostle, Gann, left around $550,000 when he died in 1955—a somewhat moderate sum for such a revered trader whose protégés went on to earn millions upon millions. "My mother used Gann's technique of swing charting," Alice told me. "She found it was the one thing that worked for her. A lot of traders do that, they find their one thing. I'm not like that. When I find something that works for me, I'm still looking for something else, for the next thing that works. It's really a quest more than anything else. Deep down I have this sort of belief that one day I'll find something that works every time. Now that's totally ridiculous, you're not going to find the holy grail that way. Intellectually, I don't believe that. But emotionally, on some level, I must, because I'm always searching for something just a little bit better."

To a trader the Market becomes something almost human—a breathing, feeling, moody being who can be lazy and slow, choppy and skittish; it can swoon and gyrate, can grow vicious, and can become vengeful. The Market is also a psychological mess: schizophrenic and paranoid, manic and depressive. In the later 1960s, a breakthrough book called *The Money Game*, by the pseudonymous economist Adam Smith, attempted to explain the Market to the mass population. "The market," Smith wrote, "is like a beautiful woman—endlessly fascinating, endlessly complex, always changing, always mystifying." In the book, Smith lunches with an attorney and high-ranking official at Fidelity, who summed it up like this: "The market is a crowd, and if you've read Gustave Le Bon's *The Crowd* you know a crowd is a composite personality. In fact, a crowd of men acts like a single woman. The mind of a crowd is like a woman's mind. Then if you have observed her a long time, you begin to see little tricks, little nervous movements of the hands when she is being false."

This feminine personification of the Market seemed a backhanded compliment. I far preferred John's androgynous philosophy, gleaned from his years on the trading floor: "The Market," he said, "goes where it can fuck the most people."

As for me, what I had suspected might happen, did—and I couldn't ignore it. The truth was: I couldn't buy into technical analysis. It wasn't definitive enough for me. Much of it seemed evasive and concocted, or just a fancy way of plotting out what should be common sense, and how could I sit there and make a decision about risking my money based on a chart I didn't believe in? That was the thing—you had to plan your strategy and stick with it. If you doubted your conclusions, or reneged on your system, you were setting yourself up for confusion, stress, and, most likely, loss. Your system was your grounding, your foothold, and I couldn't try to trade unless I had a foothold about which I was confident.

For some reason, all this made me start thinking about Anne McKenzie. The desire, the *need* to be successful at trading had cost her her life. Maybe she should serve as an example of how the Floor was a fundamental, yet dangerous, science experiment—a test of wills, perseverance, and human character. How would *you* react in the face of temptation? What about in the face of fear? Would you act quickly? Or would you freeze? How would a windfall affect you? Would money change you? Drive you? Make you? Break you? And what if you lost it all? What would you do after walking off the Floor knowing you had nothing left? Did you know yourself well enough even to be able to predict your reaction?

After six months of being in the trading world, I was finally starting to come to a conclusion about what I had set out to uncover: I was doubting that I'd make a good trader. As much as I wanted to make $1,000 in a few hours, I didn't want to have to shut off feelings and reactions that came naturally. Trading was visceral—you had to jump right in and know how to be aggressive. You had to look, act, do. Too much thought could be detrimental, and trading as a form of study could quickly become trading as a form of shock therapy. Being on the Floor gave me a reference point by which I could solidify many of my views, such as: I naturally leaned toward a conservative stance on money; I was more risk-averse when it came to money than I was with other aspects of life that involved risk; I was sensitive about monetary losses to the point that it would likely hinder my judgment; I was very conscious about the amount of stress I allowed into my life, and this affected my decisions; and, on a daily basis, I liked to feel a sense of calm and control more than I liked the feeling of an adrenaline rush. These weren't bad characteristics for other careers, but for one in trading, they could be deadly.

I had learned that possessing knowledge and command of yourself was one of the most important and difficult aspects of trading. Included in this was knowing when to walk away—that, I'd determined, was probably the most vital quality. So I decided I was going to take a step back, that instead of focusing on whether I could trade and when I was going to start trading, I'd concentrate more on the Floor in general, on learning important lessons by observing and talking to traders, and by continuing to work for Tom and soak up the atmosphere. I was not disappointed by my revelation that I wasn't going to be a trader any time soon. Rather, I felt energized by it. My decision to let go set off a spark—because I knew *I* couldn't play the game, I became even more fascinated by the people, especially the women, who could. It didn't matter that I was unsure about wanting this strange and wild career for myself; in fact, that made me all the more interested in trying to figure out why others wanted it—and how they could excel at it. I certainly had no desire to leave the Floor, quite the contrary—I wanted to learn more.

ELEVEN

Cover Your Shorts

If you've got a short position on and you fear the Market is going to reverse and go up—or if the Market seems headed toward a stop point that you've instituted—you're going to want to get out and liquidate your position. This is called "covering your shorts," and it's all about playing it safe, making sure that you don't get yourself caught in a compromising position.

One day, a twenty-three-year-old clerk named Natalie became the second woman trader in one of the financial pits. She proudly displayed her badge, NAT, on her crisp, new trading jacket, which she'd decorated with silver, glittery fringe along the pockets and cuffs. The sparkly jacket added a girlish touch to her sultry, skintight pants and skimpy top. Her shoes, however, were a complete contrast: thick, chunky black boots with rubber platforms substantial enough to crush small animals. Certainly, NAT was making a fashion statement, and it didn't hurt that her footwear had the added benefit of giving her an extra six inches in the pit. While significant lifts on men's shoes were prohibited (although many men wore them anyway), women's fashion had provided a handy loophole.

I watched as NAT stood outside the pit, flipping through her trading cards, which she held between inch-long, manicured nails. She tabulated numbers, circling them with a pen decorated with a pom-pom of pink feathers. It was a busy day and she was shaking with adrenaline, running on fast-forward, flipping her cards, the feathers wildly swaying as she circled the total here, circled the total there. She raced back toward the pit, but her shoes were so thick that she tripped on the stairs. As she helped herself up, she shot evil *watch it!* glances to the clerks around who tried to conceal their snickers. Yeah, that's right, watch it, she was a *trader* now!

Toward the end of the day, after the Floor had calmed down, I overheard another trader making small talk with her. "You didn't trade this busy market today, did you?" he asked.

She nodded, an exaggerated full-head bob. "And I'm *up*, too," she bragged. "Made back what I fucking lost this morning."

"Wow," the trader said, not so much impressed as surprised. "I just blew my day on a four-lot." He handed her a trading card and walked away. She totaled it up, pronouncing the numbers out loud, then said to no one: "Three grand on a four-lot. *Jeee*sus." As she formed the word "Jesus," I could see her tongue ring.

The rumor mill had it that Natalie had received NAT by virtue of a well-concocted bribe. The story went that she'd been having an affair with a top trader in the firm for which she clerked. One day, she said to him: "Give me a badge, put me in the pit, I want to trade." He said, "No."

So she tried it again: "Give me a badge, put me in the pit, I want to trade—and if you don't, I'll call your wife."

A pack of Marlboro Lights peeked from the pocket of NAT's trading jacket as she whispered in the ear of a frosted-blond clerk who—yellow jacket aside—could have passed perfectly for Britney Spears. Her eyes widened with Natalie's top-secret information. When Natalie finished delivering the goods, she leaned back, hands on her hips, and gave the clerk a "How 'bout *that*?" look, then she pivoted on her chunky heels and traipsed into the pit. She hoisted herself up onto a little wedge near the price reporter and maintained her balance by hanging off the rail. It was not a place I'd ever seen anyone attempt to stand, or rather, hang. A trader reached across and squeezed her waist.

"Hey, you trying to make me fall?" Natalie said, tossing him a playful dirty look.

"Be careful," he said. "Or you will."

The traders I knew had no shortage of comments regarding Natalie becoming a trader. "I give her six weeks, if that," John said.

"Oh, I don't know," his friend Kenny countered. "She's a bright one. You know she speaks several foreign languages, one of which is Vulgar."

Natalie was also notorious for an incident that had occurred last year. The events leading up to the incident were not entirely agreed upon, but the incident itself was indisputable and caught on videotape. Apparently, a male clerk walked past Natalie and muttered something to her. She turned around and decked him full-out in the face. Not a slap, a punch. He reeled back, and, of course, the reverberations of the punch rippled throughout the entire Floor—*some guy got punched out by a girl!*

As part of surveillance measures, hundreds of cameras tape every angle of the Floor. Most often the videotape is viewed by traders in cases of dispute (*trading* disputes, that is) where arbitrators need to zero in to see if so-and-so did indeed make the hand sign for fifty, even though he only intended to trade five contracts. But in this particular instance, a group of nosy traders, one of whom was John, figured out which camera covered the spot on the Floor where the punching occurred. After the Close, they raced to the Arbitration department and played the video. They zoomed in: there was Natalie, yellow jacket over skintight outfit. They ran it in slow motion: the clerk passes by her . . . she flips around . . . and—BAM! Right in the nose. They ran it again. BAM! They were howling as if it was a pay-per-view boxing match. Again . . . BAM! Again!

While Natalie's outfits and antics were diligently noted, it was agreed upon by John and his friends that one trader in particular, I'll call her Peggy, was the best-looking woman at the Merc. However, they also agreed that, as one trader put it, "she's not the brightest crayon in the box, that's for sure."

"Do you know what she also is?" Kenny asked me, his eyes wide. "She's a booger eater!" I gave him a funny look, for that was an odd, first-grade way to describe someone. "No, I'm serious," he said, and the others began choking with laughter. "It's true," John affirmed. Kenny launched into the story: "This guy on the Floor who sometimes stands next to her claimed that he'd seen her pick her nose and eat it. We're all like, Nah! So we told him, the next time you see her do it, come tell us. So last week he comes to us and says, 'She just did it!' So we figured out which surveillance camera was monitoring where she was standing and then we all go up to Arbitration. We rewind the tape, and we find it! She really did it!"

I pictured them all huddled over the monitor, much like they were with Natalie's right-hook video. They zoomed in. There was Peggy, poised, perfect makeup, trader jacket. They ran it in slow motion, her finger reaches to her nose . . . and—BAM! They ran it again . . . finger, nose . . . BAM! They cringed with disgust, all the while howling with laughter. Again, there she goes . . . BAM! Again . . .

This was not the first time I'd heard about a woman's reputation being flattened in a matter of minutes. One woman trader had started a new job at the neighboring Board of Options Exchange. Apparently, a few years prior, she'd had nude pictures taken for a bodybuilding website. It didn't take long before someone on the Floor found her pictures on the Internet and passed along the website address; and it didn't take long before she walked into work one day to find that almost every trader on the Floor who had access to a computer was ogling her naked body. She was mortified. She fled from the Floor and, despite the fact that she'd been serious about trading, never came back.

The truth is, no one was exempt from the rumor mill of the Floor—no matter how true your intentions, how much you minded your own business, or how low-profile you were. Including, I soon learned, myself. Alice informed me that after I had left her table one day a trader came up to her and warned her about me.

"Warned you about *what*?" I asked.

"Oh," Alice said in her nonchalant way, which implied that she thought it hardly worth mentioning, but that she was going to tell me anyway. "He said that you were only on the Floor to snag a rich trader and that he couldn't believe I was friends with you and let you sit at my table."

"Who would say that?" I asked. But Alice wouldn't reveal his name.

"Is it someone I know?"

Alice shrugged. "I'm not sure who you know and who you don't know," she said. "But I don't think he knew your name."

I shook my head. "It's strange that someone who doesn't even know my name could have such deep insight into my intentions."

Alice rolled her eyes. Apparently, my lack of a trader's emotional armor was evident once again. "Jeez," she said, "I wouldn't have told you if I knew you'd get so bothered by it."

To me, however, the women on the Floor who perfectly fit the stereotype of being after the men, the money, or both, were not difficult to spot—and it seemed odd that someone would mistake me for being one of "them." They typically ran in packs, and I had the tendency to bump into them on a regular basis in the women's bathroom at the Merc Club. It was fair to say that the majority of these women were clerks, and after the Close they would crowd into the small bathroom to change their clothes, slinking into spandex outfits and high heels. Then they'd reapply their makeup, glopping on layers of mascara and coating themselves in perfume. I would be at the sink, keeping to myself as I did my habitual scrubdown of Floor grime before heading to Alice's table. One afternoon, I noticed a woman fastening up a bubble-gum-pink bustier-like top. In a thick Chicago accent, she complained to another clerk how she had drunk too much. "But you only had a couple of beers," the other said.

"Yeah," she replied, holding her stomach, "but I had two White Russians at lunch."

When they were finished primping, the women would emerge from the bathroom, all done up, and head around the corner to the Club bar, where the traders were waiting, and buying. It was probably no coincidence that many of these clerks were attractive, especially when you considered that it was the traders and brokers themselves who did the hiring.

"There was this one clerk who was a model," a trader told me, "and every time she'd walk across the Floor to collect a trade, she would distract everyone."

"Why?" I asked.

He gave me a wide grin. "Because she never wore underwear."

I was a little confused. If she was clad in a bulky clerk's jacket and was merely walking across the Floor, how could anyone determine this? The trader shook his head as if there was no question about it. "Oh, she walked by and you just knew," he said, his fantasy clearly incorporated into reality. But I suppose living the fantasy was often the goal—and I was sure that many women clerks would be thrilled to know how much of the spotlight they were commanding. Moreover, for a clerk's boss, this was likely all a part of a master business plan: hire an attractive clerk and you will reap the kind of attention that every trader on the Floor craves. She was the live, pretty-smelling version of a loud trader's jacket—everyone knew the trader with the best-looking clerk.

In fact, it was amazing to me just how much the men actually paid attention. They could rattle off the outfits certain women wore, especially Natalie. I discovered this fact when I was at dinner one night with John and several of his trading buddies.

"Today, Natalie was decked out to go dancing," said Kenny, a trader who, like most on the Floor, knew Natalie, although she didn't know him.

"Did you see that one-piece zebra outfit she was wearing the other day?" another asked. They all nodded with exaggerated mmmm-hmmms and oh yeahs, as if she'd been sent there solely for their entertainment. "She was the painted lady yesterday," Kenny added, while pretending that he was applying gobs of makeup. I shook my head, for none of these traders even worked in the same pit as Natalie. But it appeared that their daily routine upon entering the Floor was to check their trading positions, check the various price-reporting boards, check their supply of trading cards, and check out Natalie.

Several years ago, John had employed a clerk whom he described as: "The hottest thing the Floor had ever seen—she was an 'eleven.' " She was a twenty-two-year-old with long, blond hair, who always wore skimpy clothes. John would get hit with $500 fines on a regular basis because she'd wear skirts that were too short, but he didn't mind—the fines paid for themselves, since everyone was so eager to check trades with her that John rarely had any errors or out-trades. John was even able to earn some spare change—other traders would pay him $100 to give her a lollipop so that they could watch her leisurely lick it. When it came time for her year-end bonus, John, initially as a joke, told her he could either give her money or take her to Hawaii. She said she needed to think about it. The next day, to John's surprise, she announced she'd take the trip to Hawaii. In the end, John decided just to give her cash, but several other men in the pit seized upon another opportunity—they offered her $10,000 if she'd go to an upstairs office and strip. She said she needed to think about it. The next day, she informed John that she would have to quit—she was going to do it and take the money, but after that she'd be too embarrassed to show her face on the Floor ever again.

Increasingly, to the horror of my inner feminist, I'd come to see all this as fair game on the Floor—traders exploited women, but women exploited traders, too. I knew several male traders who often didn't tell women they met that they traded for a living. Instead, they referred to themselves as bankers, or as being in investments, or—at worst—as brokers. The reasons were twofold: either women were turned off because they automatically thought all traders were jerks; or they were instantly turned on because they thought all traders were rolling in money.

Early on, I'd met a retired trader named Darcy Cook, who'd started as a clerk in the mid-1980s. She described to me how she'd noticed a distinct change over the years in the women who were drawn to the Floor. She said when she first began, the majority of women were down there to work, to break into the business, and maybe even to get a seat. But then, a new type of girl appeared on the scene, and Darcy did an imitation, bobbing her head side to side and faking a ditzy voice: "Oh, there's *men!* There's *money!*" She rolled her eyes in disgust and dropped back to her own voice. "These girls' whole purpose was to have a sugar daddy," she said. "These rich brokers and traders would get apartments for them, keep them happy with clothes and spending money, whatever else they wanted, furs, jewelry, just so that the men—and unfortunately, a lot of them were married—could have them at their beck and call. On the Floor, these girls hardly did any work. I would always be like, 'Are you gonna answer that phone?' and you know what they'd say?" Darcy lapsed into the ditzy voice again: " 'Oh no, that would ruin my hair!' "

But then, Darcy started noticing a little shift. The new wave of women who came to the Floor were college-educated and weren't interested in being a "kept woman"; rather, they were hunting for a rich husband, or, as Darcy called it, their M.R.S. degree. "Most of these girls were trade checkers," Darcy said, "and I'd ask them, 'Don't you want to do something else with your life? Don't you want to trade? Don't you want to even get on the phones?' And they'd say, 'No, I'm happy doing this, and I'm going to find someone who'll take care of me.' It really aggravated me because I had busted my butt for so long, and then I'd see girls sleeping with guys who'd just give them memberships."

Darcy was a tall, pretty, all-American–looking, blue-eyed blonde, and she could have easily found a swift route to a membership and a badge, but as it was, she worked her way up over many years. She'd known as early as junior high school that she wanted to be a trader. It all came about when she'd snuck into her older sister's bedroom to read an off-limits *Cosmopolitan* magazine. She doesn't remember any of the lurid Q&As, and the salacious articles went right over her head—but what caught her eye was a short piece about the first female trader on the New York Stock Exchange. It was the late 1970s, and Darcy, growing up in a western suburb of Chicago, thought, "I want to do that."

When, years later, she finally got her membership, she ran home to her mom and they hugged and cried.

Darcy knew that she was viewed with more respect than many of the other women on the Floor; however, she still experienced her own share of inappropriateness. She recalled a particular event where she had to stand on a tower of nine footstools in order to see into the pit. "So here I am on this stack," she described, "not even thinking about the fact that I'm wearing a skirt. What's behind me is the men's bathroom, and they have to walk down several steps. How stupid of me! But I always abided by the rules, so my skirt was no shorter than a trading card above my knee. So I was standing on the footstools, deep in concentration, arbing away, and this broker came out from the bathroom, came up behind me, and ran a trading card up the back of my leg and up my skirt. I knew who it was and I kicked backwards. I nailed him in the balls. He doubled over. I turned around and I said, 'You're my friend, but you crossed the line. Don't ever fucking do that again.' All the guys around were bursting with laughter. Now this broker is a guy who later came under investigation for something which I suspect was sexual harassment. I sat down with him and his lawyer, and they asked if I would be a character witness. I looked at the lawyer and I said, 'You are asking the wrong person. What do you want me to tell? The time when he did this? The time I saw him do this, this, this, and this?' And the lawyer turns to the broker and says offhand-edly, 'We can't use her.' I think they ended up settling out of court. But after that he wasn't as crude. He definitely became a bit more refined."

Darcy also witnessed a similar incident in which a trader made a com-ment to a female clerk along the lines of "Are you just showing your tits to get new clients?" and the clerk marched right up to the security guard and filed sexual harassment charges. "The guy ended up getting like a $15,000 fine," Darcy recalled. "But he just sat there and laughed about it. Of course, the clerk didn't show her face in the pit again. I hate to say it, but a lot of clerks ask for it. She was attractive, but she wore, well, she didn't need to wear such tight-fitting clothes, and she'd flirt with the guys. She'd be sitting there and the guys would be giving her massages and she'd be making faces. In my eyes, she was asking for it."

$ $ $

The exact opposite of the dolled-up clerks were the women who had accli-mated so well to this man's world that they'd lost all femininity. These women—most often traders—had strayed so far from the mean that they'd created a stereotype of their own: they were coarse, hard, and brash, and they could give back anything a man had to dish out, and then some. If a man was loud, they'd be louder; if a man was crude, they'd prove that they could be even more crude.

"Everyone can remember that type woman," a retired male trader told me. "There was one woman Local, she must have been two hundred pounds at five feet three. She was pretty bad mouthwise, lookswise, every-thingwise. She would stand on the top step, and I remember she always used to say, 'Bear grease is the best to waterproof your boots, once you get by the smell.'" He didn't remember other facts about her, such as her degree of expertise as a trader. I assumed she must have been successful, for she had a spot on the coveted top step—or perhaps she'd been relegated up there because she reeked of bear grease.

"There's no mistaking these women," Darcy agreed. "They look like they are out climbing rocks every weekend. They will make their presence known the minute they walk in the room, and they're always one-upping everybody."

Even Alice, who certainly would not describe herself as feminine, was taken aback by one such woman trader in the Club. The woman, whom I'll call J., was the guest of honor one afternoon at the table next to Alice's. The reason for the gathering: a celebration of the woman's divorce, which had been officially declared that day. Alice was not only astounded by the amount of Martinis this woman put back—around twelve by Alice's count—but more so by the words that spewed from her mouth. "It was horrendous," Alice described to me. "The level of vulgarities that came from her! She was the only woman at the table, but she had a worse mouth than all of the men combined. She wasn't a bimbo, I'll give her that, because her put-downs, especially about her ex-husband, were often rather witty. But the degree of raunchiness!" Like what? I asked, but Alice couldn't even bear to give me an example.

$ $ $

The rarest type of woman on the Floor is one who has managed to gain respect without compromising her sense of self. These women are typically the most successful traders. While other types of women try to stand out in various ways, these women didn't necessarily want to. "Never wear a skirt here," a female S&P trader advised me. "The men act like they've never seen legs before. I'm not here to be Miss Popular or Miss America, and it's very hard to erase a bad reputation down here. People don't forget."

Even though another trader, Denise Hubbard, was constantly taunted with "Hubba, Hubba!" she told me that she made it a habit to wear old, nondescript clothes and shoes. "I never wore anything nice to the Floor," she said. "Besides, all your shirts get yellow pit stains because you sweat so badly. I would intentionally wear old clothes because I always wanted to feel like I was walking in there hungry. No matter how well I was doing, I never wanted to get complacent, I always wanted to be sharp." Denise was the kind of woman other women loved to hate. She was smart, outgoing, athletic, attractive, thin—a dangerous combination. Before she'd started a trading career, she'd modeled throughout Europe. She found that her modeling experience actually helped her adjust to the Floor because she was undazzled by certain trappings. "Some of these guys on the Floor think they're going to impress you because they've got a Gold Card and drive a Mercedes. Big deal! The life I led before, with private jets and foreign royalty, put the whole money thing in perspective. It made it so that I could appreciate all that, but it didn't *impress* me."

However, getting the men to take her seriously was a struggle at first. "If you're too masculine, they don't like you, they think you're too much like a dyke," she said. "If you're too feminine, they treat you like a powder puff. It's a feeding frenzy down there, and if they find a weakness, they'll hammer on it. When I first got in the pit I had to fight to let them know that they were going to deal with me the same way they dealt with everyone else. You have to knock a few people over and stand up for yourself; I've grabbed men by the throat before. But once you do that they start realizing, well, we can't fuck with her."

Denise loved trading so much that she'd be disappointed when it was Friday. She was gutsy and often traded large size. She did well for the company she worked for and looked forward to bonus time. Only, when that time came, she stared at her check with disbelief. Her salary plus her bonus only totaled around 15 percent of the money she had made trading. The other traders—all of whom were men—had double the amount, around 30 percent of what they had brought in. "I knew I was one of their top performers,"

Denise recalled. "So I had a meeting with them. They told me to my face that I didn't have a wife and children to support so they didn't feel the need to give me a bigger bonus. Of course that's wildly illegal, but it was said in a closed-door meeting, how could I ever prove anything? And if I tried to, I would never get hired on the Floor again. I would never have another job in trading. And so I sucked it up and kept going." She shrugged. "You know how it is down there—I remember once it was ten in the morning and a trader next to me in the pit grabbed my boob. At ten a.m.! Someone wouldn't even do that in a bar! These were the days before they had video cameras everywhere on the Floor. Back then, if we had the type of sexual harassment lawsuits that we have now, I'd be living in the French Riviera."

$ $ $

It was surprisingly rare to hear a male trader speak respectfully of a woman trader. Most of the time the men griped, and one woman S&P trader in particular was a constant source of annoyance to them. Her name was Alexis—badge LEX—and she was a thirty-one-year-old, fast-talking, ex-tremely self-assured brunette who could be just as pushy and snippy as anyone, but who somehow always managed to keep her hair perfectly straight, her nails perfectly manicured, and her lip liner perfectly in place. "The Big Boys will toss her trades here and there," one of the men described to me. "Usually they're just testing the Market and are using her to pick up their small stuff." He half laughed. "But she thinks she's really trading."

"She's a vulture, a scavenger," another trader added. "She makes half a million a year begging for trades."

Of course, a third trader chimed in to dispute the half a million. "She doesn't make that much," he said, setting the record straight, as if he was somehow privy to her bank account. "But she does beg for trades. In fact, that's all she does."

I supposed I still didn't fully understand pit dynamics, for I was unclear as to why Alexis's tactics would be so bothersome. If she was able to make a good living by bottom-feeding, what was wrong with that? Many of the men were bottom-feeders. When I posed this to the men, they all dodged the question by giving the generic response they used whenever they were trying to discredit a woman: "You've heard how she got into the pit in the first place, right?"

In this case, I had heard—just as everyone on the Floor had—for rumors trailed Alexis like toilet paper stuck to her shoe. Tom gave me his concocted version of Alexis's ascension into the pit: "She slept her way right to that spot," he said. "Half the pit knows her—intimately."

By this point, I'd heard this line said about mostly every woman trader, so I wasn't buying it. "Half the pit?" I asked sarcastically.

"Okay, maybe it isn't half the pit," Tom conceded, "but it's definitely this one guy, Jimmy, who's one of the top traders down there. He took her to Vegas and then put up at least $50,000 in a T-bill for her." I rolled my eyes—his story had gone from half the pit to one guy. Baseless accusations. Besides, I'd seen Alexis in the pit day after day, screaming trades, getting in the action, sticking it out as much as anybody else. Surely Tom didn't actually believe that ulterior motives were her sole source of survival and the only thing keeping her alive on the Floor all this time? I figured this was just another example of the pit as locker room, where stories were greatly exaggerated, made up even, and where the man always emerged as the stud, the woman a slut. This time, though, I didn't want to let it go as just another unfounded insinuation—I wanted to hear the woman's side of it. I wanted to hear what Alexis had to say to all the salacious rumors. I wanted to prove the men wrong.

Since John was acquainted with nearly everyone on the lower trading floor, it took a mere mention about my desire to meet Alexis for him to get us together.

I had suggested she and I go for dinner or meet at the Club, but she instead insisted I come over to her condo. She lived only several blocks from me, and I stopped by on a Wednesday evening. Her place was a newly renovated, ground-floor duplex in the prestigious Gold Coast neighborhood. However, her building sat across from Division Street, which reeked of stale beer seven days a week, roared on the weekends until 4 a.m., and was the home of quintessential sticky-floor Chicago bars like Mother's, which played a major role in the movie *About Last Night*. Surprisingly, Alexis's place, like Alice's, was sparse, and as I casually looked around, she stated, without excuse, that she knew her place was bare and that she had no immediate plans of changing that. The noise from the street seeped through her ice-block windows, but was dulled by her television, where *Entertainment Tonight* was on. Alexis watched out of the corner of her eye, occasionally commenting on a star's looks or outfit.

"I can't believe John's trading on the computer now," she said. "I can't understand how people can trade outside of the pit. What the hell do you have your badge for if you're not going to get in there and trade? I like the jumping up and down, the screaming and yelling, I like calling the guys cocksuckers when they piss me off. That's my line, 'You fucking cock-sucker!' At first guys think they can steal a trade from you because you're a girl, and they'd be like, 'Poor Alexis, oh well.' But then I decided I was going to get right up there in their faces, exactly what they would do if I stole a trade from them. You have to do that. But I love that! I love the adrenaline. For the $3,500 I'm spending every month leasing my seat, I might as well take advantage of this crap."

I asked how she had gotten her start trading, and she eyed me suspiciously. "What did you hear?" she said.

"Nothing different than what you hear about most every woman on the Floor," I said. Alexis had baked brownies before I arrived and, instead of answering my question, she bounced up to cut them, bringing back an entire plateful, which she handed to me. Seeing that she brought none for herself, I moved the plate between us, a gesture that we should share.

"You'll eat it all," she said firmly. She dabbed at a crumb on my plate, then made a face. "I'm not interested in food anymore," she said. "I've been having a tough time at work, and I have no desire to eat." Alexis possessed an angular, perfected thinness. I nibbled on the brownie, for somehow my eating it seemed a vicarious, controlling pleasure to her, and because, I must admit, she intimidated me. Her directness made me immediately aware that she wasn't just going to gab with me the way that two girls watching TV and pigging out normally would. If I wanted her to confide in me at all and let me in on her true impressions of the Floor, I was going to have to play by her rules. Which started off with eating the entire brownie.

Throughout *Entertainment Tonight*, I tried to gently push the issue of how she made it into the pit, and from what I could gather, the rumors I'd heard did contain bits of truth. It was true that a big trader did back her—only, according to Alexis, he put $100,000 in her account so that she could start trading, while she used $10,000 of her own to actually trade with. At first, she wouldn't even speak his name to me, but eventually she did admit that it was Jimmy. "Everyone was like, 'You got in the pit because you slept with the guy,' " Alexis said. "I *never* slept with this guy, I'll take that to my grave." I wondered if there was perhaps a Clintonian context to her rebuttal, but I didn't dare interrupt. "Everyone was so convinced that he was nailing me and that that's why he put me in the pit," she continued. "I was like, 'You know what, he is a really nice guy, that's it.' I met him when I was trade-checking and he took a liking to me, whatever. The backing contract was 'I'll back Alexis and she's allowed to lose up to a hundred grand of my money,' but it wasn't like I had his money to play with. I knew that if I lost my ten grand, I was quitting. I wasn't going to keep trading and lose a hundred grand of this guy's money, because I wasn't brought up that way and I don't trade that way. A hundred grand to him was nothing—it's like 0.1111 percent, you know? At first, I was in awe of all that money, but then I was like, so he made five hundred grand today, what's he going to do differently? He's going to go to bed just like everyone else tonight."

Originally, Alexis had never possessed any aspirations to trade. In fact, her long-standing dream was to be a pop singer. As a child, she had sung with her father's band, a Greek group that played weddings, baptisms, and local parties, and later she tried to break into pop music by making her own CD. "My voice used to be all sweet like yours," she said with typical trader raspiness. The first time she saw the Floor was while she was in college at the University of Illinois at Chicago. She was dating a Cattle trader, and he brought her to visit. After that, she told him, "You guys are nuts, this is why you act so stupid because this is a stupid type of job."

But when college ended, she found herself working at the Merc as a clerk, because it was a flexible job that allowed her plenty of time to go on singing auditions. However, her music career was never realized, and Alexis turned to making commercial jingles instead while still clerking on the Floor. And then she was offered the opportunity to trade.

"When I first started trading, it wasn't that great for me," she confessed. "I didn't even want to go in the pit. I was like, there's five hundred guys in there, I don't want to be in front of them, I don't want them looking at me, which is surprising because I was used to being in the limelight. I was used to singing onstage, and when my high-school basketball team was number one in the country and we were on TV every day, who would want to be interviewed? Me! I was like, '*I'll* talk to the camera!' But when it came down to trading, I did not want to be the center of attention. I didn't want to open my mouth. I stood there and was miserable. Jimmy said, 'I look across the pit and see you, and you don't look like you want to be here.' I couldn't get myself to start screaming and yelling because it's weird."

I knew what she meant, and I recalled my pit-trading class, where I'd suddenly turned painfully shy when we'd stepped into the pit. But Alexis finally got the hang of it, and once she did, her sentiment changed completely. "Now, if I'm *not* screaming I feel like I'm missing something," she said. "Sometimes I scream just to hear myself—that can get me into trades that aren't so good, but I just like hearing my own voice. You learn how to gauge your volume, like when you want to get out of something you go from 'Two and a half!' " she said with a moderate shout, "to—" and she roared: " 'Two and a *fucking* half!' "

"Does it ever get to you being the only woman in that huge pit?" I asked.

"When I first went in the pit, I could hear people talking, 'She's a little whore.' It was really hard. And all the girl clerks talked, too, but I just thought: You're mad because you've been down here five years and nobody's offered you this chance, and here I am, down here six months and trading already. Obviously Jimmy put me in the pit because he thought I could trade. And I did, I proved myself." Alexis gave a smug nod, as if her accusers were in the room too. "I still hear the talk, but I don't care anymore because they're all a bunch of idiots anyways, so who gives a shit what they think. I know what they say," she stated, then imitated with a whine: " 'Alexis hardly trades and she wears half shirts.' " She shook her head. "The truth is," she said, her voice growing louder and faster, "I trade more than half the guys around me. Yes, I will definitely wear half shirts, with my hip-hugger pants! And they may be trading with me because of it. You think I don't know it? I definitely know it! But those guys are doing the same shit, the way they feed their brokers and take them out to fancy dinners so they'll give them fucking trades. So I'll do it my way, and if it takes a half shirt so they can look at my belly, I don't give a shit. What the hell, I got it, I might as well use it! But let's be realistic, do they honestly think that I don't trade? That brokers give me a hundred contracts a day because they think I'm cute or because I have a half shirt? Give me a break. Maybe one or two, or whatever."

It was interesting to me how Alexis, unprovoked, had addressed every one of the issues I'd heard men rant about. In most places of business, the person who was talked about had little or no clue what everyone else thought of her. Not so at the Merc. Alexis's direct rebuttal proved not only that she knew what people were saying about her, but that these things were likely said directly to her.

"You know, I still lease my seat because I really did not think I'd be trading this long," Alexis continued. "I thought I'd be married and have kids by now. But I really like to play the Market. I can't tell you how many times I've been up five grand by nine a.m., but end up walking away at the Closing bell down for the day. Why? Because I didn't want to leave, I wanted to play. A great day for me is when I'm down $15,000 and I stick it out to come back and break even. When that happens, I'm like, 'You are the Trader of All Traders!' " She held up her arms in a Rocky pose. "You feel like you just had the best day of your life because you were at the point where you were going to walk out the door, but you stayed and pushed through and got all your money back. You really didn't accomplish shit because your statement still says zero at the end of the day, but it would have been a lot worse to see a debit there with fifteen grand behind it."

Entertainment Tonight ended, and Alexis promptly flipped the channel to the teen-cult show *Dawson's Creek*. "People who knew me in high school wouldn't be surprised that I'm trading," she said. "I was always one of those people who thinks, 'You tell me I can't do this, well yes I CAN!' I like being on the edge. On my losing days I think, hey, I could be at a nine-to-five, punching in and out. But still, I would *never* encourage a daughter of mine to trade. I don't think this business is for females. It's a lot of stress and pressure that you do not need. And I'm sure my daughter will not be like me. I'll probably have a little pom-pom girl and I'll wanna throw her down the stairs."

Alexis turned up the volume on the television. "Okay, quiet now," she said. "I have to watch my show." I was poised with another question, but at her demand, I fell mute, like a silenced child. I swallowed my words and, feeling like I had no choice, turned my eyes to the television.

Midway through *Dawson's Creek* I left Alexis's place. I was somewhat disappointed that her story didn't, in my mind, effectively refute the men's views. Most everything she had said, in one way or another, actually upheld what I'd heard through the rumor mill. But was that necessarily a bad

thing? She'd admitted that her business ethic was to "work it" with everything she had—and a lot of other professional women would say the same.
So the men grumbled about that; was it because they were jealous that they
couldn't "work it" like that too? Everyone in this business was looking for
an edge, and Alexis had found hers. But the key, I was learning, was to be
conscious of the fine lines—taking careful note of the precise levels of support and resistance, which, in this case, for a woman, meant knowing when
you were "working it" too hard or not enough.

It would be over a year before Alexis was back in the spotlight of Floor gossip. The headline: she was getting married. And if that wasn't enough to
spark talk, there was a kicker: she was marrying a top broker in her pit. Just
as with any boss/employee romance, a broker/trader coupling never failed
to raise eyebrows. It could very well be true love, but it didn't hurt when
true love might also provide a handy business arrangement. According to
John, she showed up one day wearing the biggest diamond he'd ever seen.

It was also a major point of discussion that the broker happened to be
older, divorced-with-kids, short, chubby, and balding—what was seen as an
unlikely match for Alexis, which further perpetuated the assumption that
she was marrying him for the size of his wallet. But I wasn't convinced. She
was a trader too, with apparently no desire to quit working, so why was the
Floor insistent on casting her as a shallow girl interested in only one thing?
Although it seemed everyone else had immediately cast their verdict, I
wasn't about to go that far. Yes, it seemed the oldest and most typical story
there was, but I really wanted to believe there was something genuine there,
even though I knew that traders already had bets riding on how short-lived
that marriage would be.

$ $ $

I couldn't help but wonder if this was really about women using their sexual wiles to get ahead, or if it was about men feeling threatened by powerful women. Maybe the hostility between men and women on the Floor
existed because gender roles there were turned upside down.

A researcher named Michael Lewis, who was studying differences in the
sexes, designed a study with one-year-old boys and girls, where he set up a
barrier between the children and their mothers. The barrier was low

enough that the child could still see Mom, but couldn't reach her—a very troubling situation to a toddler. Most boys tried to knock down the barrier to get to Mom; most girls stood there and cried. Lewis's findings supported the existing, age-old umbrella theory: aggression and assertion are far greater in men, while women maintain greater passivity. These characteristics have a lot to do with our culture—after all, aren't we taught that men fight the wars and women sew the flags? Men earn more money per hour, and women become soccer moms. Men are CEOs, and when women reach the glass ceiling, are they conditioned to stand there and cry?

In order to survive on the Floor, women had to be deconditioned of these typical female attributes. The most successful women traders had mastered this art of neutrality. But in order for a man to accept an aggressive woman, he too had to be reconditioned—and the Floor provided little impetus for men to work at such an undertaking. Another conundrum was that while women traders likely found it freeing to be able to break from standard stereotypes and gender boundaries, many male traders still tended to codify women's success with a denigrating set of rules: "She slept her way into the pit"; "She only gets trades because she's good-looking"; "She's only here to find herself a rich man."

Because of these double standards and unrealistic expectations, I had thought that the handful of women traders on the Floor would form a support network of sorts, or at least become friends. But, in fact, quite the opposite was true. Not only did the women not bond, or look out for one another, or encourage one another, but, in the S&P pit for example, it seemed none of the women even *knew* one another, even though I could count on one hand the number of female traders who braved that pit. After a bit of contemplation, most of the women in that pit were able to at least list the other women's badges, but they told me that they'd never had so much as a conversation with any of them. Denise confided that she'd also found this surprising. "I really fight for women in this business," she said. After she retired from the Floor, she took a management position in an upstairs trading firm, where she pushed to get women traders hired. "I'm a big supporter of women sticking together, but I never got that when I was down on the Floor," she said. "The women were horrible to each other."

The pit Denise had traded in, Deutschemark Options, was one of the original homes of Bev Gelman. Bev was already established and respected in the pit when Denise had arrived. "Bev hated me when I came there," Denise said. "She was worse to me than the guys were. She was the queen of the pit and didn't want another woman there. She was such a bitch to me, for years. She would make snide comments, she wouldn't talk to me, she'd even turn her back to me."

I was well aware that Bev was tough, but I was surprised that she'd be out-and-out mean to another woman, especially a newcomer. When I mentioned Denise's experience to John, he laughed at me like I was being ridiculous. "Bev is a bitch to everyone in the pit," he said, as if it were a compliment.

When it came to women on the Floor, there was an extremely fine line between jealousy and respect. It seemed there was an unwritten rule for women who wanted to really make it on the Floor: don't turn people off, and don't necessarily turn people on. It was those few, like Bev, whose external demeanor didn't come off as threatening to the men—her looks were just average, she didn't need to be the center of attention, she didn't care one bit about what anyone else thought or did—who could step inconspicuously into the pit and little by little work her way up until eventually she blew everyone else away. It was the *Usual Suspects* syndrome, where no one had given her much thought, and no one had tried to squash her early on. She was seen as a peer, not as a sexual conquest, not as a force to be reckoned with, not as an underserving leech.

So, while the men's winning strategy was to call as much attention to themselves as possible, the most successful women on the Floor discovered their winning strategy to be exactly the opposite.

$ $ $

It had been a while since I'd visited the viewing room, and for a change I stopped in before heading to the Floor. I pressed my forehead to the glass and looked out over the pits. I remembered when it had seemed like I'd never be able to understand any of the chaos going on below, but now I could make sense of it all. I could tell where the Market was at, I could decipher what was going on in the pits, and I could pick out individuals from the mass whom I knew, and who had become friends. And yet, there was still this tingling sensation of being overwhelmed, of feeling in awe, and of seeming quite small. It was the same feeling I had whenever I would press my forehead to an airplane window to catch a view of Chicago's skyline— no matter how many times I'd seen the glowing skyscrapers lined up along the lake, it still took my breath away.

The security guard was chatty and he'd abandoned his post at the viewing room entrance to talk with me. This seemed to annoy the last row of phone clerks on the Floor, who—in the stadium-style setup—were back up against the glass wall. "They are always giving me dirty looks," the guard said. "Because they think I tell on them when they are watching pornos on their computers, or when they're reading *Playboy*, or have snuck in a can of soda." One of the clerks turned to glance over his shoulder, and the guard gave him a sarcastic little wave. Before I could inquire if he did indeed snitch, a trader hurried into the viewing room, searching for something. "Have you seen my clerk?" he asked. The guard shook his head.

"She disappeared," the trader explained as he turned to head out. "Maybe she went back into the porn industry."

TWELVE

Blowout

A trader can blow out of a losing position when she takes the loss all at once, instead of incrementally. Or a trader can blow out in the larger, fatal sense—otherwise termed as Belly Up, Tapping Out, or Going Debit. They say that no one ever leaves the Floor voluntarily; rather, it's F.R.—Forced Retirement.

There was no shortage of risk on the Floor today. It was holiday time, and on the Agriculture side, where the Markets were already closed for the day, a woman clerk was stringing twinkling white lights across the phone cubicles. On the other side of the Floor, mayhem was breaking out, the price-reporting boards already blinking like Christmas lights, the numbers flipping with amazing speed. A common Wall Street adage is: "Never try to catch a falling knife." And you knew when the Market was razor sharp because the big institutions began placing GMO orders. It stood for: Get Me Out! They didn't care at what cost, just get me the hell out. Today, the stock market was full of these orders, and was gyrating. It all sounded so dismal, and for anyone not in Futures, it likely was. Ah, but here at the Merc, traders could make money on the Up! (Swoosh!) and money on the Down! (Swoosh!)—and today they'd gotten the chance to do both because the Market bottomed out and then shot straight back up. As the Market rebounded, a trader hollered from the Nasdaq pit: "Ride the Bull!" He threw his head back and twirled an imaginary lasso. "Yee haw!"

John, however, must not have been riding on the right side, for I saw him snatch a trading card out of a clerk's hand and whip it on his desk. At the end of the day, a CNBC reporter, pink-cheeked from the excitement, summed it up: "Who needs college basketball when you have an hour like this?" Later that evening, John showed up at my apartment with hives covering his face. He had lost $100,000 and had spent the afternoon pleading with his clearing firm not to let him go. "My good days are up $20,000 or so, but my bad days are a loss of $100,000, $150,000," he told me. "So I don't exactly blame them. I'm a risk. I know this. They want me to put a million dollars in my account. But I don't want to have to tie up that much." In the end, the clearing firm suspended him from the Floor for two weeks.

After John left my place, he played a vicious round of tennis with a friend, returned home, drank half a bottle of Scotch, smoked a cigar, and nearly passed out while soaking in his Jacuzzi. He called me before he went to bed. "I wonder if it's Alice," he said. "I mean, I hadn't seen her in a while and hadn't had a losing day. And then she calls, she asks me to have lunch with her at the Club, I do, and sure enough, I get murdered."

"So all this time you thought it was me, and it's really been Alice," I said wryly.

John gave me a serious sigh. "No, it was *definitely* you for a while, Cari."

The thing about the Floor, however, was that you could always find someone who had a worse day than you. Word was that a Nasdaq trader had completely blown out, and his clearing firm had had to eat it. The clearing firm could only seize assets, and after that the trader's debt became the firm's responsibility. This was why it was common practice for traders to put their house—or houses—and cars, and whatever other large items they owned, under their wife's name.

A blown-out trader was generally news for about a day; after that, it became banal, for the occurrence was not uncommon. One-third of the membership at the Exchanges turned over every year because of blowout. A pointed example: it had been only three years since Alexis had gotten her badge, but out of the twenty people who had started out in her trading class, only she and one other still remained.

But in the odd zero-sum game of trading, one's demise on the Floor could be another's opportunity—pits like the Nasdaq were so packed that the only way to get a spot was if someone left, and it didn't matter one bit the reason for a departure, nor did a horrific blowout story serve as a deterrent to newcomers.

I was getting more daring as a clerk, and I made up my mind that I was going to command a new "spot." The one I chose was a front-row seat

outside the Nasdaq pit, and on a day when the Federal Reserve was making an eagerly anticipated announcement, I staked out my territory. With
John on suspension, I was free to take the direct route across the Floor. I
passed a woman clerk gingerly navigating the stairs, since she was wearing stiletto leather boots, but the guys had the right idea, and two slid past
me down the rails as if this were one big amusement park. I gathered up
the nerve to place myself directly at the mouth of the Nasdaq pit. I knew
it was prime real estate, but it didn't exactly occur to me that I'd be stealing someone else's spot. He was a tall, young clerk, and he stopped short
when he saw me. He crinkled up his forehead, about to chew me out, then
reconsidered. "Aw, I guess it's okay," he said, and squeezed in next to me.
I assumed his graciousness was only because I was a woman. If I were a
guy, I would have been immediately booted.

It was, indeed, a perfect spot. From here I could see the spit flying as the
traders screamed. I could feel the rumbling wave back and forth from this
pit to the S&P—one would start roaring, then, in a ripple effect, the other
would go off. As the clock ticked toward 1:15—Fed announcement time—
an order came over the loudspeaker that all clerks must leave the pits. It was
for the simple reason that there wasn't enough room for so many bodies.
Yellow jackets filtered out and positioned themselves along the stairs, where
I was standing. It was front to back, and I was feeling the stares, especially
from the women clerks—what is *she* doing here? I tried to ignore the
glares—I'd landed my spot, and I was not moving.

The Floor filled with the eerie quiet of the calm before the storm. I was
inhaling the jacket of the clerk in front of me, and I was sure the clerk
behind me was tasting my hair. I assumed an awkward position, tilting and
kinking my neck so that my nose wouldn't get smashed if someone near me
made a sharp, sudden move. The traders in the pit had to turn and twist to
all fit. The whole Floor, a sardine can, all of us jammed together, waited.
"Eye of the hurricane," I heard a trader say. And then, 1:15—the announcement flashed in yellow on the board and the twister hit, ripping through
the pit.

It had been anticipated that the rate would stay the same, but instead—
surprise, surprise!—it was increased. I had never witnessed anything like
this turn of events before. A Fed announcement typically occurs every six
weeks or so, and the entire financial world takes an educated guess as to the

outcome and, most of the time, these predictions are accurate. Not so today. All the research and knowledge possible wouldn't have made one bit of difference. It was like a horse race, you could bet with all odds in your favor, but that still didn't guarantee a win. It was just chance that your career, your livelihood, had been riding on the right side of today—but many people, including touted experts, had called it wrong. I watched the Nasdaq pit sway as everyone pushed, and I didn't even want to imagine what it felt like to be in the undulation of hundreds of jam-packed bodies. YOGI, a three-hundred-pound, top-step broker, dropped a huge order and the pit rippled as everyone careened toward him. A woman trader, Lisa, shouted, "Who'll hit me on seven on three?" She craned her neck like she was in a rising pool of water—or perhaps something worse. She yelled something to the broker next to her, but he couldn't hear her, so she grabbed his head and pulled his ear to her mouth. He nodded, and she slapped him on the back to confirm the trade. Just in time, she ducked as the guy above her bent his entire body over her to scream across the row.

The couple of hours sped by, and at the first gong—signaling thirty seconds before the Close—I watched a trader rip off his headset and push his way out of the pit. He slammed the headset on a desk and screamed at the top of his lungs for his clerk, "Frank!" No answer and no yellow jacket came running. He hollered again, his face red and sweaty. "Fra-a-a-nk!" I would not want to be Frank at this moment. Two other clerks were watching and I heard one say, "I bet you he won't be back tomorrow." I thought they were talking about Frank, but then it occurred to me that they might very well be talking about the trader too.

The final gong, and the cards hit the air like Frisbees. The traders trudged out of the pit, rubbing their dazed eyes. One trader took off his jacket and his polo shirt was sopping wet. "You can tell a nervous sweat from an anxiety sweat," Alice once told me. I began breathing through my mouth, having no desire to figure out the distinction.

When I checked in with Tom, he said he'd gotten chopped up pretty badly. Tara later told me that she'd called him for help and he'd shouted, "Don't trade now unless you want to lose money. If you want to lose, trade all you want. There, that's my help!" Then he slammed down the phone. That night, Tom sent me an e-mail: "Some days you are the windshield. Some days you are the bug."

$ $ $

Most traders go through three stages of Losing. First, you admit, Okay, I was wrong. Often, this doesn't occur until long after you've already exceeded your mental stopwatch. You should have gotten out when you had an *inkling* you might be wrong; now, it was a different story. The next stage is Denial: this can't be happening, the Market's going to come up/down, it *has* to. This is followed by the last stage, which can be broadly categorized as Panic, and may include numerous physical symptoms, racing heart, light-headedness, nausea. This is when you pull a GMO to whoever is closest—Get me out!

For traders who held positions long-term, there was the ever-present, round-the-clock risk of losing. You could lose when you were sound asleep at night. Some event in some other country—the European Central Bank makes an interest-rate move, an act of violence in the Middle East occurs, a foreign leader is ousted—would, at an odd hour, affect the position you were holding. Traders have woken up broke from situations like this—they've also woken up millionaires. In one instance, in the early 1980s, the Mexican Peso underwent a sudden devaluation. With no notice, no warning, the Peso lost nearly half its value. Traders stepped into the pit to find that if they'd been holding a long position, well, now they were holding a double-long position in a decimated Market. Alice vividly recalled the day this happened. She saw workers on ladders adjusting the price-reporting boards that listed the Peso. She saw men sitting on the pit steps, crying. Because so many traders had blown out, and the lucky ones who'd financially survived were shell-shocked, trading in the Peso pit quickly dried up. It took over two decades before the Mexican Peso was traded again at the Merc.

Most often, though, losing was not purely random, and could be pinpointed to certain, specific bad habits. The most common way to lose on the Floor was to let your ego get the best of you. "With a man, the biggest problem is way too much ego," Alice said. "With a woman, it's not enough ego. But it's equally painful to both. The male trader will tend to embrace his losses, he'll just trade harder and longer. And if it works a couple of times, he'll tend to become arrogant about it, and say, 'Oh, it doesn't matter if I'm down, I can work my way out of it!' There's a certain warning bell that should be ringing—you don't want to be down too much because it will imperil your equity, but guys won't listen to that bell. And then they start trading scared or sick. At a certain point you no longer own the trade, it owns you. Occasionally, you'll see a new guy who's afraid to pull the trigger. But usually, if a guy says in his mind, 'I'm going to risk $1,000 on this trade,' the majority of men will end up risking $2,500. If a woman says, 'I'm going to risk $1,000 on this trade,' she'll end up risking $500. Neither is being fair to themselves. The woman is panicking out at five hundred, and the men are overrisking. A guy is more likely to press his luck. Now, Bev Gelman, she can assume risk into outer space. See, when a woman is good, she's better than a man because she's not caught up with ego."

Alice's perception was quite relevant: for all the blowing-out stories I'd heard, none of them, interestingly enough, were about women. Sure, a lot of women couldn't make it or left the trading world, but none whom I knew of had gone belly-up in the dramatic, brazen, rebellious way that the men often did. And it was surprising to me just how many men went belly-up—including those seemingly together, low-key, all-around nice guys whom I'd have never pegged as ones to get swept up in the machismo of the Floor. Yet, men who appeared to be modest and level-headed confessed to me that they'd learned the hard way just how dangerous the ego could be. One was Phil, a charismatic thirty-three-year-old Bond trader at the Board of Trade. He'd started as a runner and quickly earned his badge and bought a seat with money borrowed from his parents. "When I first started trading, things were going great, the money was coming in," he told me. "I was going to look at Porsches. I was staying out all night and was always buying drinks for everyone. I didn't know if I was a broker or a rock star. And then," he said, shooting his index finger toward the ceiling, as if about to reveal a brilliant master plan, "I made a decision. I decided that I was going to make a million dollars in two months." He started trading large numbers of contracts, buying and selling with abandon. He had set out a two-month plan for himself, but the span of just two days was all it took for everything to completely backfire. He had gotten himself so caught that by the time he realized the extent of what had happened, he'd lost $400,000. "When I had to go to my clearing firm and tell them," he said, "that was probably the worst day of my life. I had to sell my seat to pay it all back. But I decided that I was still going to go back into the pit the next day, but I was going to be a changed man. And I was. I'm much more conservative now. I used to be like, 'Let's all go out, I'm buying!' Now I'm like, 'Do you want me to get you some coffee?'"

Another unlikely candidate, or so I thought, was a trader in the Australian Dollar pit named Keith. One day, numerous sell orders were being called into the Floor from the legendary trader George Soros. Keith decided to go against him and started to buy. The more Soros sold, the more Keith bought. "I don't know exactly how it even happened," Keith told me. "My ego just got a hold of me and I thought, 'I can do this!' So I started buying and buying, and it was great because everyone knew that *I* was going up against the Big One! Ten minutes later, I was throwing up in the bathroom. My life was forever changed. The rest is probably the most typical story there is—when I told my wife what I'd lost, she packed a suitcase and went to stay with a girlfriend. The next day a moving van showed up to take everything that was hers."

I relayed Keith's woeful tale to Alice one afternoon in the Club. She was unimpressed. "Happens all the time," she said. "And as for his marriage, the two of them probably deserved each other. These men do not have to stretch for women." In this case, Alice turned out to be right; the next I'd heard of Keith, he'd taken off to Hawaii to marry a woman he'd known for a month.

$ $ $

John, finally off his suspension, was at the Merc Club at around 10 a.m., biting into a turkey burger, when suddenly the entire room gasped. John instinctively flipped his head to the monitors—the Market was instantaneously, unexplainably, skyrocketing! It could only be a sign that something major had just occurred in the world. Everyone threw back their chairs and raced to the door, nearly trampling the waitresses and busboys. John didn't budge. Luckily, he didn't have a position on, and he didn't feel like battling the chaos of whatever it was that had happened. He calmly took another bite of his burger.

What he'd opted out of was one of the most harrowing days in the last several years—the Fed had cut interest rates yet again, only this time it was a completely sudden, surprise move. With absolutely no prior warning, the Market instantly soared.

The Floor pounded with the stampede of traders, and the pits were roaring. I, with lousy luck, had missed the surprise announcement by ten minutes, and when I arrived, the Market was digesting the huge move and convulsing. I had never seen such a surge of emotion—there were breathlessly ecstatic people and ashen, devastated people. There were traders who'd just lost their house and traders who'd just made enough money to buy one. A clerk told me that his two bosses had made $500,000 each in three seconds. It was only luck—it was only if you happened to be on the right side at the precise blink of an eye.

I looked up at the digital boards that scrolled the ripple effect the rate cut had had across the world: the short-term Canadian bonds were up; the Euro had rebounded; the Brazil stock index had jumped 3 percent. I thought I'd seen risky days, but this was unprecedented—if you were in the Nasdaq pit, for example, and you had one contract, you would have made or lost $40,000 when the announcement hit. Forty thousand dollars, straight up—*no mercy!*—on a single contract! But most traders had a lot more than one measly contract riding, and I multiplied a typical trading size, ten, twenty, a hundred contracts, by $40,000 to get a sense of the type of devastation or exaltation happening around me.

In came the photographers from the *Wall Street Journal*, the *Chicago Tribune*, and the *Chicago Sun-Times* with their huge zoom lenses to capture it all. Two traders next to me, both flushed and jittery, were shaking their heads. "I feel so terrible for Al," they mourned. "Can you believe it? God, do I feel bad." While carnage was everywhere here, the reality was that this was the largest one-day gain in the history of the Nasdaq. To outsiders, everything would seem rosy. The Market popped! Stocks were up! And this was yet another prime example of how the opportunity to Make Money on the Up! and Make Money on the Down! could get you fried.

Tom met me on the Floor for the last hour of trading so that he could witness what he called "the bloodbath of the morning." We sat at a top row of computers, overlooking the Nasdaq pit. I propped my feet up against the rails. Next to us, a man with weathered, wrinkled skin and white hair muttered, "Where else, besides a mental institution, are you going to see this much craziness?"

One trader, badge OCH, a sandy-haired, preppy guy in his late twenties who usually traded on Globex, got caught in the Fed's little surprise and by the end of the day he'd ditched his computer and jumped into the Nasdaq pit to try to salvage something—anything. The Closing-bell countdown was on. He screamed to his right. No one gave him a trade. He screamed to his left. Nothing. The gong sounded, thirty seconds left. His face was contorted with tension and panic, and then he just gave up. Limp, he sank down, down—I saw rows of traders' heads, shoulders, bodies, squashed up one next to the other, and then, all of a sudden, an empty spot appeared, as gaping as a missing tooth. The traders on either side glanced to see what had happened to OCH. He must have still been breathing because no one even bothered to crouch down. And then, the Closing bell, and the stampede out of the pit. As the people cleared, I saw OCH still slumped on the empty step, his head buried in his hands.

I motioned to Tom to look—it was like a car wreck, and we were passers-by trying to get a glimpse and survey the damage. "See the guy, his badge is OCH," I said, pronouncing it like the tree.

"Looks more like 'Ouch' to me," Tom said.

"I'm getting too old to deal with crazy days and surprises," John reflected the next day. But even though there were no earth-shattering announcements today, he still got caught short in a rising market. It was 5 p.m.—two hours after the Exchanges had closed—when he called me from the Floor. He was there all by himself in the huge arena, his voice echoing in the emptiness, only the clicking from the time-stamp machines and an occasional phone ringing unanswered to keep him company. He was sitting there waiting for the Market to move his way—even just slightly—so that he could cut his losses and get himself out of this position. But there was not much volume during after-hours trading, so it was proving to be a long wait.

Earlier in the week John had told me he had a blind date scheduled for tonight with the sister of a friend. "So you're going to start dating again?" I'd asked.

He sighed. "I'm beginning to think I want to get married."

"Really?"

"Yeah. I think I do. I'm tired of having making money be the main thing in my life. I think I'd like to have a family." It was a rare moment of tenderness I'd never before witnessed coming from John. I was used to the

John who always proclaimed he doubted he'd ever get married because he liked his life exactly the way it was, with the freedom to drop everything whenever he wanted and go hunting or golfing or fishing, every day, if he felt like it—even every day straight for a month, or two, or three, and he'd done just that in the past. And besides, he would say, almost every one of his friends who was married (most of them traders, mind you) was divorced or cheating on his wife. Only once before had I heard John lean toward the positive side of marriage—he had announced a standing offer of $10,000 to anyone who fixed him up with the woman he married. I had pretty much chalked up that particular "change of heart" to nothing more than trader talk—trying to come up with yet another new bet or wager simply for the sake of placing it. But in this most recent conversation, the longing in John's voice had been unmistakable, and his confession that, at thirty-seven years old, he was finally ready, seemed sincere. I'd felt proud and sad for him at the same time.

But then, from the empty Floor of the Merc, John called and canceled his blind date. "Listen, I'm a Commodities trader and I had a really bad day," he told the woman. "I'll call you to reschedule sometime next week."

"Why'd you do that?" I asked.

"I'm losing money here," he barked. "I don't have time to be doing things like dating!"

John avoided going to the Floor the following day. Instead, he bought a $1,000 fishing pole. He told me he thought he traded better when he spent money. It apparently worked, for the next day he arrived on the Floor for the Opening—a rare feat for him—made two trades, took a huge profit, and left by 9 a.m.

"Did your morning pay for your fishing pole?" I asked.

He laughed. "Yeah, I covered the pole." His intonation was such that he had covered it many times over. It appeared that his losing streak was, finally, over.

$ $ $

Several days later, at the Club, Alice dug into a triple-sized Caesar salad, specially prepared for her, with her suggested addition of cubes of turkey (the skin of which had been previously delivered to the table on a saucer, and eaten by Alice with a fork and knife, as if it were a delicacy). Our conversation today was about how it was possible—barring no major incidents in the Market—for someone to lose millions trading. "I can completely see how it could happen," Alice said. "You get a little full of yourself. You have twenty million and you lose five. You think, well I was able to make twenty—I can get my five back. But then you lose some more, and then some more, and you get into a downward spiral and you can't get out."

John arrived and slouched into a chair. He'd made money today, but it had been exhausting. Alice asked him the question of the day—he, too, felt it wasn't that difficult to rack up major losses, even in a relatively stable market. "Trading boils down to a mind game," he said. "The key is to assess the vulnerability of others and take advantage of their weaknesses." John believed a trader experienced three stages with each trade. The first was Gut. For him, his gut reaction was typically to go *against* the norm, to feed off everybody else's frenzy or fear. "If everyone thinks the world looks great, it makes me decide to sell the Market," John said. "But if everything's down and everybody's selling, my instinct is to buy."

Once he put on his trade, the next stage was Fear. "Fear allows you to have respect for the Market," he said. "And in order to be a good trader, you *must* respect the Market. This respect also allows you not to be devastated by a loss—you know the Market has the ability to wipe you out, so you can take a loss because you view it as: I'm letting the Market win for the day. Take a pro tennis player—if he loses a major match in a tournament, he's still got to be able to step on the court the next day. If he has respect for the game and for the other players, then his loss will not psychologically damage him and he'll be able to go back and continue playing. The same with trading, sure, you get depressed over a losing day, but you have to be able to go back on the Floor the day after."

The final stage was Tolerance of Pain. "If your position is really going against you, you get to this level where you know you're fucked, then you start to realize you're double-fucked," John said. "But you also know everyone else in the pit is fucked, too, so it becomes all about how long you can withstand the pain. How long can you wait it out? Can you wait until everyone else says mercy? Because if you can, then you can rape 'em. That's what Bev does best. When the last Fed number came out, Bev lost $1.4 million in thirty seconds. Everyone panicked, but Bev turned around and let them all have it. She ended up making two million off it all." John shook his head, clearly impressed. "She has the highest tolerance of pain I have ever seen. Even when everyone else is puking, she can hold out."

I decided to walk home, needing some fresh air. Midway, I stopped at a coffee shop and, over my chai tea, pulled out a book I was reading entitled *The Disciplined Trader*. A man sitting near me noticed and offered up that he owned a seat at the Board of Trade. He said he was an attorney, but instead of practicing law he used to trade in the Grains and now traded stocks from home. Over a large coffee he told me, "The owner of my clearing firm, who's one of the biggest traders at the Board, would always say: 'You should live according to your worst year.' I always thought that was the best advice. Unfortunately, many traders live according to their best year."

He was right. For such a volatile field, traders did tend to spend money with wild abandon. As Oscar Wilde said, "Nothing succeeds like excess." Every Friday limos lined up in front of the Merc, waiting to take traders to Vegas for the weekend. Once, a group of traders thought it might be fun to go to Paris for lunch. So they picked up their wives, hopped a flight to Paris, had a deliciously authentic meal, and returned that night.

Then there were the extravagant parties, the more elaborate, the better. The Merc's chairman emeritus, Leo Melamed, was thrown two retirement parties: one, a $500,000 extravaganza at a downtown hotel, with a guest list of two thousand of his closest friends; and the other, at the suburban North Shore home of a trading-firm chairman, where each table boasted a telephone that allowed you to dial up any other table. And forget an ice sculpture as centerpiece—a realistic trading forum was concocted with computer monitors that continuously scrolled stories of Melamed's life.

Of course, with a trader's hours, hobbies were a must. Cars were a big pastime—collecting them, touring rare models, racing them. John had a new hobby, which was quite apt: he'd begun collecting money. He had already acquired an impressive array of well-preserved $1 and $5 bills from the 1800s. He'd wanted to buy the very first $5 bill ever made, and had bid $100,000 for it at an auction, but was outbid by an additional $100,000. He currently had a bid riding on an Internet auction for a rare $10,000 bill.

And then there were adornments, such as jewels. In one story I'd heard, a top trader was about to start shopping for an engagement ring. One night, while dining with friends, one of the women chided the trader, "You know, it's customary to spend two months' salary on the ring." The trader, known for his austere demeanor, stoically responded: "If I spent two months' salary on a ring, the diamond would be bigger than her fucking head." (The eventual marriage ended up lasting less than a month.)

And what better way to pass the occasional Market lull than by indulging in a few bets. It's often said that if a fly is crawling on a bar, traders will bet on which glass it's going to land. The amount of money that gets laid down on ridiculous bets on the Floor is often more than most people earn in an entire year, such as twenty grand on either side of how many Big Macs/Krispy Kremes/Weiner's Circle hot dogs/Taco Bell hot-sauce packets can someone eat in a half hour? One time, the bet was to eat fifty chicken McNuggets. The trader managed all fifty; then, just to rub in his achievement with typical trader bravado, he chomped another two nuggets—which was just enough to put him over the edge, and he vomited all over himself.

Another time, nineteen tobacco-chewing traders spit in a cup, and one trader—for $5,000—drank it. Then there was the time Alice and I, along with everyone else, stared from the Merc Club window as a young guy leaped off the bridge into the Chicago River. The bridge wasn't high enough for this to be a suicide wish, but was certainly high enough to give a really good smart upon hitting the water. When the guy resurfaced, he hoisted himself from the river and raced into the underground train tunnels of Union Station, where he disappeared from our sight. "This type of thing happens occasionally," Alice had commented indifferently. Another trader offered up, "The last time I saw someone jump, it was Murphy, an out-trade clerk. He did it for $500."

I couldn't recall stories of any women traders getting caught up in such antics. When bets were taken, they'd roll their eyes, proclaim the men lunatics, and watch the outcomes with disgust.

Maybe it was because I was female, but I didn't get it—after spending all day betting for work, what was the appeal in doing so for fun too? It was definitely not about the actual dollar amount, because anyone who could afford to risk $20,000 on someone else's gastric system wasn't likely in need of the winnings. And it wasn't necessarily about winning, either, because there was always some "investment" that traders were talking up too—oil wells, real estate, yachts, even expeditions to dig for Genghis Khan's tomb. It was, I believed, about the risk—the *need* for risk. It seemed almost like a chemical addiction: traders were hyped on an elevated level of risk all day, five days a week, and how do you come down from that? The answer was: You didn't. You surrounded yourself with more risk. You made your life outside of trading just as heightened, just as sensory, just as risky. You became accustomed to the thrill, to the speed, to the adrenaline rush of living on the edge, to the nerve-tingling, sensory-enhancing possibility that everything could blow up in your face.

Back in the coffee shop, as I read my trading book, the trader at the next table leaned over with some final thoughts. "I've been sitting here thinking," he said, "that really, trading is the purest form of money. This alcoholic I know said, 'Alcoholics are people who absolutely love risk, but who are, unfortunately, inept at handling it.' And I think that can describe traders as well. We keep doing something that may feel good at the time, but over the long run, well, it might just destroy everything."

THIRTEEN

Short Squeeze

Occasionally, when the Market is quiet, the Bulls will sneak in and do a
Short Squeeze. This is a combined effort, where a bunch of bullish traders
suddenly begin a buying spree in hopes that they can pressure those with a
short position to succumb. It's a scare tactic, and because of it traders have
a common warning: don't sell short a dead market. The opposite of a Short
Squeeze is a Bull Trap, where the Bears sneak in and squeeze the Bulls out
of the Market.

For all those who disappear from the Floor because of blowout, there are just as many who leave because of burnout. This was the case with a woman named Ricki Lane Sutton. Before Ricki ever considered trading, she was bartending at a no-frills hangout in Chicago's Lincoln Park. She liked the people she worked with and she liked the people she made drinks for, all the neighborhood guys—many of whom, coincidentally, traded at one of the Exchanges—and the students from nearby DePaul University who would tip well with Mom and Dad's money. Ricki liked the money—the money she made, and the money she skimmed off the top, or the bottom, or whatever little loophole she could find. This was not the first time she had stolen from an employer. She had stolen from just about every job she'd had since she came to Chicago at age eighteen.

If you saw Ricki, and were to get to know her, you would never suspect this type of behavior. She was a tiny sprite, with straight brown hair; she was not especially pretty, but not *not* pretty, either—somewhere in the nondescript middle, where average sounds too generic but was exactly right. But the thing about Ricki was, she was smart. So smart, in fact, that she knew she'd better not let you onto her. She stole because she was paying her way through school at the University of Chicago. Although the money she made bartending was good, it wasn't good enough to cover tuition to the expensive and elite U of C, where Ricki was one of the atypical ones on campus for whom attending the school was not considered an honor by her parents, and for whom there was—never mind a trust fund (laugh!)—not a penny put toward her education. Her father, a supervisor at a large car manufacturer, had watched his daughter perusing all the glossy college catalogs with Ivy League crests on the covers, then told her she wasn't getting any sort of monetary help, so she might as well spare herself some agony and just go to State U.

And so Ricki went ahead and picked the priciest school on her list.

This knee-jerk reaction was to become a pattern for decision making in Ricki's life. The word "no" would prove the impetus for her to instantaneously make up her mind to do whatever it was anyway, with more force and fortitude than ever. That single word would project her down paths that she never would have turned had she been left to her own volition.

Ricki had spunk, and it was enough to more than compensate for her tiny five-feet-two-inches, 105-pounds-soaking-wet frame. She was also smart enough to figure out a plan for how she was going to get things in life: she was going to try not to be noticed. She was average enough to just blend in, she'd never be a threat, she'd never be the center of attention or someone you'd be wary of—and that was exactly how she liked it. The world was her game, and she was going to play it that way—and no one would ever know.

I had met Ricki in one of those roundabout ways that made me realize that when it came to trading, it wasn't just Chicago that seemed like a small town. She was living in Los Angeles, and I was there visiting a friend who'd met Ricki at a University of Chicago alumni event. My friend described her as a trader turned filmmaker/writer, and he thought the two of us would have a lot in common. Of course, I was intrigued to meet her—from my own experience, I'd found that the qualities that made me successful with writing were likely the same qualities that would burn me at trading, and I was curious to see how she'd balanced the two.

At first, Ricki was wary of me. Just the fact that I worked at the Merc seemed to open a padlocked trunk of memories that had been stowed away in an attic somewhere, with no intent of ever being found. But once the layers of dust were swept clear and the lock broken, it all came spilling out like an upended shoebox of old photographs.

Ricki had grown up in Atlanta and still had a soft Southern drawl that was occasionally detectable. "People are always telling me my accent returns," she confessed, "when I talk about money." During her first summer after college, one of Ricki's regular customers at the bar was a guy who clerked at the Chicago Board of Options Exchange. He told Ricki that his boss was ready to give him a badge and that he needed to find himself a clerk. He offered her the job. Ricki had heard a lot about clerking because the night doorman at the bar was a clerk at the Merc, and he'd introduced her to a clerk friend of his, whom she had started dating. She'd also had a taste of the trading world four years earlier, through her college boyfriend, Brandon. Brandon's father was a top accountant who boasted many of Chicago's big traders on his high-profile list of clientele. For a holiday party one year, the traders took a group to Las Vegas; Brandon and his family were invited, and Brandon was even allowed to bring Ricki.

"I was eighteen years old, and I'd never even been to Vegas, let alone seen money being tossed around like that before," Ricki recalled. "They even gave us $100 each to gamble with. Well, Brandon was this rich kid who was also amazingly brilliant—the kind of person who could get all A's at the University of Chicago without having to study at all. He also was wild and rebellious." He persuaded Ricki into buying cocaine with their hundred dollars. It was the first time she'd ever done drugs before, and wouldn't be her last. "We were just living it up, putting all of our tab on the company and going to the big dinners," Ricki said. "It looked really good, and imagine it from my perspective—I mean, there I was, literally stealing to survive, and barely surviving at that. And here were all these big-money people and it just looked so damn good to me."

Ricki took the job clerking. But she continued bartending at night because the clerk's salary was hardly enough to live on, let alone put a dent in her student loans. The year was 1985, and the Board of Options Exchange was just settling into its new home—a massive, cutting-edge technological wonder that boasted the dubious distinction of having more computer screens under one roof than any other building in the world; so much heat was generated from all the screens and electronic reporting boards that the air-conditioning ran year-round, even in the dead of a Chicago winter.

Ricki was fresh from completing her bachelor's in economics, and ready to conquer the world—but, as it turned out, she wasn't going to be clerking for her friend, but rather, his boss, a three-hundred-pound, would-be philanderer, except for the fact that his appearance often prevented it. As a pastime, he was a bookie for sporting events. He had Ricki deliver envelopes full of cash, and it didn't dawn on her until much later what she was actually doing. Forget conquer the world; instead, Ricki was running down the street to pick up the huge hoagies that her boss loved to eat, sauce dripping down his chin, shredded lettuce hanging from his teeth. All the guys would attack the sandwiches that her boss would spring for, and he'd invariably get around to asking Ricki—with his mouth full of pastrami and onions—why the hell wasn't she eating? It was quickly evident to Ricki that she wasn't going to be one of the boys.

She wasn't going to be one of the girls either, although she was trying. But these girl clerks looked so pretty and put together all the time. The more she tried to buy into it all, the more she disintegrated into her usual self—screw it, she thought, she'd blend in in her own way. She'd put on khaki pants, like the guys, and a button-up shirt, and, because men had to wear a tie, she'd wear a thin leather tie, which was stylish then. She'd grab her clerk coat, run a comb through her hair, and that was *it*. Her uniform was a protection of sorts—if she could blend in enough, maybe they wouldn't see her at all.

However, her boss noticed her; and he was starting to get irritated with her. She wouldn't eat the big sandwiches or go to any of the games he was always superciliously offering tickets to. Ricki disliked sporting events and besides, she tended bar at night. She felt like a defiant little child around them all, as if she were being contrary just for the sake of getting attention. "No! I don't wanna eat the subs! No! I don't wanna go to games. I hate-hate-hate them!" She just wanted to do her job and be done. She didn't want to be friends with these people—or, worse, she didn't want to risk becoming one of them.

And then, the final straw: at the end of work one Friday, her boss said to her, "We're going to go to the hot tub at my condo. Come on." Several others gathered around, and Ricki suddenly felt trapped.

"Uhh . . . well . . . what am I going to wear?" she stammered. Everyone started laughing, patronizing ha, ha, ha, has, "What's she going to wear? Why, didn't you bring your bikini to the trading floor today? Oh, you forgot, well now, what do you *think* you're going to wear?" Somehow, she begged out of the situation, which was nothing short of a catch-22. The next week, her boss sat her down and said, "You're not cut out to be a trader. It's not going to work. You can stay here through the summer, but then you're going to have to go." There it was again, someone telling her no, which made Ricki's temperature boil and her eyes narrow into vicious slits. Her boss stared at her, then condescendingly said, "I thought you might cry."

No, Ricki recalled thinking, *I just want to fucking rip you into shreds!*

At the bar that night, as she pounded a few in between serving a few, she talked to everyone who had some connection to a trading floor. "I need a new job," she said. "I want to trade." But the predominant thought in her head was: *I'm going to fucking trade because that fucker is going to see me be a trader!*

Ricki began interviewing with many different trading companies. She received a few offers to work upstairs, in an office. "But I want to be on the Floor," she'd say. "Well, that takes a certain type of person," they would respond. But Ricki knew that what they *really* wanted to say was: "Small women like you who are not especially pretty and who have voices that don't carry have no business being on a trading floor."

In one interview, things were going well. The interviewer was discussing aspects of trading and said, "You know, like Vegas, like the roulette wheel." And Ricki, simply making conversation, said, "You know, I've only been to Vegas once, and I didn't even gamble." The interviewer's face went blank, and then he swiftly closed his notebook and rose from behind his desk. "This isn't going to work for you," he said, and hastily ushered her out.

Finally, Ricki found a company at the Merc started by a guy named Singer and a guy named Wenger, which took college graduates with no trading background and turned them into traders. All you had to do was sign a binding three-year contract that relegated you to a salary of their discretion, as opposed to a percentage of what you earned trading. If you were a lousy trader, then they'd take the hit, but if you turned out to be adept at trading, it was a shoddy deal. Ricki signed anyway.

It had been only two weeks since her corpulent boss at the Options Exchange had his little talk with her and had graciously extended her date of termination, when Ricki walked onto the Floor, gathered together her few personal items, said good-bye to the few people she'd actually come to tolerate, and left.

Her job with Singer-Wenger began with practice trading sessions and daylong classes in a classroom, learning in-depth theory—the majority of which Ricki would never end up using. By the end of the summer, Ricki, with her badge with her initials—RLS—was placed in the Yen Options pit, and was ready to make her first real trade. She wore the Singer-Wenger red trading jacket, which was too big and made her feel as if she were a little girl playing dress-up in her father's coat.

"I can viscerally still feel that first day on the Floor," Ricki told me. "And the most overwhelming feeling was that I was in this role. It was like I really didn't belong, and somehow I was there anyway. It was a pretty incredible moment." As part of the program, Ricki had a Singer-Wenger trader standing over her at all times, guiding her through the process. For the first few days in the pit, Ricki was silent. She needed the time to acclimate, to figure out who was who, and what he was doing, and why he was doing it. And then, Ricki made a trade.

It was a two-lot. She called it out, she got it. And then she got a jab in the back—she flipped around to face another trader.

"Hey, I was right behind you," he said. "One of those should be mine." Ricki stared at him. "Give me one," he said.

It had been weird to hear her own voice calling out her trade just a few seconds earlier, and it was weird to hear it again, the way it came out oddly steadfast: "No."

The guy from Singer-Wenger leaned over and said in her ear, "Just give him one."

The trader pushed. "Come on, give me one!"

Ricki said: "No, it's mine." The Singer-Wenger guy grabbed her by the arm and, pushing through the sea of people, led her directly out of the pit. Her cheeks flushed with embarrassment as he parked her just outside the pit entrance and began lecturing her—scolding her—for all to see. She held her ground, held it until the thought occurred to her that it was in the realm of possibility that a ridiculous one-lot could actually cost her this job. With her body quivering with frustration and her eyes beady and unforgiving, she reentered the pit and gave the trader the one-lot. But that was IT—no one was telling her no again. "I became a whole different person," Ricki said. "Like a little tiger. I mean, I'll scratch you—don't get too close! I was a fucking wildcat! I was there to prove that girls could do this, too, and fuck you!"

Only one other woman worked for Singer-Wenger at that time, Karen, who was hired right after Ricki. "She was something," Ricki recalled. "I mean, she was this very attractive and went-out-of-her-way-to-be-attractive type of woman. Whereas I was like, get out of bed, don't even look in the mirror, throw on shit, and go." As haphazard as it sounded, Ricki's lack of caring about her appearance was actually purposeful, it was her way of thumbing her nose at other women on the Floor. "I *had* to look like shit," Ricki told me, "because if I started worrying about how I looked, I'd be dead, all right? But Karen, she always worried about how she looked, and she always looked great—and she slept with everybody. *Every*body. Somehow, she was able to do that and maintain respect. I don't know how she pulled it off, but no one ever was like, 'Slut!' She was good-looking, so it wasn't a detriment to be associated with her. It was almost like if you hadn't had a fling with her, then what's wrong with you? She was always careful and wise with the terminology, to call it 'dating' or something like that."

Ricki, however, didn't want anyone to know her business—especially that she was dating a clerk, even though she'd been seeing Kevin long before she'd started on the Floor. She was so determined not to give any-body even a snippet of information to gossip about that she refused to talk to Kevin during the trading day. "I wanted to be seen as an equal," she recalled, "and I felt the only way to maintain that was to keep my personal life very, very separate from that place. And I just didn't trust those men. They were attractive . . . but"—she hissed for emphasis—"*dangerous*. You could get eaten alive—I saw the danger of that immediately."

Ricki soon discovered that she was good at trading. It clicked for her, and she began making money. All the things that had seemed so compli-cated in the classroom she was now pulling off without a second thought. "It had only been a few months," Ricki said, "but I turned to one of the older traders, and said, 'All these different kinds of spreads, they don't really mean anything—it's just buying low and selling high.' And he goes, 'It took me a long time to figure that out. You're way ahead of the game.' I was so disappointed! I realized that even trading was just another machine, and I was in it." Ricki stomped out a rhythmic beat with her foot. "This machine just paid better than most assembly lines." She stomped again, like march-ing to a drum, one foot in front of the other, just look straight ahead and follow the leader, no need to think. This was what she'd struggled to put herself through one of the priciest universities for?

Ricki hadn't been in the Yen Options pit for too long before Singer-Wenger decided to move her. One of the reasons may have been a little incident: a Futures trader was trying to make the transition to Options and was assigned by Singer-Wenger to clerk for Ricki so she could help teach him. "I don't even know what precipitated this moment," she told me, "but I said something like, 'Here're my cards, go run my sheets, I need them now.' And for some reason, he calls me a cunt. It was one of those moments where you feel like everything goes silent and the word reverberates across the room. You know, it goes *cunt, cunt, cunt*. And everybody's looking at you like, what are *you* going to do? I felt that moment. And despite the fact that I was my angry little self, I knew it was a pivotal moment. I knew it was very important how I reacted to that word. So, I did not react. I acted like it didn't happen, and I turned and went about my business. And the more moments that passed, the better it got." She chuckled. "I think that really confused him. The other thing was, I didn't tell on him. Not a word to anybody, just like it never even occurred.

"Well, the next morning, the boss calls me into his office, and he says, 'I heard that you've been treating your clerk badly.' I got up and I closed the door. And I said, 'Listen, yesterday in the pit, in front of everybody, he called me a cunt and I wasn't going to say anything about it. But let me tell you I am not treating him badly and I am not doing anything wrong and I don't want to be, and I should *never* be called that.'"

Ricki was soon informed that her new home would be the British Pound pit. On one hand, it was a fantastic opportunity because she was the only Singer-Wenger person in the entire pit, which meant there was no one constantly looking over her shoulder, checking what she was doing, critiquing her, or telling her no. Then there was the flip side: being in a pit completely on your own could be treacherous.

The British Pound pit, at that time, had its own set of unwritten rules, which included the use of some questionable trading tactics. Ricki was astonished that this type of trading went on. "I felt like I was supposed to be the police—'Hey, wait! You guys aren't supposed to do that!' " she said. "I didn't realize that I was supposed to shut my mouth and just do it, too, and make the money." Others in the pit began resenting Ricki for spouting morals. Finally, a trader named Wayne took her aside and explained, "Now, listen, this is the way we do stuff in here, and if you play your cards right, we'll let you in." Ricki took Wayne's advice, and just like that, she chucked her morals. "I got back in the pit and I just started rip-roaring," she said. "But the truth was that the British Pound pit was really hellish and horrible. It was very small, only a few people, and there were these two brokers who ran the pit. One, I couldn't stand—he was nasty and misogynistic— and the other drove me crazy—he was an insane and repressed homosexual who was always screaming and throwing a fit. And the two of them hated each other, and they both hated everyone else. You'd have to do all this mind manipulation just to get a trade from them."

Finally, Ricki had had enough. She went to Singer-Wenger and said, "You need to get me out of that pit, because if you don't, I'm just not going to show up anymore!" Ricki was making Singer-Wenger nice money, although she didn't know exactly how much. She was on a salary—$30,000 a year at that point—but she knew the amount she was bringing in was far, far greater. She had clout, and her request was taken seriously; she was promptly taken out of the British Pound pit and sent to the Soybean pit at the Board of Trade.

The Soybean pit was huge, and home to a lot of the Big Old Boys. But by the sheer ebb and flow of the Commodity market, it just so happened that when Ricki got there, business was slow and the pit was virtually empty. She'd sit on the steps most of the day, daydreaming and thinking. She thought and dreamed about what she *really* wanted to be doing: making documentary films. One day she decided that she owed it to herself to follow this dream, and that now, financially, maybe she could. She pretended to be studying charts or doing crossword puzzles as she filled out her application to film school. Not long after, she was accepted and enrolled in a graduate film studies program at Columbia College in Chicago. Ricki was on her way to finally feeling happy.

And then in April 1986, Chernobyl happened—and the Soybean market, which had been unbearably dead, took off. Unlike most Locals, Ricki had sat in the pit day in, day out, even though the Market had been stagnant. Because of this, she had secured a spot for herself and had also gotten to know the brokers who *had* to be there every day. So when the Market kicked into action and all the big—but fair-weather—Locals returned,

Ricki was right in the middle of it all. And it was great! Singer-Wenger upped her salary, and by her third year, she was making $80,000, which still paled next to the amount she was bringing in, but was, in her eyes, a ton of money.

Ricki's success, however, began straining her relationship with her boyfriend, Kevin. Here she was making it trading—what *he* really wanted to be doing—and he was still clerking. But if her prestige and salary intimidated her boyfriend, it was exactly those things that impressed her father. By Ricki's third year, she was making as much money as her dad. And, for what seemed like the very first time, Ricki's father was proud of her.

"Suddenly my relationship with my father shifted," Ricki said. "His whole life he had subscribed to this: 'Work is going in at this time and staying until that time and working *hard*, and how hard you work and how many hours you spend working equals how much money you make, and you must move up, and you must kiss ass, and you must keep your mouth shut, and you must do this forever.' And suddenly all of his ideas about work were just fucking blown out of the water. In my version, you went in to work and you were crazy, and you shouted, 'Fuck you!' at people, and you did what you wanted—and then you left at two o'clock!

"The sudden respect I was getting from my father was very shocking because it wasn't expected. Oh, I realized it was about the money I was making. We went on a vacation—I took us—and I still found him a really disappointing person. Our family was a dysfunctional, fucked-up, getting-divorced family. And my father was really emotionally distant, and a perfectionist. You could never do good enough for him. If you got a 98, why didn't you get 100? If you got 100, well, you'd better get 100 next time, too! You know, it just didn't end." Finally, Ricki was pulling A-pluses in her father's eyes. Only, it really had nothing to do with her as a person—and those really weren't A-pluses he was seeing, but dollar signs.

Ricki began attending film school part-time and loved it, although there was no denying the discrepancy between her school world and her trading world. Her film school friends had no concept of what trading was, so Ricki would explain it like this: "Let's say you go by a gas station and notice the price of gas. Just do that today, right? And let's say it's $1.29. Do you think it's going to be higher or lower tomorrow? If you think it's going to be higher, you want to buy it; if it's going to go down, you want to sell it. And decide to yourself that you've done one or the other. Then tomorrow, look at the price of gas and decide what you are going to do again. Tell yourself that you lose $100 every time it goes up a penny, or down a penny, whichever position you are in. And if you could make it real, so that every time the price changed you had to give a dollar to a friend or they had to give you a dollar, I think you'll start to feel something. If you don't think you are attached to money, you'll discover that you are."

But even if her school friends got the basic concept of Futures trading, they still were *artists*—or at least art students—and they wore clothes from the Salvation Army, and braided their hair, and listened to vinyl records, and lived in the seedy yet artsy part of town where rents were cheap. But most of all, they despised the big-money culture. Ricki, to her benefit, was always the type of person who was satisfied with the bare minimum, she was used to living frugally—and the money she was making trading didn't much change that. "I saw too many people who, the minute they made some money, would suddenly run out and buy a really expensive condo, and a new car, and a boat," she told me. "I wasn't like that, I saw the opportunities to make money like a sort of harvest. It's time to harvest, and that's what you do, you sock it away. You don't spend like there's no tomorrow. And besides, I didn't want to have this beautiful condo with a chandelier, and have my film school friends be like, Oh my God! They didn't want to deal with anybody like that. So I was living in this crappy, little apartment down in Wicker Park with everybody else."

On the flip side, when the handful of traders Ricki had befriended saw where she lived and what few belongings she had, they felt sorry for her, assuming she was sticking it out on the trading floor, but not doing well. So they would end up taking care of her. One wealthy trader in particular would always say to Ricki: "You fly and I'll buy." Their relationship consisted of Ricki driving him around to swank places that were well beyond her means, but he would foot the bill, so long as she was there to accompany him. This dynamic set an odd precedent for a relationship— did he like her as a person, or was he just needy and in need of company—especially company who would revere his success and be grateful to him for opening all these gilded doors? And did Ricki like him as a person, or was she just in the relationship to Get, to Take—to dine and see movies and pop open champagne and sit front row at concerts—to Take, Take, Take?

The conflate of Ricki's two disparate worlds was near impossible, and because film school was her passion, she began to side more with that realm—only not to the degree where she considered quitting trading. She couldn't walk away from the money, yet her day job was becoming a topic of conversation she tiptoed around as if it were a source of embarrassment. She even found that it was coming awfully close to the point where she— the girl who used to steal from her employers—was starting to feel a twinge of guilt for how she earned a living. Here were her school friends, working full-time minimum-wage jobs in addition to attending class. If she could just teach them all how to trade, they could double, triple, quadruple their money by working a measly four hours a day. But that was not possible, for it all circled back to their refusal to be associated with anything that had money as its driving force.

Roles and relationships were so upside down for Ricki that in her romantic life, she broke things off with Kevin—who had finally gotten his trading badge—and became involved with a financially starved film school student. Ricki assumed the breadwinner role, and her new boyfriend, the housewife. "It was not an equal relationship," Ricki told me. "For some reason it felt safer for me to be with a man who was not as financially successful or as together as me, because I was afraid of an equal man. An equal man was going to screw me over. I needed someone below me that I could safely trust, you know? Maybe how much he needed me was how much I could trust him. He would stay at my house and get up at the crack of dawn to make me coffee and bring it to me in bed, then he'd drive me to work, and pick me up. I mean, he did everything for me. And I paid." Ricki paid for rent and groceries, and if they wanted to go out to eat, she'd treat. In fact, she'd often treat several film students because she liked to go out to dinner, but knew they weren't able to afford it. It was the juxtaposition of her relationship with the traders. They'd taught her that it was great to do something for another person—so long as you were guaranteed something out of it, too.

During baseball season, Ricki's new boyfriend worked as a beer vendor at Wrigley Field. "It would be blasphemous to people from the Floor if they knew," she said. "I mean, here they are in the box seats. They'd be like,

'You're going out with that guy? We're calling him for beer.' " Eventually, that relationship ended, and Ricki began seeing another film school student, although the dynamic was much the same—she had the control. "It was unhealthy," she said, "but in a strange way it made me able to step onto that trading floor as an equal—in a sense, I had a wife at home, too. And not only that, I mean, those men could talk all they wanted, but you know what, I got coffee in bed and a ride to work. Did your wife or girlfriend do that for you?"

It was approaching the end of Ricki's three-year contract with Singer-Wenger, and it hurt her head just thinking how much money she'd made them. Several of the other contracted traders had become so disgruntled over what they viewed as sweatshop tactics that they complained, and when that didn't work, they threw a fit, and when that didn't work, they quit. But that was where the noncompete clause kicked in, and they couldn't trade for the specified period of time until the clause expired. Ricki wanted to get mad, she wanted to quit, but she couldn't—she needed money, and she needed this job to give it to her. And besides, trading had afforded her the great opportunity to be in film school.

The way it usually worked with Singer-Wenger was that at the end of three years they'd make an offer to the trader to stay on with them, and the trader would usually say, "No, that's not good enough." So, there'd be some negotiating, and some of the traders would stay on, but most would go their own way and trade for themselves or for a firm that gave them a decent percentage of all their earnings.

Ricki was waiting, waiting, waiting for that offer. She had even rehearsed different versions of her response: "I'm sorry, but I think you omitted a numerical figure in this offer"; "I'm sorry, but before I sign I'd like to go over the records of my trading account so I can determine what percentage of my trading profits are reflected in this offer"; or "You must be out of your minds, there's no way in hell I'd ever accept this!"

Finally, it was her day. She went upstairs at the scheduled time and waited for the owners, Singer and Wenger, to welcome her into one of their offices. Only, it was the manager who came walking toward her. He motioned for her to take a seat. "Usually, we all meet together," he said, shifting uncomfortably. "Listen, Ricki, they're not going to ask you back."

Her eyes glazed over with vitriol and her hands tightened into fists. *They* were telling *her* no? She walked out of there and didn't set foot on the Floor for an entire month.

During that time, she busied herself with school. Little by little, reasons for why she might not have been given an offer popped into her mind. Many of them had to do with being a woman and not really fitting in. She didn't want to hang out with them after work and drink, or go to the bars, or go to games. She didn't show up for company get-togethers, and in their eyes that wasn't a very team-player thing to do. But what they didn't realize was that Ricki couldn't let herself be a team player, she had other commitments, other agendas, with school and her films, and in order to be good at trading she needed to nurture her film school world—it gave the trading world meaning. "Trading wasn't my life," Ricki told me, "and they knew it, but they didn't like it. It was probably very threatening—I mean, how could this girl not want to just be trading? It's just not in their way of thinking."

During this respite, Ricki got a phone call from a trader, Wayne, whom she had worked with in the British Pound pit. They'd had their rough times—Wayne was the one who'd told her she'd better wise up to the ways of the pit—but they had managed to put all that aside and become somewhat friendly. But for Wayne, there was one instance he never forgot: a friend of his who traded in another pit had come into the Pound pit with a rather large order. "I'll sell fifty!" he had yelled. And there was Ricki: "I'll buy 'em." The trade turned out to be a huge loser for Wayne's friend, but a huge winner for Ricki. Wayne had been impressed with Ricki's sense of the Market, so impressed that now he was calling her with a question: would she like to become his trading partner? He outlined his plan: he would trade in the British Pound and the Yen pits, and Ricki would trade in the Pork Belly Options pit, and they would split everything fifty-fifty—profits and losses—unless one, or both, of them surpassed a certain level, then it would switch to sixty-forty of their respective earnings. Ricki couldn't even remember her dead-on trade that had impacted Wayne; it had been made with Singer-Wenger money and had earned Singer-Wenger money, not her. But she said yes to Wayne, and the next week she returned to the Merc and stepped into the Pork Belly pit.

Wayne himself had tried to break into Pork Bellies, unsuccessfully. But he felt Ricki could do it. It was a small pit with mostly veteran traders and was open for only four hours a day. Ricki went in, and made it. "I found that I did well with the old guys," she said. "I mean, first of all, they're older, they're not as fast. I can be fast! And second of all, they've been there for years and they're bored. So if you've got a young woman there, they're just a little bit more, you know, up for that. Besides, I didn't like being in the big pit with everybody screaming and all the pushing and shoving, and I wanted to stay far away from that."

Ricki's mind-set was also different this time around. She still knew deep down that she didn't want to be there, but she also knew she wouldn't find this combination of money and freedom at any other job. She was going to adhere to two philosophies. Philosophy Number 1: she would try to be the first person in the pit every morning so she could get a spot close to a broker, and then she wouldn't leave. Others would go to breakfast, or to get coffee, or to the bathroom, but she would guard that spot from bell to bell. She knew traders would come in late and try to squeeze in, edging someone out of a spot. She also knew their "lean" tactic, where they'd just stand there and lean on you, and lean and lean, hoping that you'd get so aggravated, you'd give. But she'd get her footing and hold it because the second she faltered, that was it, someone else would be standing in her spot, and she'd end up one body removed from where she wanted to be.

Philosophy Number 2: she would avoid confrontation whenever possible. To Ricki, that meant, keep to yourself, keep quiet, and don't call any attention to yourself. "I learned to hold a lot in," Ricki said. "And when I did that, I started grinding my teeth. But I actually got a lot of pleasure out of not letting people know how much they bothered me or how much I hated it there. And I would even do weird, psychological things—like, I would actually be nice to people who were really mean to me. It was my own little game, like a way of being in control of an environment you can't control. As a result, I changed a lot as a person—but I had to if I was going to stay there, I had to adapt. It gave me a lot of bottled-up stress, though, and I'll admit that during that time I was a complete pothead. Went home and had to have it, but it probably helped me. A lot."

Ricki's two philosophies served her well. She no longer resented the Floor for trying to twist her into someone she wasn't—she was doing that all on her own. But it didn't matter because she could be herself at film school. "Let those men from the Floor think what they want, as long as

I'm going home with my piece of it," she said. "I don't need them to respect me, because I'm using them to the fullest. I was in the pit for one reason and one reason only: to make money, and I wasn't going to feel bad about it."

One day after work, Ricki was crossing the street when coming toward her—from the direction of the Options Exchange—was a large figure that looked slightly familiar. Then it dawned on her: it was her old, hoagie-chomping, hot-tub boss. Her first instinct was to turn the other way, but she was wearing her jacket, her *trader's* jacket, with "RLS, Ricki Lane Sutton," right there on a badge. No, she was not going to turn around! She sucked in her breath and walked right past him. Out of the corner of her eye she saw him turn his head to look back at her.

A few years later, she'd feel vindicated even further when she'd hear that he went bankrupt.

Ricki traded Pork Belly Options for four years. And for that entire time, she was the only woman in the pit. She typically traded small—one-lots, two-lots, an occasional ten-lot. This went along with her goal of blending into the landscape—the men would want to be big, fifty! one hundred! They'd toss her a one-lot, hardly taking notice. And Ricki, sneaky and sly Ricki, would do that all day long—a little here, a little there—and by the Closing bell, she'd have a full basket. She had acquired a gut feel for the Market and could trade on instinct, and *trust* that instinct—and, she believed, she had the men there wrapped around her finger. "They were a little bit onto me, but they liked me," she said. "I was playing my old, I'll-be-nice-to-them routine. And I was. I listened to them. Listened to their talk about some sports game—and I learned to talk game without even having seen a game. 'How about that last few minutes?' That's all you've got to say. 'Oh, the last few minutes were incredible!' I treated them well. I acted like I cared. Sometimes, I did care . . . but it was definitely for a purpose." At the end of each day, she'd go home, fix herself a leisurely lunch, and then, in a marijuana haze, she'd convince herself that she'd achieved success, and that that was all that mattered.

The end of Ricki's time in the Belly pit came about suddenly. She, like many traders, leased her seat. One day the owner of her seat called and told her seat prices had jumped and that he'd sold his seat for a nice profit—

and, oh, by the way, the new owner didn't want to lease it out. Ricki panicked and shouted, "Oh, my god, but I've got positions down there!"

"Sorry," was the extent of what he offered Ricki.

She frantically tried to lease another seat, but there were none available. She couldn't get onto the Floor and trade without a seat! Finally, she was able to secure one—for an astronomical monthly sum. It scared her how her career was so hinged on somebody else's impetuous decisions. She could have lost everything by leaving her positions riding like that. Such was the zero-sum game she was playing—for every winner, there was a loser.

But the new seat lease was killing her, so she told Wayne it was time for her to move on. "Besides," she said, "I couldn't stand to look at the Belly traders for a single day more."

She wanted to stick with agricultural commodities because those pits were open the shortest amount of hours. For someone who didn't really want to be there in the first place, and who made it a rule not to leave the pit—even for a bathroom break—short hours were key. She also preferred a small pit, with the old men. She found exactly what she was looking for in Soybean Options at the Board of Trade.

Trading pits have somewhat of a revolving door, so it was not unusual to see new faces—but it was unusual to see a woman's face. Once again, Ricki was the only woman in the pit. Whenever she caught the Who-is-this-little-girl? glance, she'd make sure to mention that she'd just had a good ride in the Pork Bellies for four years. It was easy to make the old men flinch with that. They'd scatter back to their spots and leave her alone, their own insecurities painting scenarios in their minds: "This little girl must know something . . . what if she knows more than I do?"

Again, Ricki followed Philosophy Number 1, Go in Early and Stand There All Day. She stood there when it was dead and boring and when people were doing nothing but waiting, waiting for another minute to bring them closer to that final bell when the agony would end—at least until the next morning. And she tried to follow Philosophy Number 2, Be Nice Even If They're Being Mean to You, but that was difficult, given that the Soybean brokers were anything but fair and enjoyed pitting people against each other. It was customary for brokers to divide up each order so that everyone could make a decent living. But these brokers tended to lazily give a large order, in its entirety, to the first Local they saw. And it was usually the same veteran. This method had a way of turning a pit into a war zone, where the Locals would become vicious.

The competition proved overwhelming, and Ricki began thinking of walking away from trading for good. She was almost done with school and often found herself smoking more pot and daydreaming about her next move. She wanted to go to Los Angeles and start a serious film career. But did she have enough money to make the move? And would she have enough money to tide her over if it took a while to get her career going? She'd been saving money, and if anyone knew how to hoard it was Ricki, for her father had taught her well. She now had a bank account bigger than she ever thought she'd have, but was it *enough*? And, really, what was *enough* anyway? Compared to most on the Floor, what Ricki had was paltry. And maybe it was . . . maybe she *should* be taking more, should be risking more to get more. Or maybe this talk was trading floor influenced, where everything was skewed, where people complained, complained, complained, "It was such a lousy day, I only made a thousand bucks, why even bother coming in?"

All these thoughts were running through Ricki's mind as she stood in the middle of the trading floor one day, having up and walked out of the Bean pit unable to stomach any more. Despite the roaring chaos around her, she stood there picturing Topanga Canyon in California, with its winding roads and panoramic views of the San Fernando Valley. She envisioned the little cabin she'd live in and write in, and the rocky bluff where she'd shoot scenes for her next film. She could almost smell the pine and touch the wild golden poppies. Only, she'd have all these expenses—she'd have to buy a car. And how much would rent be? And she'd have to pay for all her film equipment and hire technical people to work with her, and, and, and . . . her beautiful daydream was like a balloon with a slow leak, and the wonderful little world was starting to fizzle, becoming misshapen and limp. Suddenly, a hand was on her shoulder.

She looked up to see an unfamiliar man in a trader's jacket. "Are you all right?" he asked. How long had she been standing there with a glazed, faraway look? "What do you trade?" he asked.

"Beans," she said. "It's horrible." She couldn't help it, it was the truth.

"You ought to go over to Wheat Options," he said. "They like women in Wheat." And with that, he walked away.

Ricki hadn't even taken notice of his badge acronym, let alone his name.

Later, she'd wish she had, for this simple bit of advice from a stranger who'd felt sympathy for a woman getting the squeeze would ultimately set off a profound course of change in Ricki's life. Before she could even think about what she was doing, she found herself heading to Wheat Options. The first person she saw there was Virginia McGathey. She came right up to Ricki and held out her hand. "Hi, I'm Ginni, nice to meet you." Ricki was stunned. No one *ever* did that to a newcomer—you were supposed to be wary of anyone new, and you were supposed to try to prevent them from taking even a sliver of your piece of the pie. But here was Ginni, welcoming Ricki to what would become her new home.

The Wheat Options pit was small enough that it shouldn't have been a big deal when Ricki was sent to the last step in the back, except for the fact that she was tiny and couldn't see anybody, even on tiptoes, nor could anyone hear her. It took her about two seconds to realize the spot was worthless, and two more seconds for a young trader to shove his way over and brazenly proclaim, "You can't stand there, it's my spot." Ricki wanted to roll her eyes and say, "You're making a fuss about this terrible spot?" But instead, she put on her sweet-as-pie face. "Okay, I'll just move over, if I stand over here a little bit, then is this okay?" He'd been prepared for a battle, not meekness, and, unsure what to do, he reluctantly nodded and squeezed in. He was lucky he did, for, as the days went on, he proved to be even more clueless than his first impression, and he constantly turned to Ricki for help when he was confused about even the most basic of Options tactics, such as Puts and Calls. But Ricki would always take the time to help him. Maybe it was because Ginni set the tone for the pit and that was the kind of thing she would do.

Ricki knew she needed to work on moving forward in the pit, but every morning she'd come in and go back to her spot next to Clueless, and the day would begin with Ricki straining to see Ginni dole out trades.

One day, the guy who stood on the step in front of Ricki was late coming in. She saw him heading across the Floor—but she also had her eye on his spot. She thought, *If I just take two teeny steps forward, I'm in that spot. But he's coming, and the bell's ringing, and I have to decide.* It was one of those split-second resolutions that your body determines more than your mind. It seemed so small and insignificant—two baby steps—but she sensed that that foot-wide spot would change the scope of everything. She knew this would be one of those pivotal moments that she'd look back on, gratefully, but also with disbelief that she'd actually *done* it.

"I took the two steps forward!" Ricki recalled, "and of course, everybody's like, 'Arrgh! What are you—?!' I just ignored them. I pretended I was invisible. I just stood there and tried to be as small as I possibly could. And the trader gets there, and the thing was, everyone was always complaining anyway about how his voice was too loud, so the others were technically on his side, but they weren't really sticking up for him too much. He said to me, 'You can't stand there.' And in this pathetic little voice I say, 'I've got nowhere else to go.' There was something about that statement that just shut everyone up. *'I've got nowhere else to go.'* So he squeezed into my old spot, and there was his big, loud voice behind me, but I didn't care. From then on, I got there first thing every morning and I stood in that spot, and it was mine. And let me tell you when that place hit big with the drought, if I hadn't been in that spot . . . well, it was another couple hundred thousand, if not everything."

The drought of 1995 was a stunner, the likes of which Ricki had never seen. The days were frenzied, insane! Ricki could hardly write her trades fast enough to keep up. When the drought first hit, Ricki put on a long-term position and watched as the money compounded. She would come in every morning and note that her account would be up an additional $20,000. It was as if she had dreamed during the night that she was making money, and lo and behold, it wasn't a dream at all! Her position was relatively small—other traders were coming in every day to find themselves up $50,000, $100,000. Ricki had always been a conservative trader and had been completely satisfied making around $100,000 every year. But now to be making that in a week's time? Without really doing anything? For every emotion you'd think you'd have in a situation like that—you'd think you'd be exhilarated, right?—some unexpected feelings tended to bubble to the surface. At first, for Ricki, it was shock. But that quickly wore off, and good old Greed and Fear started to set in—the money that had initially seemed like a gift, now felt very much like *hers*, something that she had to protect and guard—she'd tasted it and now she wasn't going to lose a crumb, not one single penny of it. "That was the year that scared the shit out of me," Ricki recalled, "because all I could think about was, What if the Market moved against me? And what if it moved really fast and really big and I couldn't get out? Then, I'd be bankrupt! And then I would have spent ten fucking years of hell for not only nothing, but less than nothing! And I just wasn't going to let that happen."

The drought frenzy lasted for over three months, and by the end of that time, Ricki was numb. She had never made so much money in her life, and she felt like it was a message, like some higher power was saying, "You wanted it—here it is! Now what are you going to do with it?" Ricki had spent enough time struggling to recognize exactly how great she now had it. So how could she rationalize leaving at the highest point? How do you leave the party while it's still fun? How do you walk away from the black-jack table when all your hands have been winners? Everyone in that pit had made a killing, and no one else was leaving; they weren't seeing this showering of fortune as some prophetic sign. Ricki came to convince herself that she was being a neurotic miser.

The money cloud that hung over her began to darken her other life as well, despite the fact that things had been going wonderfully—she had completed her degree, and she'd even won a Student Academy Award for her thesis film. But her first independent film project turned into a disaster. The producer she'd hired made decisions incongruent with what Ricki wanted, most of which had to deal with the budget. Having to work closely with someone who was so inefficient with money drove Ricki crazy. By the end of the project no one was getting along, and the Chicago film community was so insular that Ricki knew this experience would haunt her for some time. She retreated from the world that was once her haven, and without that to turn to, she found it increasingly difficult to get out of bed every morning and go to the Floor.

One sweltering August day was to be her last as a trader—although she had no clue of that as she kept hitting the snooze button. Finally, she dragged herself out of bed. Her stomach was doing flip-flops. She drank a large cup of coffee; it didn't help. So she turned to the only way she knew how to console herself. She smoked some pot as she watched the sun rise. While getting high was something she did regularly, she had never, ever done it before work, and it crushed her to realize that not only did she need it to calm herself after work, but now she needed it to get herself to the Floor in the first place.

Twenty minutes later, she was standing in the pit and the Opening bell was ringing, when suddenly, everything went dark. "I could hear the voices around me," she recalled, "and I was trying to see, but it was black. I was going to ask the broker in front of me for some water, but then I felt like I was falling, and I just grabbed him and said, 'Something's really wrong.' So they called the fucking paramedics. People helped me out of the pit, and my vision came back. But they wanted to take me off the Floor in a wheelchair, and that was too embarrassing for me. I was like, 'No, no, I've *got* to walk out.' So I walked out, and the paramedics were like, 'Did you have any breakfast today?' 'No.' 'Have you used any substances?' 'Yes.' And I thought to myself, what the fuck am I doing? And they were like, 'Listen, you have two choices. Either we're going to take you to the hospital or you're going to go home. What do you want to do?' And I said, 'I'm going home.' And that was the last day that I traded. What an embarrassing fucking last day. And I'm sure there was all this gossip about why I didn't show up after that, they were probably all making fun of me.

"You can mentally push yourself so far, but when these physical things happen, you really need to pay attention. I knew I had to make a change. I knew I had to leave."

The question was, where should she go? She was serious about a film career, so she narrowed it down to New York City or Los Angeles. But she feared that if she was in New York, she would get sucked into trading, that no matter how much she coveted the artist's life, Greed was insidious. "If trading was down the street, I was going to be there," she said, "because I couldn't stand the idea of other people making that money. *I* should be there making that money too. And I knew that every day I'd think, 'Why the hell am I working for peanuts when there's money just waiting to be taken?' I knew I had to make a complete break from trading, and the only way to do that was to be nowhere near it. I didn't tell many people what I was going to do. I just got in the car and left."

By the time Ricki made it to Topanga Canyon, rumors were spreading like wildfire back on the Floor—only it was the opposite of the demeaning, mocking chatter Ricki had imagined. When she called one of the traders who had become a good friend, he said, "Ricki, tell me if this is true! I heard you made three million dollars and that's why you retired." Ricki sighed and bashfully admitted to him, "Oh, I wish I had made anywhere near that.

I wish I had made *one* million. Boy, if they really knew what an idiot I was to have left for so little. We better just keep this rumor going, because it would be too embarrassing if everyone knew the truth."

When I met Ricki in California, she had been making documentaries there for five years. She had moved from Topanga to Reseda and bought a little blue stucco house with a tiny brick wading pool in the backyard. Reseda—made infamous by a Tom Petty song, "It's a long day living in Reseda, there's a freeway running through the yard . . ."—is commonly considered the armpit of the greater L.A. area. It's as New Jersey is to New York, often the generic punch line that never fails to get a laugh—such as in the joke I heard at a comedy club the evening after I'd met Ricki: "So you come to a four-way stop at an intersection and how do you determine who goes first? The person who got there first, right? Not here in L.A. Here, it's the most beautiful person who gets to go first. So when I'm in Beverly Hills, I know I might as well just put the damn car in park, I'm gonna be at this stop sign for a while. But then I go out to Reseda, and I'm at the intersection, and I look right, and I look left, and I just cruise right on through."

When Ricki and I had first spoken on the phone, she invited me to her home to meet her, which, when I arrived there, I was glad she'd done, for it was quite meaningful to see her environment. While the traders Ricki had stood next to in the pits were living in monstrosities in the pristine North Shore suburbs, Ricki liked Reseda because it was quiet and affordable. Her house was sparsely furnished, but what was there was warm and saggy and comfortable. On her fireplace mantel were two framed pictures: one of her with her mom and younger brother, who was an engineer in San Diego; and the other of her dogs, two white miniature schnauzers.

We headed out to Ricki's backyard to talk. She loved to sit at the table on her tiny slab of concrete patio, drinking herbal tea while her dogs played at her feet, and reading books like the Dalai Lama's *Meaning of Life*. But I noticed that Ricki began clutching her lawn chair as soon as she started talking about the Floor.

"The trading floor, to me, was like a bad parent," she said, "and you keep going back—give me love! Give me love! Give me love, you motherfucker! It can still drive me crazy to know that people are there right now making all of this money! I wish I could make that kind of money now, you know? If I could just make half of that, I'd be really happy. I'd make a quarter of it and be really fucking happy right now." She shook her head in disgust. "See how my language goes as soon as I start talking about trading? Until very recently, I used to beat myself up over old trades that I should have, could have, would have . . . if only, you stupid idiot, if you had done this or that, you could have another $20,000 right now!" She sighed and leaned back in her chair. Her dogs scurried over to sniff her toes.

"Letting go of money is so difficult," she said, her voice contracted. "I mean, my God, you grow up in the household where every penny is counted. And then, you go into this world where you're trying to get the best price, the best deal, the only reason why you're there is to make money. And then I go into independent filmmaking where you've only got a certain amount of money that you have to make work for you, and money is *still* really fucking important. But money comes and it goes, and I'm trying to be more comfortable with that. But it's taken me a long, long time.

"It's difficult for me to think about those years trading," she admitted. "The Floor is like a battle zone. Without downgrading war, I did feel like being there was like war. Truthfully, I can't really stand to be in crowds anymore. I really want quiet now, above all. I almost want to say I'm not as ambitious as I used to be. But I am, only I want to work on things where the process itself is pleasurable. If it never turns out to be successful— whatever that means—it doesn't so much matter, because at the end of the day, I will have enjoyed it. And I'm constantly coming more and more to terms with what I'm willing to do to just lead the life that I want. But I did make a promise to myself after I left trading that money would not be my motivation anymore for things that I do.

"I think one of the hardest things about that place was that no one really cares if you succeed or not. Nobody's going to coddle you. 'Okay, I'll hold your hand while you just step down in here,'" she said, making her voice tiny and shaky, as if she were talking to a kindergartener. Then she whisked her hand through the air. "Forget about it! They're like, '*Don't* do it! We don't need another person in here!'" Ricki was leaning in close now—her voice filled with ire. The memories churned and registered as lines and tightness on her face. For ten years, she'd dragged herself to a place she didn't want to be. It occurred to me that a prostitute might speak the same words—"But the money was so good, how could I walk away from money like that?"

Ricki and I talked for the rest of the afternoon as she led me through the chronology of her trading career. As I listened, I wondered if I could allow her experience to stand for what might possibly have been my own, had I chosen to pursue trading. Was her burnout the most likely outcome when one tried to force an artistic brain to conform to an antithetical world? I wanted to view her story as foreboding, and I saw our time together as my way of vicariously experiencing a life that, from the outside, sounded oh-so-appealing, but, had I truly pursued it, would have likely wrecked me.

Since I was going to be in L.A. for a couple of weeks, Ricki and I made plans to hike Topanga Canyon. But when I arrived at her house a few days later for our hike, Ricki, instead, led me to the back patio. We sat and, to my surprise, she pulled out a tissue and dabbed at her eyes. Uh-oh, what had I done? I felt twinges of guilt, as if my presence had set off some sort of post-traumatic stress response—what was it about the trading floor that could affect someone's psyche on such deep levels? Ricki wasn't the only trader I'd known who'd had this reaction. A friend whom I hadn't realized had traded on the Floor a decade earlier had cried for days after she started reminiscing about her time there—she'd told me she had no idea she possessed such pent-up negative feelings. Other retired traders I'd met flat-out refused to talk about it, they didn't even want to let their minds go there. It was as if they were survivors of a bizarre experience that they could never quite reconcile with.

But Ricki tried to reassure me that she was okay. "Don't be afraid of these tears," she said. "They're sort of like tears at a wedding. You know, after we had talked, it definitely brought up a lot of stuff. It was just like, oh my God, I can't believe how much this all still affects me. That trading floor was just such a big part of my life, and it was so powerful an experience that it *does* still affect me . . . a lot. And I found myself having all these conversations, kind of with myself but as though I was talking to you—and it was really getting to me, because I felt like I couldn't get out of the negative memories, that they just kept swirling around. And I've just been wanting to get out of it for so long!"

The tears streamed down her face. I wished there was something I could do to comfort her, but I realized that having someone who would just *listen* was what Ricki really wanted.

"I tried writing about it, I thought about doing a documentary on it," she continued. "I've tried in so many ways to let it go, and it's just been impossible. Yesterday morning, once again, it was still with me. And I came and sat out here and, you know, I really started thinking about how many people were good to me there. And what I realized is that I went in there a very hurt and neglected and angry little person who was really searching for, I think, a father figure. And the truth is, every step of the way, there was someone there to help me, whether it was those men who said, 'We're going to believe in you, even though there are no women here, we're going to teach you how to trade, and we're going to put up our money for you.' Or my partner, Wayne, who had been a rival, but who said, 'I know you got fired from that company and I'm going to take my own money and I'm going to believe in you.' Or the many, many people who actually put money into my film projects for school—they did, even though they knew they'd get nothing out of it. There were a bunch of guys from the Soybean pit, and I really didn't even like a lot of them, but they would come over to my house on a Saturday and help me do these little film projects for school. They wanted to be playing golf, yet they were at my house—you have to admit that's really pretty cool. And in fact, one of my very first film projects for school was about a broker in the Bean pit, whose mother was supposedly crazy." At her recollection, her face lit up through her tears, and she clapped her hands with the hilarity of it. "The broker was this farm boy who must have weighed three hundred pounds. He stood next to me in the pit and I hated it and hated him because he was so huge and didn't know when he was invading your space. He was also really stupid, so I wanted him to be his stupid self in my film. So, there he was, over at my house, and of course, I was completely ungrateful at the time, I was just going to use him and do whatever I wanted. We went into his whole little family history about his mother being crazy, and he participated and gave me all of these family photos. He did that for me.

"So yesterday, as I was sitting here thinking, it suddenly came to me just how much I had gotten out of that place. It healed me from being this kind of woman who needed support and acceptance from men, and who needed financial help. I really got everything that I needed there. And I'm grateful for that, so, so grateful."

She took more tissues, then half laughed. "I know it doesn't make any sense, and that I'm contradicting myself, I mean, I described that place as hell, and I certainly had enemies there because that's what that place is about, it's all set up for aggression and competition. But that's what makes it so amazing that, in spite of the atmosphere, there were all these people there who were giving and supportive and caring beyond what was necessary. And it wasn't about them wanting to go out with me or having sex with me, I mean they weren't going to get *anything* from me in return.

"There are a handful of men from the Floor who are going to be my lifetime friends. I went back to Chicago for one of their weddings and everyone else showed up too. My date was a friend from film school and he didn't know anything about the trading world or that kind of life, but he was off talking to some of them, and he came back to me and said, 'Ricki, those people really admire you, they were bragging about what you were like as a trader.' That felt really, really good, you know?" She nodded with a contented satisfaction.

While Ricki's words might have made me think this was nothing more than regret for having derided people, and that she was now trying to take it all back for fear that I'd gossip when I returned to Chicago, the earnest emotion in her face made me rule out such shallow tactics—she was more real than most people would ever allow themselves to be. The Floor had shaped her, then unshaped her. She'd arrived there angry, and the Floor had allowed her to remain that angry girl—and to profit from it. It had nurtured that anger, encouraging it to thrive. But just like any craving that gets oversatisfied, you eventually stop wanting it. Her anger had gorged long past the point of fullness, and it was only then that she could realize that she didn't want it—didn't *need* it—anymore. And that's why she could now look back and see the Floor for what it had provided her: a much-needed outlet.

We hiked in near silence. Up, up, up the canyon, along the winding path to the peak. A light fog rested over the valley below, making the scenery blurry and surreal, as if it were all a movie facade. Everything that Ricki had told me made me view her as a sort of old soldier, trying to process all her flashbacks and find a place for them where they wouldn't haunt her anymore. Finally, I spoke. "What do you think allowed you to be a successful trader?" I asked.

"I would always say: I know nothing," she said. "And knowing I knew nothing was the best edge I had. If I made money, well, I just got lucky. And when I was wrong, I had the discipline to get out. And that's all it was," she said, shrugging, "admitting you're wrong and knowing when you're lucky." I smiled at her conclusion. All those years of personal torture, followed by years of trying to mend herself, all over a job she could sum up in one sentence—which included the word "luck."

"I make so little money now," she continued. "And it's really ironic because as my income has slowly gone down the drain, I've been able to let go of money. You would think that when you had a lot of money, that's when you can really let go. But, the truth is, I've only been able to realize how much I really have by kind of getting down to nothing. I realize how much one needs and how much you don't need. For so long, I felt like I hadn't gotten enough from the Floor, that I should have more, that I was *owed* more. But I think I'm at the point now where I can mentally conclude that I have gotten enough. I *see* how much I have. I feel a peacefulness in that." She sighed. "It's something I've been working for, for a long time."

At the end of the day, as we pulled up in front of her blue house, I realized I'd probably never see or talk to Ricki again. She clearly needed this door to be closed, and she wanted it to be closed on this note, where she was finally grateful, and not bitter.

"Is there anything about it all that you still miss?" I asked as she turned off the ignition.

She shrugged helplessly, then answered as a recovered addict would, still idealizing the very thing that had nearly caused self-destruction. "Oh," she sighed, "just the money." She stared out the window. "I'd take that money."

FOURTEEN

Average Up/Average Down

This is a snowballing tactic where you add to your position even though it's going against you. Let's say you think the Market is going to go up. You buy a contract at 10. The market drops to 8. You are convinced it will eventually go up, and if you liked it at 10, you like it even better at 8, so you buy some more. The Market drops to 7 and, still a believer, you buy more. The flip of this is when you think the Market's going to go down, and you buy it all the way up. This is a risky practice, one that can have big payout if it's successful, but this type of trading can also get you into a vise and squeeze you. Usually, the term Averaging Up or Down makes its way onto traders' Top Ten lists of Don'ts.

On a Monday morning, in a surprise move, Bev Gelman walked off the Floor and said she wasn't coming back. She promptly flew to a house in the Hamptons that she had rented for around $1,000 a day.

She'd been grumbling about work for some time, but no one had expected her to actually up and quit. I had always found it surprising that she hadn't retired years ago. And yet, the suddenness of her departure sent the Merc reeling. The Eurodollar volume dropped so drastically that the Merc began offering monetary incentives to Eurodollar traders to beef up the number of contracts they traded each day. The Merc also drew up plans to enlarge the pit to include twenty-five new spots in an effort to make up for the loss of one woman—one $100 Billion Woman.

Bev's spontaneous retirement reverberated not only across the Floor, but across the country, all the way to Wall Street, where brokerage houses, hedge funds, and international trading firms, which had revered her and relied on her, mourned the loss and speculated as to why she quit. One unfounded rumor was that she'd had some recent seven-figure losing days—although when your yearly earnings were in the double-digit millions, it wasn't too unexpected, nor too difficult, to digest losses of that size. Others said she was tired of the out-trades she had to consistently eat, and that when she came in on Monday morning and saw an $80,000 error on her account, she threw up her hands in frustration and walked off the

Floor. Another version was that this was all premeditated—she came in, made a couple of trades, and then slipped out, without having previously told anyone this was to be her final day.

And then I heard a theory that initially seemed the most far-fetched to me: that her departure was for personal reasons. Bev's boyfriend, who was her protégé in the pit, had recently ended their relationship, and she found it increasingly more difficult to stand next to him and try to work with him day after day.

How could anyone buy *this* explanation, I wondered. I mean how could a powerhouse like Bev, who single-handedly became one of the top traders the Merc had ever known, be influenced to walk away because of matters of the heart? And yet, I kept hearing this as the "real" reason—from Chicago to Manhattan. Wall Street hedge-fund managers believed this to be her motive; so did Harvard MBAs from Goldman Sachs, as well as numerous Merc traders, many of whom were in Bev's circle of friends.

Perhaps it was true, perhaps loss of love was the major factor for her retirement, and maybe I'd been jaded by watching her command a pit full of raging, hulking men. It was a rare and potent and conflicting notion, and maybe my unwillingness to believe that her reason could be that simple, that visceral, that *vulnerable* said something about how the Floor had changed me.

And with that I realized that despite Bev's power, despite her money, her language, her reputation, despite all these domineering and material forces that had kept her in the pit, it just might be that in the end, the fragile human side had won.

$ $ $

About a dozen clerks and a few traders from the Merc were living it up at a new hot-spot bar that happened to be on the ground floor of my apartment building. I was there, by coincidence, for a drink with Tom, Tara, and a couple of other friends.

It was one of the first warm evenings in what had seemed like a never-ending winter in Chicago, and with the patio doors wide open, the trendy bar had a South Miami Beach feel. The Merc table only added to this scene—with young guys with bulging muscles and charming smiles and spiky-flip, gelled-up haircuts. They all wore silky shirts, collars opened to reveal single gold chains around their necks. A few female clerks were there too—all young, thin, bleached blond, and in tight clothes. I spotted Natalie, the recent clerk turned trader. Spotting her was not difficult, for she was done up like 1980s Madonna—hot pants and a strapless top that she kept absentmindedly hiking up, a chunky metallic belt at her hips, and slicked-back hair that was normally chin length, but had been created into a full, cascading ponytail of fake-hair extensions that draped to her mid-back.

"She's still in the pit?" Tom asked incredulously. "If she was trading on her own, she'd last two weeks, but since she's screwing somebody big, I give her six months."

Tara rolled her eyes. "Of course, Tom's philosophy: every woman on the Floor must be screwing somebody." I watched Natalie as she slinked, cat-like, through the group.

My friends and I had yet to order anything; we'd been trying to flag down a server, but no one would even look in our direction. While over at the Merc table, they had their own private champagne and vodka bar, with their own personal cocktail waitress pouring and mixing drinks just for them. After twenty minutes of waiting, Tara and Tom decided they'd had enough, and headed out.

One of the clerks happened to look my way with a spark of recognition. His name was Kyle, and from the couple of times we'd chatted on the Floor, I'd found him disarming and charmingly smooth all at the same time. He invited me to their table and, after I pulled up a chair, gave me the lowdown of the evening: "It's the baby of the group's birthday, that guy right over there, Benji, he's twenty-one tonight."

"Twenty-one, huh?" I said.

"You say that like you're old or something," Kyle said, then told me I looked all of twenty-three. Kyle, along with most of the other clerks here, was twenty-four. They had all grown up within several blocks from one another in Bridgeport, a blue-collar Italian neighborhood on the outskirts of the city. "We used to run around on the playground together," Kyle said. "Now our playground is the trading floor. See Billy over there?" He pointed out yet another clean-cut, dark-haired, nice-looking guy who wore a light blue silk sweater that just happened to cling perfectly to every muscle in his chiseled chest. "Billy was the first one of the group to come to the Merc. He started as a clerk, now he's a trader, and doing really well," Kyle said. "He just turned twenty-six."

"Do you have aspirations to trade?" I asked him, and he responded with an enthusiastic yes. "But not anytime soon," he assured me. "I'm having too much fun clerking, I mean, all my friends are there, we all grew up together and now we work together and party together and live near each other in Melrose Park. You know Melrose Park?" I shook my head. "It's like a ten-minute drive from here," he said. "It's kind of greasy, but I like it. You know, I'll trade eventually, but I'm not rushing into it. Besides, I'm doing well for myself."

I wondered exactly what he meant by "well," since a trade-check clerk typically earned minimum wage. His point was well emphasized, however, by the way all the clerks were dressed to the nines and tossing around premium vodka drinks from their private bar; and, just to provide a point of contrast, my other friends who'd remained at our table—two attractive women, both doctors, no less—had to wait forty-five minutes before a server even appeared, only to inform them that the bar was backed up and it would still be a while before they could get a drink.

"The secret to success on the Floor is to swallow your pride," Kyle told me. "My main guy is one of the biggest traders at the Merc. Luckily, I work for nice guys. But still, you've got to eat a lot of shit. You take it. You swallow it. You accept the blame. And you'll do well."

"Do you think it's as easy for a woman?" I asked.

"I don't want to sound like a chauvinist, but if I had a girlfriend I wouldn't want her to work there. Women have to deal with a ton—comments, looks, come-ons. And I'd be lying if I said that a lot of the women down there didn't have things going on on the side. If you asked the women, most would deny it, but trust me, there's a lot of that going on." His eyes subconsciously darted to Natalie. "I know for a fact," he added.

Kyle introduced me to Joe, another childhood-buddy-turned-clerk. Joe stood out because he was lanky and had a mop of curly hair. He wore thick glasses and, based on looks alone, he'd seem to be more comfortable in a computer lab than a trendy bar. He quickly proved me wrong, however, by joining in a round of shots—only, he took his directly from the bottle.

"It's okay," he told me, after chugging what seemed like a third of the bottle. "I live just a couple of blocks away, on Oak. I can just stumble home. I usually do." I knew Oak; it was a pricey street in the heart of the Magnificent Mile. "I own a condo," he said, then gave me a boyish, hopeful grin. "I have a hot tub."

"Joe, do you do something else besides clerk?" I asked.

His hopeful grin turned to a devious one. "Yes and no. . . . See, my uncle is a big trader on the Floor, and I help him out. We have sort of an arrangement with trade checking. So, anyway, about the hot tub . . ." I was saved by another clerk, who rushed over. "You're going to Vegas, right, Joe?" he asked.

"Hell, yeah!"

"Kyle here can't go. He's got a wedding!"

"Screw the wedding, Kyle, it's Vegas!"

"I can't screw the wedding, I'm fucking walking down the aisle in the wedding!"

"Billy, are you going to Vegas with us?" Billy, the lone trader among the group, contemplated for a second. "Yeah, I'm in, but forget the weekend. I'm going Friday through Thursday, man!"

Joe turned to me. "Cari, you comin' to Vegas?"

The group was polishing off the vodka, and when more arrived they showered their cocktail waitress with a round of applause. They were as friendly as they were flirty—and it was all with an air of good fun. That's what life was about for them: let's have fun! It was almost this reverberating buzz—*I'm making cash, I'm young, and I'm living it up!* It was refreshing in a way to be around people who had grown up in working-class, gritty, city outskirts, and who were thrilled with the idea that they now were making the money and enjoying the money, and enjoying it with the kids from the old neighborhood. They were throwing it around, exactly like they'd dreamed they'd do when they swore they'd never slave the way their fathers did, and that they'd provide all the things their mothers had stopped wanting long ago because what was the point of wanting something you knew you'd never get. And now they were doing it. They were 22, 24, 26, and they were doing it. God bless the Merc!

From what I'd seen and learned, I knew it would only be another couple of years or so before all that changed. Before making money and spending it got old. Before what was once enough money was suddenly no longer enough—not because you'd spent it, but because if you had made crazy money last year, then you should be making double-crazy money this year, and if that wasn't the case, if the money was not growing exponentially, then there was something wrong. And hey, it wasn't exactly pleasant to learn that the guy who stood next to you in the pit was making more money than you—and so was that guy there, and that guy over there, and you knew you were a better trader than that jerk over there, but dammit, you heard he was making more than you too. You should be making more, you deserved to be making more, you WILL make more, you promised yourself. No matter that you were making nearly seven figures a year. You were 29, for goodness sake, you should have broken the million mark already. Half these other bozos in the pit had.

Maybe there was something wrong with you. Were you not on the ball enough? Not quick enough, not astute enough? You would have to change this. Who cared if that meant that you'd be so exhausted that when you weren't on the Floor all you'd want to do was sleep for days? Who cared that when you did finally sleep you'd have terrible dreams that the Market kept going against you no matter what? Who cared that all of your personal relationships would suffer because you were so tense and grouchy all of the time? None of that mattered because you absolutely had to prove yourself. It didn't matter that, materially, you already owned just about everything you could want. No, you needed to make more to prove you weren't a loser. You'd do it. You had to.

It also didn't matter that it wasn't fun anymore.

In this world, there was always someone who was better than you, faster than you, richer than you. And even if you *were* pretty damn good, fast, and rich, well, there were plenty of examples—most of whom could be found tossing back shots at the Club bar—of how easy it was for all of that to just disappear.

$ $ $

It was Valentine's Day, and since neither John nor I had a date, we decided to go to dinner. Just after the close of the Market, John left me a message: "I got killed today and I still have a position on. Probably have to cancel for tonight." Click. I called him later on his cell phone. He was still at the Merc. "How are you?" I asked.

"Surviving," he said. "I'm short the Nasdaq and long the S&Ps, and I'm having trouble getting out of this spread. I'll try to make it over in an hour." Two hours later he called. "I can't get out. There's no volume, no liquidity." He was all alone, staring at a screen of lifeless numbers and waiting, waiting, for them to move. But they were not moving. It was Valentine's Day and everyone was having candlelit dinners, not sitting in front of their Globex machines and trading after-hours Futures. It was just John, waiting out his own anachronistic version of the holiday, more akin to the St. Valentine's Day Massacre. Just him and a listless market that wouldn't give anything up.

At 7:30, I called to check on him. He'd finally left the Merc. He was able to get out of some of his position, but was letting the rest ride. He was sitting down to eat his Valentine's dinner—a Big Mac and fries.

A couple of days later, John called me from home. His voice was scratchy and stuffed up. "I'm sick," he said. "I've been getting no sleep because I was all stressed out about that huge position. I could have made a lot of fuckin' money if I had held it till today, but, no, I got out yesterday. I just couldn't take it anymore." His voice trailed off, and I could hear the Market update from the Bloomberg channel in the background.

"You put too much stress on yourself," I said.

As I could have predicted, he brushed it off. "It only happens every three or four months or so." Every three or four months was, in my mind, too frequent to be playing chicken with a bulldozing market. Bodily stress was a huge risk factor of trading, and the main reason why there weren't too many traders in the pits who were over forty. At the New York Stock Exchange, paramedics and defibrillators were immediately on hand, and the financial canyon there had been dubbed "Heart Attack Alley." Some of the biggest charitable donations to the nearby NYU hospital were from the Exchange, J. P. Morgan, and other large trading firms. Trading also boasted occupational hazards of throat polyps, hearing loss, back problems, high blood pressure, and ulcers. One Merc chairman had a bubble-gum machine in his office that dispensed Tums.

Oh, but these Peter Pans believed it was all worth it. And somehow, the ones like John who managed to last on the Floor seemed to average out pretty well—even with fluke situations, like the time John had an error in the pit that could have been disastrous, but ended up fortuitous. He had put on one side of a trade—bought a hundred contracts—only, unbeknownst to him, the trade was somehow registered as if he had made two simultaneous, identical trades. When the price was right, he'd sold his hundred contracts and took a nice profit. But it wasn't until after the Close, when he went to review his account at his clearing firm, that he saw the erroneous trade. It was still riding and, to his disbelief, was a million-dollar winner. But John, in an upstanding act, told his clearing firm, "That trade is not mine."

They responded: "No one else is claiming it. You own it." So John waited to see if anyone would lay claim. He checked in the next day. Nothing. The trade had dropped some in value, but was still a huge winner. He waited some more, and when no one had claimed ownership by the third day, he raced to the Floor and got out with a $650,000 profit. He then offered to split the earnings with the broker whom he'd originally traded with, which was a remarkable thing to do and something that most people on the Floor wouldn't even have considered. The broker gladly accepted. (Would the broker have been so eager if the trade John had been asking to split was a loser?) Despite the money John took home, he still kicked himself that he'd acted so darn honestly and hadn't just taken the trade when it was worth a million.

Errors like this, to me, seemed nothing short of winning the lottery. Several years ago, another trader had a colossal error—he didn't realize his hands were facing the wrong way and he sold instead of bought. And the order was huge, a thousand contracts! He went before the arbitration committee and they ruled that the unintended trade was his responsibility. As only luck would have it, the Market broke, and his error turned into a winner. The unintended trade had been one side of a spread, and the day he decided to leg the other side, he brought his entire family down to the Floor. They watched him shoot his hands into the air and shout to buy a thousand contracts to leg the spread. He made a million dollars before their very eyes.

At Alice's table today the topic was job satisfaction. "You know, I heard somewhere that the highest job satisfaction was among firemen," Alice said. "At first I found that hard to believe, but when you really think about it, a fireman can crawl into bed every night thinking, I fought a fire today—and we all universally agree that fighting fires is a very honorable, noble thing. Look at policemen, they have to spend a lot of their time on mundane things like writing parking tickets. Rarely is there a mundane fire. Doctors, they have so much else to deal with, HMOs and malpractice cases, and they see a lot of people who don't get better or don't heed their advice, and that's not very satisfying. With trading, there's not a lot to feel satisfied about except the money. But those firefighters, with all the risk, they are the happiest."

Career goals were an odd thing—what compelled someone to devote his or her life to certain fields was often admirable, perplexing, and sometimes curious. Trading, out of all jobs, quite likely offered the most immediate gratification. You could put on a trade and within seconds, see the result. And at the end of every day, you had a rating of your performance. If it was bad, oh well, tomorrow would be a brand-new chance to start over—you didn't have to try to piece together fragments from the day before; you didn't have to bullet-point your new, improved plan of action; you didn't have to apologize or defend yourself to a boss; you didn't have to swallow your pride, risk demotion, or fear for your bonus. No, if you were an independent trader, you got right back in there and you traded.

And when that bell rang, you were done, and it was still the middle of the day, you had no work to take home and no meetings to attend and no corporate dinner that you had to suffer through. You were free. Your bank account was your accomplishment. And what an accomplishment it could be! Only, trading was a one-dimensional job. Money was put ahead of creative, intellectual, or emotional satisfaction. Here, there was a direct line between you and money; while in most every other job that line veered first to some other point—the people your job enabled you to help, the service you provided, the task you completed, the item you manufactured—something in addition to the paycheck. It was this added dimension about which a person could feel a sense of achievement, a sense of worthiness, a sense of satisfaction. True, in most jobs, the paycheck still motivated you, but it wasn't solely about the paycheck, there was an incentive separate from that—it was first about doing your job, doing it well, reaping praise, garnering respect, and *then* it was about the money. This was why, I believed, it was possible to find people in low-paying jobs who were extremely happy—they simply loved what they did. I'd heard only one trader, Trish, who'd been trading Bond Options for eighteen years, express that she'd continue trading regardless of the money. "I am addicted to trading," she'd told me. "If I knew I would never make over thirty grand a year for the rest of my life, I would still trade." But for most traders, there was no love unless there was money. Alice said that people like her and John *needed* to make money, they needed it to make themselves feel good. It was all wrapped into their self-esteem. I asked Alice what she thought of the adage: It is not money that's the root of all evil, but the love of money. Her reply, in true Ayn Rand fashion, was that she didn't think money, or the want of money, or having money, or wanting to have more money, or doing something just for the money, was bad at all—and certainly nothing close to evil.

One thing was for sure, and I had to see it to fully believe it: Money could vanquish everything else—even the fact that the President of the United States was standing next to you. It was a momentous scene at the Merc the day that George W. Bush visited. Security was ubiquitous, from snipers on the roof; to divers in the Chicago River, which flowed alongside the Merc; to Secret Service agents lurking around every corner. My bag was searched, and men in crisp, dark suits, wearing the telltale clear spiral wire around their ears, gave the nod that allowed me to pass.

On the Floor, television crews were constructing huge scaffolds to hold strategically placed stage lights. Cameramen inched along the rails, doing nothing short of tight-rope balancing acts to get the lighting just perfect. The pit was growling, although directly above it, in the glass-enclosed viewing gallery (shut off from the public today), I watched the serene scene of the president, surrounded by suited men, emerging from a private room.

"Hey, Al," a trader next to me called out. "I thought you were having lunch with the president?" "No," Al shouted back, "I'm just paying for the president's lunch."

As soon as Bush stepped onto the Floor, a roar erupted. Forget the normal pushing-and-shoving match to get by, now, with Bush's entourage, it was a mob, which moved in a swelled mass, seeping toward the S&P pit. Bush entered the pit, and something miraculous happened. "Are there guys still trading?" a trader near me asked. "Not a two," another said, They both nodded with impressed disbelief. It was true, trading had, amazingly, ceased—for five entire seconds.

And then, the arms shot back up and the shouting resumed: "Buy five!" "Sell two!" "Buy ten!" From behind me a trader quipped, "That sure didn't take long." I knew that the lack of interest—or perhaps you could call it lack of respect—wasn't meant to be some sort of political statement. The Floor historically has had a Republican slant, and I rarely heard naysayers. As the president weaved toward the Meats, clerks and traders held out trading cards for him to sign. At the Cattle pit, a stage and podium had been constructed, since trading there was over for the day. Bush took the stand. "A cash cow!" he announced with his trademark throaty chuckle. Apparently, the action of the Floor had significantly awed him. "I thought I had seen just about everything in life," he said, "until I came here."

All the while he spoke, the pits remained half full. Traders were working as if it was a normal business day and certainly not as if the President was in the same room. The traders yelled and screamed at each other, and half of the Globex traders were still at their terminals, eyes glued to the screen, fingers hitting buy and sell and sell and buy. Money was at stake, no matter who was in the next pit over. I'd heard numerous stories of people so determined not to leave the pit that they had wet their pants—and worse. It was money, money, money, trade, trade, trade, the Market wouldn't wait and the Market didn't care.

The next day, things at the Merc were back to normal. At the regular security check, I sent my bag through the X ray. The security guard looked troubled. "Did you hear them?" she asked, motioning to two traders waiting for the elevator. "It's f—— this and f—— that. Disgusting. Absolutely disgusting." I hadn't even noticed. I'd actually come to tune it out—or worse, had become accustomed to this level of profanity. On the Floor, certain words were not relegated to specific emphasis, they were simply common adjectives. Traders played a game of catch with the worst of words, tossing them around, regardless of the content of the conversation. And, like an accent rubbed off, I was finding a carelessness in my own language. Even in my head, the words that popped into my mind were far more caustic than before I'd come to the Floor. My reaction to a stubbed toe was now also my reaction to something far less painful, such as a broken pencil lead, or spilled water, or a missed green light.

I headed onto the Floor. Just as I no longer noticed the foul language, I also no longer noticed many other aspects of the Floor that used to terrify me—the people running at me from every angle, the mass of trash, the winding staircases, the flying trading cards that often dinged me in the head. I no longer felt intimidated by the Floor. Instead, I felt an odd sense of power—I was still just a lowly clerk, but I'd come to realize that being a woman far overrode the yellow jacket. I could distract. I could attract. I could get attention. I still had the occasional daydream of just walking into the pit and making some trades, working it with everything I had before anyone could figure out that I didn't really know—tradingwise, that is— what I was doing. But this attention from men was deceiving. After a while, it no longer seemed flattering at all, but rather, an odd game where the goal was for the man to maintain the power by steadily breaking down a woman, making her feel as if she were there to look at, praising her for all the wrong things, and encouraging all the wrong behavior. As much as the attention was an initial boost, it could begin to make you feel cheap—only, it often happened with the subtlety of a subliminal message. A woman on the Floor needed to be immensely tuned into reality not to become trapped by those dull, yet frequent, signals that gnawed away, gnawed away, gnawed away at her sense of self.

Recently, I ran into a group of traders at a bar and they invited me to hang out at their table. I was having fun until they had to go and do something stupid: they offered me $100 to lift up my shirt. I thought they were joking, and I joked right along with them, saying that was far from enough. They told me to name my price.

Was this behavior a man's way of reminding everyone who was really boss, who really deserved the respect? I met a woman clerk on the Floor who'd been the recipient of a large birthday gift from the brokers for whom she worked. They all pitched in and paid for breast augmentation surgery for her. Was this generous? Or was this degrading? Should she be happy? Or disgusted? Perhaps all of the above, which confused a young, or needy, or eager-to-please, or insecure woman all the more. But in the end, it was still a woman's personal choice as to how much she wanted to feed into it all. It was the woman herself who would decide to take that money and actually go get implants.

"The Floor magnifies things inside you," Denise Hubbard warned me. "If you're greedy, it will magnify your greed. If you're timid, it will make you more timid, if you're a loudmouth it will make you louder. I always tended to be very athletic, so I think it pushed me there—I was in the gym three hours a day. Being on the Floor is such an unhealthy, artificial environment, and I needed to do all that to cleanse myself of it. I stopped eating meat, I began taking a ton of vitamins. A lot of people, though, if they have a tendency to drink too much or to do drugs, they'll be pushed in that direction. The Floor brings out the best and the worst in you." She chuckled bitterly. "It pushes you to either become a vegetarian or an alcoholic. And there's nothing in between. It will demoralize you and make you feel like you can't do anything, or it will make you feel like, if I can do *this*, I can do anything I set my mind to."

For the record, no, I did not lift up my shirt. I walked out of the bar. I would never have done it, although, I must admit, during the cab ride home, my mind did wander to the new DVD player I had been wanting, the one I could have afforded if I had just let them have a quick glimpse of me in my bra.

$ $ $

A clerk on the Floor was getting reprimanded, which was not an unusual sight, only this time, the Nasdaq broker was castigating the clerk so outrageously that I, along with everyone else in the vicinity, couldn't help but stare.

"Did you write this?" the broker shrieked, waving a trading card in the clerk's face. "Are you an f——in' idiot? Are you?" The clerk was about as clean-cut as a guy could be, baby-faced, with brown hair neatly combed and conservatively parted at the side. He silently hung his head. I'd seen plenty of other clerks get yelled at, but not with this much intensity; and usually the clerk would try to deflect the blame, saying it *had* to be someone else's fault, or the clerk would assume an eye-rolling, pouty attitude and spout a string of obscenities the second the broker walked away. In this case, however, the clerk stood there and respectfully took it, all the while looking as if he might cry. I couldn't stand the sight of it, whatever he'd done, it was obviously a mistake, and couldn't the broker have handled this by pulling the clerk aside, allowing him at least to maintain some dignity in front of his peers. It occurred to me that I could just step in, and no one was here to stop me from doing just that. And yet, my feet wouldn't budge. It reminded me of when I was pledging a sorority and was constantly hazed by the sisters. Once, another pledge got caught in the seemingly innocent act of eating a leftover piece of pizza at the sorority house. The sisters seized on the moment with brutal force, screaming at the pledge in front of us all and calling her the most hurtful word one could call a college freshman girl: fat. The sisters each took turns pointing out various sections of the pledge's body and detailing the fat. The pledge had hung her head in the same way the clerk was now, and started to cry. I had wanted to step in then, and I remember watching it all and envisioning what I'd say and do. But instead, I stood frozen—just as I now did, watching and cringing like everyone else.

After the broker finally finished his tirade and huffed away, a Market reporter stepped over to console the clerk with a pat on his back. From the clerk's mannerisms, he seemed an all-around, polite, gentle kid. Although distraught, he tried to collect himself and get back to work.

The scene bothered me for the rest of the day. Had I witnessed a pivotal moment in that clerk's life? I couldn't help but imagine him in five years when he was a trader and *he* was the one who was screaming obscenities, having had it drilled into him that it was okay to act this way, having been put down so many times that it gradually transformed him into someone who wanted to give it right back to some other undeserving, helpless clerk. It was the vicious cycle of hazing, one monster bred another, and everyone did it—because they could. Almost immediately after my college hazing experience had ended and I'd been initiated, I dropped out of the sorority. The new pledges were coming in and we were expected to act as cruelly to them as we had been treated. We were told to take out our aggression from the months of hazing on these helpless new girls. Others in my pledge class relished the thought. I didn't want any part of it.

"The power gets to you," Tom told me when I called him from the Floor to check in. "After I became a trader, there was one time I pushed a clerk halfway across the Floor. He'd always been a jerk to me, and he was resentful that I was this college kid who came in and clerked one summer and then became a trader. One day he gave me a little shove, and I just launched him!" Tom let out a wicked chuckle.

In this world, the selfish, impulsive, temper-tantrum side of one's personality was nourished—if you met enough people who readily acted on their tyrant tendencies, you would soon start to think it normal, acceptable behavior. For the rest of the day, I felt as out of place as I had the first time I'd stepped onto the Floor by myself. The normal obstacle course of elbows and shoulders seemed sharper and pointier. And all the bodies and flying trading cards and mass of debris seemed to be firing directly at me. I felt claustrophobic, even though there was 70,000 square feet around me. By the time the Closing bell rang, I was spacey and frazzled. In a haze, I rode up the escalator to the clerks' floor and mindlessly followed the crowd— which, being all male, headed straight into the men's bathroom. The security guards came running after me, shaking me from my daze with their shouts, "Ma'am! Ma'am! You can't go in there!"

Red-faced, I checked my jacket and headed out. Just off the escalator in the lobby was the antithesis of the trading floor: women were stationed at a conference table with cans and posters, collecting for the charity of the week. Traders who, just a few moments earlier, had been ready to strangle someone over a trade were now sliding bills into the collection-box slot. They didn't accept the brochures or cards that accompanied a donation— it was all just superfluous paper to them. One woman at the table declared, "These kids are something." Once, I had overheard a Red Cross volunteer at a mall declare that the best place to collect was from the Exchange on a Friday. "They were shoving $20 bills into the can," she had exclaimed. "I even got a $100 bill! I guess the Market was up that day." So here it was, Friday afternoon, and it really didn't matter if the Market was up or down, it mattered if you had called it right—and, apparently, many traders had. A trader in a white jacket with the badge CUJO snatched the collection can. "Come on, you big spenders!" he shouted, cajoling everyone as they stepped off the escalator. "Put your money where your mouth is!" Another trader folded a bill and put it in the can. "That's what you're giving? A buck, Tommy?" Cujo scolded. "Now we all know you're cheap!" The charity women were in awe as Cujo shoved the canister in others' faces. It was his little Friday afternoon shtick. He was loud and raucous and the others joined in. "Hey, Cujo, you going to do a little song and dance?"

I leaned against the wall and watched the scene for a few minutes. It was then I realized another odd juxtaposition: across from the charity table was the board where the disciplinary actions were posted. Traders often read the listings as a form of entertainment: someone was fined for "using undue force while entering/exiting the pit"; another was written up for exhibiting "unbusinesslike behavior"; and a trader was fined as well as suspended for "fraudulent trading." In other words, some guy started a fist-fight, another spit on someone, and someone else got caught fixing trades.

One veteran broker, Bill, whom I'd met at Alice's table, had summed up the Merc this way: "I've been on the disciplinary committee and have seen the worst, and I've been on the charity side and seen the best." The extremes were about as far apart as you could get, but, as with most things in our culture, it seemed that the positive side tended to be a lot less visible than the negative—or at least a lot less salacious. The headlines about prearranged trades, misreported profit figures, and customer violations far overshadowed those about the Merc boosting their self-policing efforts, expanding their investigative staff, and increasing the number of fines. For all the misdoings, there were likely as many—albeit unnoticed— benevolent acts. Many traders' names dotted the city as major benefactors of hospitals, museums, and schools. Regarding this, Alice's mother had come to a dependable conclusion: "Traders come in two varieties: Princes and Pricks."

$ $ $

I was out for coffee with two friends of mine, Will and James, who knew each other from when they'd traded at the Board of Trade, long before I'd met them. While James was waiting in line, Will let out an intentional yelp. James, as if it were a conditioned response, jumped, then turned to give Will a dirty look.

Will was bent over, laughing. "Ten years later and he still leaps," he said, slapping his knee. James, I learned, couldn't help it. His response dated back to when they used to trade together in the pit —Will would always yelp whenever he took money from James. And James still flinched on cue.

Both of them had left the Floor several years ago. James had started a manufacturing business, but Will ended up in a string of random jobs and was currently unemployed. He was reluctantly considering going back into trading. "I used to make good money, doctor money, with an unfinished college education, and working only four hours a day," he told me, then sighed. "But I just couldn't take the stress of trading anymore. Now I'm thinking of applying for a clerk job."

"It's been rough for him," James confided to me later. "What do you have to put on your résumé after you leave the Floor? There aren't too many other jobs that you qualify for just because you were a trader. The skills are very specific." It was true that trading was a trade, as unstable as it was narrow. History had exemplified this, for the New York Public Library experienced its busiest time ever—where there was standing room only and people were frantically researching—in the winter of 1929, immediately following the Great Crash.

Traders tended to describe those who left the business as people who "*got out*." Like they escaped. And, interestingly, every woman I'd met who had been an astute trader but who'd gotten out of the business gave the same reason for why she left: it was because of the bullshit. They all used that identical phrase: *the bullshit*—all the bullshit of the Floor, the bullshit in the pits. I had never really understood what they meant until my second year at the Merc. I had taken some time off, and when I returned and stepped onto the Floor, it hit me just as harshly as the locker-room, dirty-sock, musty fraternity-house smell. The majority of people in this cavern of a place hated each other, or feared each other, or were jealous or vengeful, or disgusted with each other. Those who were friends were so outside of the Exchange—inside, business was business, money was money, and it didn't really matter that this one was the best man in that one's wedding, not when it came down to a trade. There was little if no trust there; there was little loyalty; there was extreme paranoia; there was insane, intense competition; and there was the notion that if you were having a bad day, then everyone else around you should be having a bad day, too. But in a zero-sum game, there was always a plethora of others wielding the salt for your gashes.

It used to be that the Floor left me awestruck, but now, as I stood there taking it all in, the feeling of exhilaration that I once had was replaced with a queasiness. I felt as if the Floor was rigged with volts of negative energy, frustration, and agony that zipped across the room like an electrical storm. All these Masters of the Universe, all the bravado and hierarchy and insecurities and cliques; the gossip, rumors, and indiscretions; the disingenuousness, self-centeredness, and backstabbing; the egos, rites of passage, and hazing; and the whirlwind of ups and downs and downs and ups, cash and debits and debits and cash. It was then that I discovered what every trader knows, even if solely on a subconscious level: there's but a subtle difference between attraction and repulsion.

Traders like Bev—as well as many others—could have walked away years ago, monetarily set for life. Why did they stay? Why did they choose to do this every day when they clearly had achieved the pinnacle of success?

In an old psychology textbook from college—unopened since then—I stumbled upon the closest thing to an answer. It was a description of a laboratory rat study: two cages filled with rats were rigged with a sort of "magic button," which the rats could push at will. In Cage One, the magic button would produce a treat every time it was pushed. In Cage Two, however, the button would randomly produce either a treat or an electric shock. Opposite from what one might think, scientists discovered that the rats in Cage Two pushed the button with far more frequency than those in Cage One. The results were bizarre from an intellectual standpoint, and yet they aptly captured the essence of animal behavior: intermittent reinforcement was—for whatever reason—addictive. Translate that to human terms: it was all about the thrill of risk. It applied perfectly to the microcosm of the trading floor—triumphant days, abysmal days, and everyone kept coming back for more.

I'd come to believe there was no group more fun to be around than a group of successful traders just off a good day. They welcomed you into their world, where you could have whatever it was your heart desired and where the night was always young, and there was nothing more to think about until tomorrow—except for living it up. When the sun shone, it was beautiful and warm. It was easy to get pulled along for the ride—and just as easy to get pulled down when the ride was over. When the shadow was cast, it was a cold, dank, lonely place. William Eckhardt, a founder of the Turtles, summed it up this way: "Addictiveness is the reason why so many players who make fortunes leave the game broke."

Thanks to good old intermittent reinforcement we are no better than the lab rats—we stick around because when it's good, it's really good, and we think that just might make up for, well . . . maybe equal out, well . . . maybe make us forget all the bad.

It had been nearly two years that I'd been on the Floor. And I was tired of the bullshit.

Tom and I decided on a nearby date that would be my official last day at the Merc. When that date arrived, instead of heading to the Floor, I opted for my old haven, the viewing room. In the elevator on the ride up, a clerk behind me was lamenting, "How good does it look on a résumé that I get my boss popcorn?"

At the viewing-room window I stood next to two men in suits. From their conversation I gathered that one had been a clerk years ago for a large S&P trader. "There he is," he said, pointing to the pit. "See the big, fat, bald guy in the white jacket? He's staring straight at us. He can't see in here, can he? Nah, he wouldn't recognize me anyway, it was years ago, I was a scrawny kid right out of college. Look at him. You know how much he makes? Take a wild guess."

The other guy shrugged.

"Ten million a year. Yep. He's got a house in the suburbs with a rotating garage. The thing turns and it spits out whatever car he wants." He shook his head. "Just look at the big guy. He's picking his nose. I come back here after what, six, seven years, and he's still picking his nose."

It was almost paradoxical to look out over some of the wealthiest men in the country who also happened to be some of the most uncouth. They could buy anything, but they couldn't change the fact that they were products of the pits, that the place that enabled them to succeed also taught them to behave in ways that seemed to negate their success.

My eyes strayed from the pit and up toward John. He was fiddling with his laptop, which he often used to display additional charts of the Market. Something seemed to be the matter, and later, after the Close, he filled me in that his laptop had suffered a nervous breakdown. He'd been charting away, moving this baseline here, extending that one there, projecting, comparing, estimating, when suddenly the screen went blank. He called over the Globex tech guys to see if they could figure out the problem. A half hour passed and they couldn't determine what was wrong. John was growing frustrated because Alice had spent three weeks programming a $20,000 trading module onto that laptop. And then—the screen flashed and the culprit revealed itself: up popped a box that opened into a full-screen picture of a nude woman with her legs spread, her toes reaching toward the corners of the monitor. John froze.

The mouths of the geeky tech guys dropped. "I think you downloaded a virus," one said quietly.

"I have no idea where that came from," John said defensively. "I don't download that shit!" He tried to clear the screen by hitting some buttons—any buttons!—but the computer would only allow the user to enter the porn site, no other programs or files were available. Even the guys who stood near John who downloaded pornography all day long were quite impressed by the raunchiness on John's screen. John's face was deep red, and he contemplated just picking up the laptop and throwing the whole thing in the trash. Instead, he shut it off, thanked the tech guys, and promptly walked off the Floor. Of course, in any other profession, he'd likely have been terminated over such an incident. On the trading floor, however, it would get him nothing more than a week's worth of jabs.

$ $ $

It had been several months since I'd been to the Merc, but it was difficult to go too long in Chicago without meeting someone with a connection to the place. At a recent brunch, I struck up a conversation with a man named Marcus, who was in his 30s and who used to trade. Our conversation began just like most others I'd had with retired traders. "Oh, the things I saw, the things that took place, you wouldn't believe!"

I nodded, for I now felt I'd seen it all too and could say the same.

"No," he said, his voice growing serious. "I mean, there were things that *happened*. Things I can't even talk about here."

"You mean like sexual harassment, that kind of thing?" I asked.

He half laughed. "Worse."

Worse? For some reason, Anne McKenzie popped in my mind, even though I hadn't thought about her in some time. "Like . . . suicide?" I ventured. His eyes immediately widened. Then he leaned in and lowered his voice. "Let's just say people *called* it suicide."

Others made their way toward us, and Marcus deliberately changed the subject. Later, I made a point of meeting up with him in the kitchen. I asked if he'd tell me more.

"I don't know if I should," he said. "I mean, there are some dangerous people out there. It might just be something that's better left alone." I didn't know him, so I couldn't gauge if he was being a sensationalist or if these were legitimate concerns. But what if it *was* Anne McKenzie to whom he was referring? Then again, what were the odds of that? Thousands of people had been through the Merc—and there were likely to have been a handful of suicides over the years.

He did know *something*, though, and his discomfort was reminiscent of the initial trader who had told me of Anne. For some reason, I knew it was her—so I played my card. "I heard about a young woman trader who jumped from Sandburg," I said.

He froze. "How did you hear about her?"

"Through a trader," I said, "but I promised I would never use his name in connection with the story."

Marcus looked over his shoulders to make sure no one else was listening. "I believe," he said, "that someone *helped* her jump."

Marcus's speculation caught me off guard. I had to follow up, had to see if I could gauge his credibility, had to see what else he knew. Marcus was still involved with the markets—now on the technical side—and he agreed to meet with me at his office after everyone had gone home. Over a glass of Scotch, he filled in the story that I'd grasped onto since the very first day I had stepped on the Floor. Her name wasn't, of course, Anne McKenzie—I hadn't even been close. It was Diane DeLuca. She had worn a purple trader's jacket. She didn't much like it in the pit, and she preferred to sit at her firm's desk, a few feet away, and watch the action from there. She sounded to me a lot like Ricki, for she didn't want to be friends with anyone there, she wanted to make her money and leave. Marcus was a summer clerk, since he was still in school at the time. He knew several people who traded on the Floor, and he'd been bestowed the yellow jacket so that he too could learn the craft. He was a small kid, short and skinny, and, although he loved the business, he didn't much like it in the pit either. Diane was always friendly to him, and they would hang out together and talk. She took him under her wing as if he was her little brother and offered advice about trading. "Never take free trades in the pits," she'd instruct. "They act like they're your friends, and they'll offer you trades, but, trust me, don't take any favors—or they will own you forever." Marcus listened wholeheartedly, for he planned to get a badge as soon as he finished school. "Don't risk too much," she'd warn, and she'd follow it up with what Marcus would come to think of as her motto: "Stay small, stay alive."

He echoed the words to me now. "Stay small, stay alive." He had a faraway look. "I wonder if she was somehow trying to tell me something," he said.

Now that I had her real name, I was able to find a copy of her death certificate in the dingy basement of City Hall. She had jumped from the forty-fourth floor at 2:40 a.m., and was pronounced DOA. I also ran her name by everyone I knew, and the pieces of Diane's life and death began to fall together in an odd way. Here were the facts: Diane traded Deutschemarks for a large, powerful trading firm at the Merc that had previously been brought up on charges of illegal trading. One of the partners in the firm—I'll call him E.—was a tremendously successful trader who'd been on the Floor for some twenty-five years. He was known for having a shady past and a fierce temper. He'd made headlines in the 1970s for alleged customer violations and for an alleged attempt to squeeze the Wheat market—whereby the government regulatory agency, the Commodity Futures Trading Commission, declared an emergency and forced him and other traders to liquidate their Wheat positions. But despite this situation and the numerous allegations, E. was never charged. Until 1987—Diane's last full year.

The Merc charged E. for making prearranged trades and for withholding customer orders during the prior year. He was fined $250,000 and suspended for one year. Oddly, one of the brokers with whom E. had made some of these prearranged trades was nailed with a $500,000 fine and suspended for ten years for the same offense.

News articles described E. as extremely wealthy, yet ferocious. According to the *Chicago Tribune*: ". . . his aggressive style hasn't always made him popular on the trading floor or in other business matters, associates said. On one occasion, the well-heeled trader wanted to sue a cleaner over a $110 bill, said [a former associate]. 'Most people give and take in life,' [the former associate said]. '[E.] immediately escalates any dispute. . . . He wants you to believe he's the toughest guy out there.' " Marcus knew this firsthand. He remembered receiving a phone call from E. after a trading dispute, in which E. said that he wanted to bash Marcus's head in with a baseball bat.

With the information I'd now collected, I began to string a hypothesis together: Diane was always sitting at the desk where the orders were coming in. E.—and possibly others—were fixing trades, withholding trades, and maybe even creating dummy orders or, perhaps, an entire dummy account. Had Diane seen these fraudulent orders? Did this woman stumble across more than she was supposed to know? Diane was young, but she was savvy. Her words of advice to Marcus proved that. But had she reached her breaking point? Was she about to come clean with what she knew? Adding an even more compelling element was that at that time, undercover FBI agents were scoping the Floor as part of a wide-scale, two-year investigation of illegal trading at the Merc and the Board of Trade, which would eventually result in almost fifty indictments. Had they been questioning Diane? It was the agents' habit to focus on the smaller traders and try to persuade them to leak information about the Big Boys.

The agents were successful at this with another young woman trader at the Board of Trade. Her name was Melanie Kosar and she was just twenty-five years old when the agents showed up unannounced at her home at 10 p.m. They told her if she didn't become an undercover informant in the Bond pit where she traded, that they had her on charges of undoing a one-lot trade with another trader. Her alleged crime was the trader version of a right turn on red—the smallest violation one could commit. The agents told Melanie that if she didn't cooperate, she would lose her job, her house, her car, everything. No one knows for sure if she supplied information about anyone else in the pit, and it didn't so much matter since a *Wall Street Journal* article outed her—the headline alone was a dagger: WHILE CHICAGO TRADERS ARE EYEING THE MARKET, ONE TRADER EYES THEM. BOND BROKER MELANIE KOSAR TAKES ON UNENVIABLE ROLE AFTER FEDS CONFRONT HER. SHUNNED BUT STILL WORKING. The morning the article hit the stands, the traders turned their backs to Melanie as she entered the pit. For a half hour she tried to trade, but she was invisible to the hundreds around her. In tears, she gave up and left. Twice she tried to return, but the booing and hissing were so extreme she couldn't even step into the pit.

Melanie had been quoted in the article as saying that trading was her life, that it was the only thing she knew how to do. And yet, when no one will trade with you, it's impossible to trade. She gave up her seat and her dreams of trading and went to work for her father in his suburban dry-cleaning store. She ended up pleading guilty to prearranged trading, was expelled from the Board of Trade, and barred from all trading for three years. It might as well have been for a lifetime.

At this point, Diane was already dead. Had she been put in a similar predicament? Had agents been pushing her to leak information on her big bosses? Were her bosses onto what was happening and afraid she might sing?

A former Merc president, Everette B. Harris, described the Market as being there "to harness human greed for the good of all." And yet what happened when that backfired, when greed got so out of hand that it lived up to its reputation as one of the Seven Deadly Sins? "Infectious greed," Alan Greenspan had termed such a thing, and blamed it for the burst of the high-tech bubble. But this was more than just infectious—E. and his cohorts were extremely wealthy, they had no want for anything, and yet they still stole. It was insatiable greed—or maybe something even beyond that, something more visceral, like a conditioned response that the brain could no longer control. They'd discovered how to pickpocket the most bulging wallets, and they couldn't resist.

A few people I spoke with remembered the last time they saw Diane— a day or two before the jump. They all described her as happy, normal, and appearing like nothing out of the ordinary was going on. They also said that when they'd heard she had committed suicide they'd been very surprised she'd do such a thing. But what I found to be most odd was that the majority of traders I asked hadn't heard of the suicide. Instead, they had varying stories as to Diane's fate. Alice thought she'd heard Diane was killed in a car accident. Others knew that *something* had happened, they just didn't know what—Diane's was just another face on the Floor, there, then gone.

"Oh yeah, Diane, DeeDee," Denise, who'd traded in the same pit, said. "What *did* happen to her?" Denise made some calls to her former pit-mates. Everybody had the same response: "Yeah, where'd she go? She just disappeared."

"I believe," Marcus told me, "that she took the fall—literally speaking— for the big guys." He chuckled the way one does in a hopeless situation. "The Merc is the most expensive club to join. It's a secret-handshake society where people learn to protect what they have, at all costs."

Diane's building, it turned out, was along the outermost block of Sandburg Village, just down the street from my apartment. I had unknowingly walked past the scene hundreds of time. One typical windy Chicago day, I entered her building. I asked around and finally found a maintenance man who'd been there for twenty years. He'd known Diane. "Never in a million years would I have thought she was the type to do that," he said. "But I think she had a very stressful job. Maybe that's what made her troubled." I asked if he recalled if anyone else had been around, if she'd had any visitors, or if someone may have been spotted leaving the building at that odd hour. He shook his head with certainty. "Was there any sign of a fight or struggle?" I asked. Again, he shook his head.

"Only weird thing was," he said, "is that that part of the roof is locked at all times and no resident has the key. We have no idea how she got up there."

$ $ $

There were some aspects of trading that I'd concluded I would never understand. Such as how you could be so passionate about something that felt nothing for you and could easily squash you. How you could devote your every day, your hopes, your future, and, often, the future of your family to something that could turn on you as suddenly as lightning striking—and yet there were thousands of people who would give anything to place themselves in that vast, open field while the electrical storm was raging, and throughout the tempest, they would diligently, relentlessly—recklessly?—reach toward the metal key.

Trading was the most typical romance: the chase, the rush, the infatuation, the incredible highs, the near-debilitating lows, and most of all, the jolt from the constant newness—and from the occasional win. "Trading is better than sex," Alice said. "Because after it's over, you've still got all that money."

One retired trader, whose father had been one of the most successful Pork-Belly traders, described to me how torn he felt about trading. His father's job had enabled the family to live an incredibly lavish life, and yet he said: "My father spent his life determining the price of bacon—hundreds of millions of dollars over the price of bacon. Fortunes made and lost over the price of bacon. All that agony over bacon. It's bacon! How in the world can that be fulfilling? Well, it's no secret that it's not. People there are not fulfilled by their job, so they use the money as a means to fulfill themselves—only, this doesn't work for the long term. But I'll tell you, it really is amazing the things you can buy, and have, and do, all because of hamburgers and corn and soybeans, and even bacon."

$ $ $

Less than a year after Bev Gelman had left the Floor, she returned to her old spot in the pit. At first I was shocked at the news. Why would she subject herself to the pits again when she could live worry free and luxuriantly for the rest of her life? And then I remembered something she'd once told me. It was after a party and, to my surprise, she'd asked if we could share a cab. During the ride, we began talking about her sisters, and she described them as incredibly talented and successful in a variety of different areas—unlike herself. All she believed she knew how to do was trade.

"Oh, come on!" I had moaned.

"No," she insisted, "I am an idiot savant."

I'd brushed off her comment and all but forgotten about it until I heard she'd reappeared on the Floor. She'd reclaimed her spot and, just like that, she was back trading, as if she'd never left at all. It somehow, at that point, all came together for me, making an odd sense: during her brief retirement she'd traveled the world, but how could that compare with having the financial world hinge on your every move? How could spending time as an anonymous tourist in, let's say, Australia, compare with knowing that the largest international banking institutions were waiting on the line for you to call out your trade? How could straining against the language barrier in France compare with having the Market react whenever you uttered a number? And how could you bear to sit on a deserted beach when there was such money and prestige and action waiting for you if you just stepped back into the pit?

Most of us will never know masterdom as Bev did, but all I could assume from her return was that power must not only be addictive, but all-encompassing. Even Alice marveled at what it must feel like: "Can you imagine the thrill of knowing you just stuck it to the three largest male traders in the pit? You watch their mouths drop open! You can't beat that rush."

I eventually took off for New York, leaving my yellow jacket crammed somewhere in my closet back in Chicago, gathering dust and, likely, a fine on Tom's account. And yet, I still found myself visiting Times Square to gaze in awe at the Nasdaq banner. Around and around the ticker scrolled and looped. Despite the leaps and plummets, the scandals and lies, the money that materialized, and the money that evaporated, this was what made the world go round. Stare at it too long, and you'd get dizzy.

I didn't have much desire to return to the Merc anytime soon. I missed the action, but not in the way that I wanted it back. I had originally stepped onto the Floor trying to break into a man's world. But as the numbers flashed and the adrenaline surged, as the Pepto-Bismol was chugged and the deals were made and the little cards were ripped up and thrown into the air like confetti, I realized it wasn't really about that, that the concept of Mars and Venus was just a bunch of five-and-dime psychobabble. It was about something that traders had that I didn't—as Alice liked to say: "It always surprises me how greedy I really am."

I think Darcy Cook summed it up well: "What is it that keeps people in a business where their stomach is always in knots? Where you sweat wondering if you are going to make your margin call? Why would you put yourself through that every day, unless there is something deeper inside, some desire, some kind of drive, some kind of intrigue? It's like there's this main catalyst and we're all magnets drawn to it." Darcy's eyes lit up. "Is it something that's all covered in glitter? Is it something like an eclipse where they say, don't look at the sun, but you still always do?" She then paused, as if waiting for an answer to hit her, although she knew, as did everyone on the Floor, there was no answer that could be put into words. "It's just something about this place," she said. "And you know, in other walks of life they say, 'You can't take it with you,' but that's not how it is in this business. Here, it's the one who dies with the most toys wins."

Acknowledgments

There's a common trader quirk: everyone loves to talk, but no one wants to be singled out for it. The pit is akin to a fraternity, where what happens there tends to stay there. Divulging stories is as frowned upon as showing an outsider the secret handshake. Couple that with trader superstition, and this list of acknowledgments could go on for pages. So I have to leave this as a general thank you: I'm grateful to everyone who granted me an interview; it took some brave and committed people to let me into their lives and careers, and I'm indebted to them for their honesty and candidness.

A big thank you to Theresa and Jim, who introduced me to trading and were my inspiration for this book; Jim was also kind enough to point out that when I wore a particular blue V-neck top into the pit, the traders on the upper steps could see down it. Neal Weintraub, author of *Trading Chicago Style*, gave me my first real introduction to the Merc; he wants it on record that if there's an afterlife, he hopes to be reincarnated as a Swedish-bombshell Bond trader. Next came Alice Kelley, who became not only my prize source and lunch benefactor, but a good friend. Also, just for the record, Alice was not thrilled with my description of her eyeglasses as "blue plastic frames"; they are, she's informed me, $1,200 tortoiseshell frames. The men who frequented Alice's Merc Club table were all genuine and helpful; one in particular wants to remain nameless, but was a wealth of information, as well as my blind-date coordinator. John Anton became a good friend, screenwriting partner, and sparring buddy, and he's also the brains behind the title. Ginni McGathey and "her girls," Melinda and Nicole, deserve much thanks and respect; and they would like it noted that, although they agree the Soybean Oil and Meal pit has "The Most Dickheads per Capita," that this most definitely excludes Melinda's father-in-law, who happens to trade in that pit. Ginni would also like to apologize to her mother for all the bad language. Romey and Michelle were great fun; and I wish Romey luck in pursuing his dream of writing a memoir. I met Denise Hubbard, oddly enough, through an acupuncturist, who, I do believe, had ulterior motives and a romantic eye for Denise; while that didn't pan out, a great friendship with Denise and me did. Denise was my voice of reason, and did a great job of looking out for me.

On the publishing side, my agent, Dan Mandel, took my idea and ran with it, and there's no greater feeling than knowing someone's truly interested in what you have to say. Along that line, I'm indebted to my editor, Ann Campbell, and to the wonderful Gerry Howard, who together snatched up the book and made my idea a reality. Ann was not just my editor, but also a friend, and I'm sure she knew to block out a chunk of time whenever she called me because we talked like we'd known each other for years. Also at Broadway, Ursula Cary, Laura Pillar, Catherine Pollock, David Drake, and Louise Quayle did wonderful jobs. Thank you to Amy Schiffman of Gersh, who is always a refreshing dose of real generosity. And thanks go out to Sarajane Avidon, Dick Simpson, Alison Witkin, Karen Holmes, Dennis Kroner, Ethel Hammer, Erinn Huttas, Jeff Gordon, and fellow journalists Sheryl Kennedy, M.B.A., and Mark Warnick, J.D., for all their time and help.

A very special thanks to my parents, and since this book is about money, it's worth it to doubly thank them for all that they kicked in when my advance ran out. And also, to my brother, Jason, whom I fear I inspired too much with all my talk of trading—he's trading on the computer now, and I wish him the best of luck!